END-TIME SECRETS

OF

DANIEL 8–12

Revised Edition

THE GREAT "PREFACE"

TO THE

BOOK OF REVELATION

FRANKLIN S. FOWLER JR., M.D.

Director, Prophecy Research Initiative
Christian Heritage Foundation, C.S.

Publisher:

Christian Heritage Foundation, C.S.
4256-B Mockingbird Lane
Banning, California 92220-1123 USA

END-TIME SECRETS OF DANIEL 8–12

Franklin S. Fowler Jr., M.D.

First Edition, 2005
Printed and bound in the United States of America.

Library of Congress Control Number: 2007922209
ISBN 1-4120-6144-x

Published by the Christian Heritage Foundation, C.S.
4256-B Mockingbird Lane, Banning, California 92220
www.endtimeissues.com

Unless otherwise indicated, Bible quotations are taken from the King James Version by Oxford University Press, Great Clarendon Street, Oxford ox2 6pd, England; "Containing the Old and New Testaments translated out of the original tongues and with the former translations diligently compared and revised by His Majesty's special command."

Cover design and layout by Jeanne C. Fowler

ACKNOWLEDGEMENTS

This book would not have been possible without the faithful support and intuitive insights of William and Marjorie Allen, Robert Sochor, Franklin and Florence Fowler Sr., Raymond and Gail Cress, Kenneth and Olga Fowler, Douglas and Pamela Stilson, Vonda Stilson, plus the loving and tireless support of my wife, Jeanne Fowler. To each one, along with a myriad of others, a forever thanks!

CONTENTS

FOREWORD

There are many commentaries and prophetic works that address the varied messages of Daniel. That book, perhaps more than any other, is the subject of amazing diversity of opinion and scholarship.

Some schools of thought conclude that this is more of a literary work than a theological discourse. Others relegate it to the work of many authors with a lack of cohesiveness. Some feel it was written 200-300 years later than is generally believed. With such varied views on Daniel, its place in the sacred cannon has been compromised. Disappointingly, many expositors begin *interpreting* before they contextually analyze or exegete.

This book represents only an introductory approach to the wonders of Daniel. It is vital to discover the repetitive imagery in God's many contacts with Daniel. There is a progressive reinforcement of thought, continually adding details to clarify truth. Highlights of the conflict between good and evil are especially vivid in light of the end of time.

The first half of the book relates to God's sovereign rule over secular powers. The last half addresses specifically God's sovereign interest in His people, with the desire to see everlasting righteousness among them.

Our focus is on Chapters 8–12 and the great themes conveyed to all those who are written in the "Lamb's book of life" (Daniel 12:1). Those chapters are so crucial to grasp. In fact, heaven was so concerned that Daniel understand the issues with precision that Jesus personally visited him three times, presenting some of the most profound language and thoughts in all of Scripture.

Though it's full of meaning and spans the next 2500 years, the majority of the visions and themes relate to the final generation to live on this earth.

INTRODUCTION

In Jesus' day the Pharisees were sequestered by a narrow base of knowledge, performing ceremonies without understanding and filling their lives with acts of tradition devoid of meaning.[1] This acted to thwart spiritual growth and create barriers to eternal life. Jesus told John that at the end of time many who would call themselves committed Christians (Laodicea) and feel satisfied with their knowledge would be spiritually naked. Its sanctifying power would never be experienced.[2] They would be just like those ancient leaders. Vast fields of truth yet to be discovered were at hand but never seen. Their spiritual capital was spent on valueless knowledge. Truth would be static and not progressive.

Few Christians today go beyond the very first level of Biblical understanding they had at baptism. Often the path that follows is littered with revolving door *opinions* from that *simplistic basic knowledge.*

"When God's people are at ease and satisfied with their present enlightenment, we may be sure that He will not favor them. It is His will that they should be ever moving forward to receive the increased and ever-increasing light which is shining for them. The present attitude of the church is not pleasing to God. There has come in a self-confidence that has led them to feel no necessity for more truth and greater light."[3]

Truth was never meant to be grasped with cursory study. Saving truth was designed to ever expand before the inquiring mind. This was the burden of the apostle Peter, once naive and very satisfied with himself. "*Grow* in grace *and* the knowledge of our Lord and Saviour Jesus Christ" (II Peter 3:18) he admonished. Continued advancement is required in the Christian life.

"The truth is an advancing truth and we must walk in the increasing light. We must have living faith in our hearts, and reach out for larger knowledge and more advanced light."[4]

"Whenever the people of God are growing in grace, they will be constantly obtaining a clearer understanding of His word. They will discern new light and beauty in its sacred truths. This has been true in the history of the church in all ages, and thus it will continue to the end."[5]

Truth does not change. Light on truth increases as it advances. Remarkably, new light will also be discerned and beauty of old truths will be seen. "The time for the unfolding of special truth in relation to the closing scenes of this earth's history is during the last generations that shall live upon the earth."[6]

When the disciples asked Jesus those three pivotal questions about *the end* (Matthew 24:3), their minds were to grasp the great duality of truth between the physical temple and the spiritual temple.

Before Jesus answered them, He made it clear that correct knowledge was

---

[1] White, Ellen G.; *The Desire of Ages,* pp. 278-279.

[2] White, Ellen G.; *Faith and Works,* p. 82.

[3] White, Ellen G.; *Testimonies,* vol. 5, pp. 708-709.

[4] White, Ellen G.; *The Review and Herald,* March 25, 1890.

[5] White, Ellen G.; *Gospel Workers,* p. 297.

[6] White, Ellen G.; *Testimonies,* vol. 2, pp. 692-693.

vital to a saving experience for that time. "Take heed that no man deceive you" (Matthew 24:4). Increased light is a barrier against deception. Does this apply to prophecy?

"The prophecies of Daniel and of John are to be understood. They interpret each other. They give to the world truths which *every one should understand*. These prophecies are to be witnesses in the world."[7]

Not only are they to be *understood* but understood so well that they can be a witness to truth through our teaching. Why?

"The study of the Revelation directs the mind to the prophecies of Daniel, and both present most important instruction, given of God to men, concerning events to take place at the *close of this world's history*."[8]

This was penned after 1844. What in Revelation speaks of the close of this world's history? Virtually the whole book. What speaks about the very end of time in Daniel? Most messages in chapters 8–12. That is why *this* book was written.

"There is need of much closer study of the word of God: especially should Daniel and Revelation have attention as never before in the history of our work."[9]

Daniel "bears his testimony, that which the Lord revealed to him in vision of the great and solemn events which we must know as we stand on the very threshold of their fulfillment."[10]

We are also warned regarding the book of Revelation.

"The solemn messages that have been given in their order in the Revelation are to occupy the *first place* in the minds of God's people. *Nothing else is to be allowed to engross our attention.*"[11]

Then a warning about Daniel: "Let us read and study the twelfth chapter of Daniel. It is a warning that we shall all need to understand *before* the *time of the end*."[12] (1903)

Was that warning simply that probation would close and the great time of trouble would then begin? Was it about three time prophecies that *ended in 1843,* as so many have erroneously concluded? Absolutely not! It is the "twelfth chapter" that we are to understand *before* the end of time. That chapter is so important, those time prophecies so vital, Jesus *personally* appeared to Daniel to give them. They are to be part of the final Loud Cry that will clearly tell the world in specific terms that time has almost ceased.

"A message will soon [future to 1906] be given by God's appointment that will swell into the loud cry. Then Daniel will stand in his lot to give his testimony."[13]

[7] White, Ellen G.; *The Seventh-day Adventist Bible Commentary,* vol. 7, p. 949 (emphasis added).

[8] White, Ellen G.; *The Great Controversy,* p. 341 (emphasis added).

[9] White, Ellen G.; *Testimonies to Ministers,* p. 112.

[10] White, Ellen G.; *Manuscript 32,* 1896.

[11] White, Ellen G.; *Testimonies,* vol. 8, p. 302 (emphasis added).

[12] White, Ellen G.; *Manuscript Releases,* vol. 15, p. 228 (1903); *Last Day Events,* p. 15 (emphasis added).

[13] *Ibid.,* vol. 2, p. 20 (*Letter 54,* 1906).

PREFACE

Standing unique among Old Testament books, Daniel is written with predictive messages that carry one forward to the very *end of time.* That era unequivocally ushers in the kingdom of God in heaven (2:44; 7:13-14, 27; 8:25; 12:1). Daniel portrays a *point* in time when victory over evil will finally come and God's people will be forever delivered from its heinous influences.

Most fascinating, this book is written in two languages. Chapters 1 through 2:4a is a historical introduction in Hebrew. Chapters 2:4b through 7:28 are in Aramaic and describe the succession of nations that were specific challenges to God's people. Finally, chapters 8–12 are once again in Hebrew and outline the final conflict between apostate Christianity and God's remnant people.

It is this latter section of Daniel that is the focus of this book. Those Hebraic messages present great themes to guide God's people right at the end of time. It also serves as an introduction to the whole book of Revelation. The imagery of Jesus in 10:5-8 is a segué into His portrayal in Revelation 1:12-17.

Jesus tied these great truths to the *end of time* in that great eschatological discourse, "When ye therefore shall see the abomination of desolation, spoken of by Daniel the prophet ..." (Matthew 24:15 and Mark 13:14). Making sure that this period of earth's history was fully understood, Gabriel repeatedly told Daniel that those prophesies were for the *eth qets,* Hebrew words denoting *the end. Qets* is from the root word *qasas,* meaning "to sever." *Eth qets* denotes a period when the final severance of time will come. Uniquely, it comes in a *judgment* context when the finality of all issues occurs [Genesis 6:13 (metaphor for the end); Ezekiel 7:2-3, 33:11]. This is in great contrast to God's kingdom which will know "no end" (Isaiah 9:7).

When will God execute judgment? Daniel opens to the student exactly when this will occur. Carefully and progressively one can see it is *after* the 42 prophetic months of 7:25, *after* the 2300 prophetic atonement years of 8:14 and *during the* 1260 literal days of 12:7.

"A wonderful connection is seen between the universe of heaven and this world. The things revealed to Daniel were afterward complemented by the revelation made to John on the Isle of Patmos. These two books should be carefully studied. Twice Daniel inquired, How long shall it be to the *end of time*? ... The book of Daniel is unsealed in the revelation to John, and carries us forward to the last scenes of this earth's history.... Teach these things."[1]

Daniel 8:19, with great precision, states that the *eth qets* will occur at the *appointed time* or *mowed.* After many years (at least seven and possibly as long as 19) Jesus personally came to Daniel and told him when the *mowed* would end. There is no date setting or timed prophecies that *lead up* to these periods. God said that was not for us to know (Acts 1:7). Daniel is event-driven. Those events come at the *eth qets,* which, when they begin, come within a timeframe described in Daniel 12.

There is a great deal of prejudice and bias related to Daniel 8–12 based on misapplication of quotations from Ellen

---

[1] White, Ellen G.; *Testimonies to Ministers*, pp. 114-115 (emphasis added).

G. White. This book sweeps aside that restrictive focus of the past and, with Biblical firmness, points forward to the time these passages will become part of the Loud Cry.

"The prophetic periods of Daniel, extending to the very eve of the great *consummation,* throw a flood of light upon events then to transpire."[2]

"A great work will be done in a short time. A message will soon be given by God's appointment that will swell into a loud cry. Then Daniel will stand in his lot, to give his testimony."[3]

Paul made it impeccably clear that Jesus will not come as a thief in the night to those who are children of the light (I Thessalonians 5:5). He then challenged God's people to "Let us watch and be sober." Watch for what? His coming? That is *not* the message. It is for the signs that give His people light that summer is near (Matthew 24:32). It is almost time for the harvest.

This study will not move forward sequentially verse by verse. The structure of Daniel 8–12 finds a message, explanation, then repetition of those messages with added insight. These chapters reveal the final rise of the papacy. To make sure this message is not missed, chapter 11 is inserted. Thus, an approach will be taken to highlight informational clues that build upon each other until a whole of end-time truth is opened up.

Daniel 8 and 9 present special everlasting covenant themes. Since the King James Version fails to correctly present several key texts, they will be dealt with in special detail as this study progresses.

Though at times in-depth study must be taken to make certain that truth is upheld, all attempts to simplify the veracity of these prophetic messages in unpretentious language is made.

---

[2] White, Ellen G.; *The Review and Herald,* September 25, 1883 (emphasis added).
[3] White, Ellen G.; *Manuscript Releases,* vol. 2, p. 20 (*Letter 54,* 1906).

CHAPTER 1

CHRIST'S DISCOURSE BEGINS WITH AN END

– Unfolding Matthew 23 and 24 –

No, Jesus didn't make a mistake. The Jewish leaders did. They twisted and skewed the meaning of one of the Old Testament prophets so badly they rejected their nation's probation and failed to welcome the Messiah when He arrived. Jesus (that Messiah) would later remind the disciples of what those leaders missed. That Old Testament writer did predict when the Savior of the world would make His début! Then he gave stunning details, in a timing formula, of how to know the "when" regarding His *next* coming – the second Messianic arrival! The day and hour? No. But periods so close it comes to the "eve of the consummation." We're going to listen in on that profound discourse with those disciples. But before we do that, let's take a look at the *background* event that immediately preceded that session.

Denouncing Apostasy

Like an unflinching warrior, Jesus had just boldly pronounced doom upon the Jewish leaders (Matthew 23:2-39). Never before had He given those priests and Pharisees such a signal warning that their corruption would be followed by unrestrained woes on themselves and the nation. "Woe unto you, scribes and Pharisees, hypocrites!" – He repeated over and over.

The curses included:

1. ***Guilt*** of all the seed blood of the righteous from Abel to Zechariah (Matthew 23:35).

2. "***Damnation*** to hell" [implied] (Matthew 23:33)

3. The "house" of Israel, the Jewish nation, where God had dwelt, would be left ***desolate*** (Matthew 23:38).

4. The temple would be totally ***destroyed*** (Matthew 24:2) (private notice given to the disciples).

5. Then, as with all prophecy, a timing statement: All these things would happen ***within one generation*** (Matthew 23:36).

Solomon's temple had stood there on Mount Moriah for over 350 years when it was destroyed by Babylonian armies in 586 B.C. With that fearful loss, the glory of God's presence left forever. The Shekinah had bid farewell. Later, Cyrus gave permission to rebuild the temple; this was accomplished by Zerubbabel. That stood for nearly 500 years when Herod the Great came to power as king of Judea. He lavishly rebuilt and refurbished the edifice, starting in approximately 19 B.C. The work was still progressing during Christ's life, extending right up to the onset of His ministry (John 2:16, 19-21). But there was no ark of the covenant.

Some of the stones Herod used were over 600 tons. The Most Holy Place was

1

30 x 30 ft. and veneered with 22 tons of gold. The structure was supported with massive beams of cyprus and cedar.[1] The outer walls were made of white marble.[2] As Jesus left the temple on that fateful day of woes, it was the last time His sacred form would grace its precincts. He announced to the disciples its fate. Its destruction seemed mystifying and almost impossible. It was a fearful prediction. They would later see that His departure and prophecy symbolically represented heaven's abandonment of the Jewish nation as His chosen people.

The fate of Israel and its glory – the temple – was now on the disciples' minds. Undoubtedly, they were stunned at Christ's words. The great symbol of the Jewish nation, the world center of its seven annual feasts, the administrative hub of all Semitic peoples, was at that temple. Four of the disciples finally had a chance to query Jesus about the anticipated catastrophe. The questions they posed seem so simple, but that's all Jesus needed to begin an awesome story. We can be quite certain that it wasn't long until every ear would be riveted on what He would convey.

Timing Issues

With unquestioned intensity they asked, "When shall these things be?" "What shall be the sign of thy coming?" "What shall be the sign of the end of the world?" They associated these questions with those fearful curses. Jesus was immediately responsive to their concerns. But He also had far deeper issues to share. Two of their queries related to *events;* the other to *timing.* All prophecy has timing markers. It is also event-driven. It would be meaningless if predic-

tive history didn't have that time association. Time brings motivation and urgency to a message. It sets truth in a proper context. Jesus wouldn't disappoint their request. He answered all three questions.

The Savior unfolded a critical truth that ties to Biblical prophecy: *There are two ends of time!* Both relate to when God has two distinct groups of people: one, the Jewish nation; the other, the 144,000. Each relates to their terminal history!

His event-driven answers show us two fascinating *sequences.* Amazing – both can be *joined* through information from that wonderful Old Testament prophet the Jewish leaders abandoned: Yes, it was Daniel.

Time of Sorrows → Persecution → False Prophet → Hatred among Men → End (Matthew 24:7-13)

Abomination → Tribulation → False Christ → Celestial Signs → Second Coming (Mathew 24:15-30)

What about the "timing" of those two ends, these two sequences? For the Jews, one would occur in their generation, of which Jesus was a part. For the other end of time, Jesus had other clues associated with His second coming. They too, when started, would occur within one generation! He did say, "of that day and hour knoweth no man, no, not the angels of heaven, but my Father only" (Matthew 24:36). Could that mean He dismissed a timing answer related to His second coming? Jesus cautioned us to "watch!" several times. He said that we could know *when* it was "even at the doors" (vs 33). That means we will know what to watch for! Just how far *can* we go in "knowing" that second timing? So close we can see

---

[1] biblia.com/biblekings15.htm
[2] en:wikipedia.org/wiki/Herod'stemple

confirmatory events and, when associated with Daniel's *time periods* which go to the eve of His coming, we can know He is *at* the door.

Years ago expositor E. G. White thought so much about what another author wrote that she quoted him. This is what Joseph Wolff, Jewish writer and missionary said: "Did our Lord say that that day and hour should never be known? Did He not give us signs of the times, in order that we may know at least the approach of His coming, as one knows the approach of the summer by the fig tree putting forth its leaves? [Matthew 24:32]. Are we never to know that *period,* whilst He Himself exhorteth us not only to read Daniel the prophet, but to understand it? and in that very Daniel, where it is said that the words were shut up to the time of the end [which was the case in his time], and that 'many shall run to and fro' [a Hebrew expression for observing and thinking upon the time], 'and knowledge' [regarding that time] 'shall be increased.' Daniel 12:4. Besides this, our Lord does not intend to say by this, that the approach of the time shall not be known, but that the *exact* 'day and hour knoweth no man.' Enough, He does say, shall be known by the signs of the times, to induce us to prepare for His coming, as Noah prepared the ark.'–Wolff, Researches and Missionary Labors, pages 404, 405."[3]

It was a time of great religious awakening when she penned the above. White was telling that awakening story when she quoted Wolff, who was expecting
Jesus to come then. He didn't. But Wolff enumerated an important principle – the *extreme nearness* of the second advent

can be known with precision. Wolff misinterpreted one verse, Daniel 8:14, which led to his (and thousands of others') misapplication of "when" to 1844. Our understanding today of Jesus' answers to the disciples and the book of Daniel helps us *know.* How? They are filled with *additional* end-time timing clues that we now understand.

Here is one interesting example: "For when they shall say, Peace and safety; then sudden destruction cometh upon them, as travail upon a woman with child; and they shall not escape" (I Thessalonians 5:3). As labor pains progress, they become *more frequent* and *more intense.* That can be plotted on a graph and is called an *exponential curve.* The sudden destruction that occurs *just before* Jesus comes is just like that. Jesus really warned that the *time of sorrows* would be like an exponential curve. Luke 21 (a companion chapter to Matthew 24 along with Mark 13) says: "And when these things *begin* to come to pass, then look up, and lift up your heads; for your redemption draweth nigh" (Luke 21:28). Why? It will follow a predictable path modeled after that curve!

The events Jesus outlined as part of the "time of sorrows" *collectively* include:

1. Wars
2. Earthquakes
3. Famines
4. Pestilences
5. Celestial signs

When these destructive elements *begin* to occur *together,* in an exponential fashion, "look up, and lift up your heads, for your redemption draweth nigh" (Luke 21: 28).

---

[3] White, Ellen G.; *The Great Controversy (Pacific Press Publishing Association,* Mt. View, CA)*,* p. 359.

Natural disasters reported

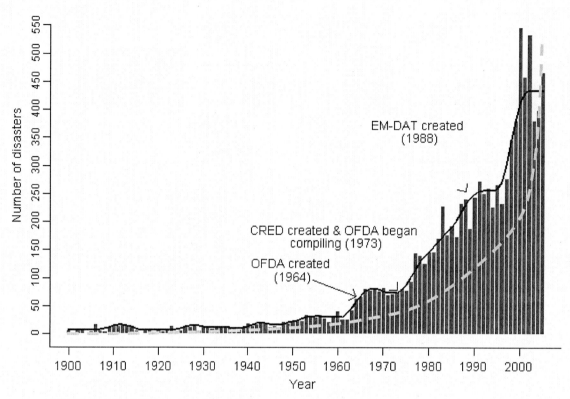

EM-DAT: The OFDA/CRED International Disaster Database - www.em-dat.net - Université Catholique de Louvain, Brussels - Belgium

Jesus also said that when these things **begin** to come to pass, they would occur within one generation (Matthew 24:34; Mark 13:30, Luke 21:32). Have we moved into a period when these five issues have **begun** to occur in an exponential curve?

It's amazing – that gives us another "timing clue." The "chosen people" will soon be faced with terrible strife. When an exponential curve is moving almost straight up, a crisis or some dramatic event occurs. Painful woes, in turn, with eternal consequences are about to come to those in rebellion. Matthew 24 outlines the issues that Jesus wanted to highlight to the disciples and for us today. Only by heeding a special call in which Jesus

warned **when** to "flee" (Matthew 24:16, Mark 13:14, Luke 21:21) will a remnant be saved. Yes, the details are given by that misunderstood prophet Daniel. What was his message?

A Message Related to the "When" Factor

Jesus gave another incredible "timing clue!" One that Christians today seem to take lightly. Stunning as it may seem, He began by saying "when" – that's a timing word – a significant event is unveiled, the signal to "flee" comes. Here it is:

"**When** ye therefore shall see the abomination of desolation" then "flee" (Matthew 24:15). That's a divine order. It

Natural disasters reported

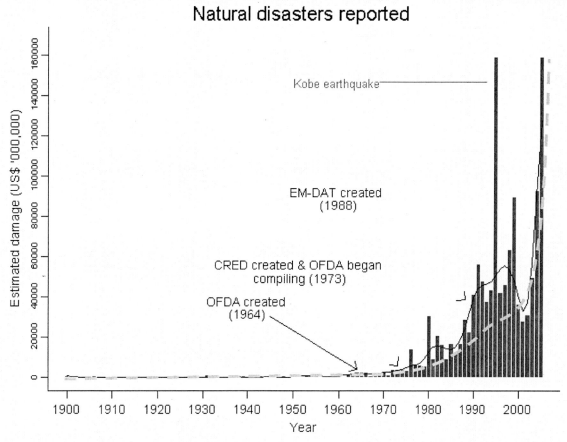

EM-DAT: The OFDA/CRED International Disaster Database - www.em-dat.net - Université Catholique de Louvain, Brussels - Belgium

must be very significant! The Greek word for "abomination" is *bdelygma*. It refers to something God hates. It is a gender-neutral word. In Mark 13:14 He notes that the abomination is "standing where it ought not." That participle is masculine. Thus, many scholars have concluded that it must relate to a person. The anti-christ or something associated with him is often portrayed as a person who steps into a place reserved for God (cf. II Thessalonians 2:4).[4] Yet, the word *bdelygma* insinuates a detestable idol or some false standard. Could some person symbolize that terrible wrong? Luke clarifies even

more this timing issue by describing it as *when* "Jerusalem [is] surrounded by armies" (Luke 21:20). Jerusalem is to be encompassed by powerful forces, an anti-Jerusalem contingency carrying a false standard. There will be an *individual* who leads or is a great symbolic head. With the word "armies" being used, that force will be out to demand submission (surrender) or be destroyed.

How do we tie all this together? Is it literal or figurative? Will it be a middle-eastern issue? What does "Jerusalem" mean? What about those two sequences? What exactly is that false standard or abomination? Who could that "head" be? We will begin to address these questions next.

---

[4] Brown, Colin; General Editor; *New International Dictionary of New Testament Theology* (Zondervan, Grand Rapids, MI), vol. 1, p. 75.

IMPORTANT PROPHETIC METAPHORS

– Symbols Jesus Used in Matthew 23 and 24 –

First – Understand "Jerusalem"

Between Christ's bold denunciation of the scribes and Pharisees and the time the disciples questioned Jesus, came a plaintive cry. Jesus articulated His heart-wrenching response to His people's rejection: "O Jerusalem, Jerusalem" (cf. Matthew 21:43), personifying the city. This lament follows the rhythm of a funeral dirge.[1] He then described that city as His chosen people who were to represent Him. He talks of its children, "I have gathered thy children (cf. Deuteronomy 32:12, Psalm 91:4), "even as a hen gathereth her chickens under [her] wings, and ye would not!"

Here, the city is seen as a special mother (cf. Isaiah 54, 62:1-4), a female symbol. God's gathering together of them was for their protection. They were to be forever part of His family. But now, because of apostasy, He said, "your house is left unto you desolate," announcing that there is no longer a place the mother and her children, the Jewish people, can call home. Something would destroy that "lady" symbol. Though that did not materialize until A.D. 70, this proleptic statement portrays its irrevocable doom! Though the Jewish people have now set up another "state," it is fragmented geographically, occupancy is shared with others and it is controlled by secular interests. Jesus declared its favor with God

---

[1] Keener, Craig S.; *A Commentary on the Gospel of Matthew* (William B. Eerdmans publishing company, Grand Rapids, MI), p. 557.

at an end (cf. Isaiah 64:10-11). The word "Jerusalem" continued as a great metaphor for *God's people* through all subsequent ages. A *woman* is symbolic of a church, His chosen, a remnant (e.g. Genesis 3:15). Again, the warning to *His* people (Matthew 24:15) relates to *when* they are surrounded by a militant false standard, preparing to force them to submit. *When* that occurs, He passionately said, "Flee!" A deeper study will show the issue relates to a false religious standard threatening His church. The Middle East related to its first literal and symbolic meaning. That, in turn, became a metaphor for the whole world at the last end. When the "gospel of the kingdom shall be preached in all the world ... then shall the end come (Matthew 24:14).

The "Abomination" – Historical Background

In Matthew 24:15 the abomination that leads to desolation is a warning to *flee*, separate, come away from or, as in Revelation 18:4, "come out of." If the armies are surrounding Jerusalem, how do you flee or "come out of?" "There hath no temptation taken you but such as is common to man: but God [is] faithful, who will not suffer you to be tempted above that ye are able; but will with the temptation also make a way to escape, that ye may be able to bear [it]" (I Corinthians 10:13). Its first "end-time" application helps us understand the final one. God made a way of escape.

In August of 66 A.D., a major Jewish revolt against Rome occurred. Twice-per-day required sacrifices honoring the Roman emperor (Nero) were stopped. They then assaulted and murdered the Roman garrison at Masada. Judah's curator and king, Marcus Julius Agrippa II, sent a Roman contingency of 3000 cavalry into Jerusalem to quell the unrest. Most of those troops were killed or captured by the Jews. Agrippa and his sister/wife queen, Bernice, barely escaped. News of the Roman defeat went quickly up the chain of command to Cestius Gallus, Governor of the Roman province of Syria. He was asked by Rome to intervene. Cestius was slow and indecisive and had no battlefield experience. It took several months for the Twelfth Legion, under his leadership, to leave Antioch and attack Jerusalem. He had 33,000 troops; 5680 were killed, forcing him to retreat in defeat.

Roman General Vespasian was then asked to take charge of operations. His son, Titus, and Legio XV Apollinaris from Alexandria joined him with a total of 55,000 troops in the spring of 67 A.D. By March of 68 A.D. most of Palestine was taken, except for Jerusalem. Vespasian carefully avoided that city until the country was secured. Meanwhile, Jerusalem suffered an internal reign of terror. Jewish factions had been fighting each other. Many of their military leadership lay dead.

The Roman efforts were suddenly halted with the news that Nero had committed suicide. Several Roman emperors followed in quick succession. Vespasian decided to wait for the Roman leadership to be stabilized before marching on Jerusalem. In 69 A.D. Vespasian was unexpectedly named the Roman emperor. He immediately left for the city of Rome.

Titus assumed command and was sent in early 70 A.D. to capture Jerusalem. During the siege the Jews resisted with an outside surprise attack. Titus nearly lost his life. He temporarily withdrew the Roman forces.

The armies that had surrounded the city were now at a distance. The Christians interpreted the words of Jesus as referring to this moment. It was at this time that they escaped. Not one was killed. *BUT – how could those armies ever be interpreted as an "abomination," a detestable standard standing in the Holy Place?*

Wherever the Roman armies went, they carried a Roman ensign of loyalty. This was a straight staff capped with a metallic eagle. Immediately under the eagle was an image of a man's head, signifying the Roman emperor, who claimed to be divine.[2] The eagle was a Roman symbol representing its bearers as messengers of the gods. It portended death and destruction (Jeremiah 48:40-42, Hosea 8:1). It was a symbol of the power of the Roman Empire (cf. Ezra 11:1–12:30). In the Apocalypse it was further a harbinger of expected judgment.[3] The man's head showed that they were loyal to a man – the leader of Rome.

In the four living creatures (Revelation 4:7), the fourth had the head of an eagle. It was this creature that asked John to "come and see" the pale horse of the fourth Seal. That pale horse symbolized death. The eagle was also a symbol of the tribe of Dan. His tribe was an abomination to God. Later, that tribe was represented by a serpent. Dan is not found

---

[2] Carroll, B. H.; *An Introduction of the English Bible* (1947) (http://www.preterism.us/abomination.htm).

[3] Osborne, Grant R.; *Revelation* (Baker Book House; Grand Rapids, MI), p. 360.

in the "twelve tribes" making up the 144,000 (Revelation 7). He is a great end-time symbol for an evil power who wants to be like God. He was positioned north of the sanctuary and is a fit symbol for the antichrist – a bird and a man on the Roman staff, a beast and its head, a Roman power situated within seven hills that calls herself "MOTHER." In God's plan, Jerusalem was to be a mother and, in the apocalypse, the bride. Rome tries to usurp that.

The armies were obviously an abomination. But what or who they represented are key to the deeper issue Jesus wants us to see. As Titus surrounded Jerusalem, so were the Christians surrounded with symbols that were abominable to God. It all related to worship. Those symbols elevated honor to man, not God. They also bore allegiance to gods other than God. The retreat of *what mocked God* was the Christians' signal. They knew Providence was at work and they

it, they were standing in a place they did not belong.

This is a great metaphor for the final and ultimate threat, which will be to God's church – the temple. When standard(s) that honor man and not God stand in its sacred precincts, eschatological urgency comes. By May, Titus' attack was resumed, the city was finally taken and the temple burned. Desolation followed, just as Jesus predicted.

The "Abomination" – End-Time Application

There is a stunning contemporary application to Christ's prophecy. It is crucial to observe that He was referring to events future to the time He spoke! Yet, the majority of expositors who go back to Daniel's chapters (Jesus' request – Matthew 24:15), which describe that abomination and desolation issue, suddenly revert to the B.C. era, making a literal

Transgression Abomination associated with desolation (tribulation begins) (Daniel 8:13, 11:31)	→	Time of Trouble such as never was (Daniel 12:1)	→	Resurrection associated with deliverance (Daniel 12:1-2)

fled.[4] The Qumranites also viewed those Roman standards as the epitome of idolatry (1QpHab6.3-4). Many felt it would be better to die than to permit these "standards" to enter the temple's precincts. To where did those precincts extend? Several furlongs outside the city walls. That's why it was called a holy city. That's why, when the armies surrounded

Medo-Persian and Grecian application. That is where the tragic Antiochus IV Epiphanes application comes into so many discourses. The fall of Jerusalem in A.D. 70 was future. The prophetic allusions to the abomination were also to be associated with His second coming. Twice He refers to it in this discourse (Matthew 24:27, 30)!

In Matthew the tribulation follows the abomination and concludes with Jesus' return. This eschatological re-application

---

[4] Schaff, Philip; *Creeds of Christendom*, with a History and Critical notes (Baker Contemporary Publishers – Vendor), vol. 1, pp. 397-398.

lies directly to the tribulation messages noted in Daniel 8 and 11 through 12:2.

How can we define more clearly the abomination associated with the desolation related to the second coming? If we were limited to Roman history in Matthew 24, Mark 13 and Luke 21, it would be fodder for endless speculation. In a breathtaking warning, bound only to a simple phrase, Jesus indicated that a deeper understanding of the end of time is found where "the abomination of desolation, spoken of by Daniel the prophet" is (Matthew 24:15). It is as if He were saying: "Look, the scribes and Pharisees didn't know of My coming because they didn't study Daniel. Anyone can now learn about My second coming if they also go to Daniel. Where? Where it talks about the abomination of desolation!" Amazing! Those exciting prophecies are then the preface to the book of Revelation. They are apocalyptic. They are filled with incredible details of earth's final months. Way beyond that, they clarify who that "man" will be and tell of the struggles of God's people right to the end. They also describe the final victory when God's people will be delivered.

All that became the catalyst for writing this book. Those desolation messages begin in Daniel 8:13. Gabriel describes a sin that leads to desolation – the *pesha*. He will once again address it in 9:24, where he notes that it must be eliminated, even by God's people, to bring in everlasting righteousness!

Thus, the *pesha* is the sin or act that brings in the abomination – God's declaration. This book introduces the setting and general issues for that *pesha*. That is a signal to "flee" or "come out" of Babylon. The abomination issues weave their way from chapter 8 through chapter 12. It is to those areas that Jesus said, If you really want to know the second advent story – "the rest of the story" – study Daniel! That's what we are now going to do!

THE SETTING

The book of Daniel is made up of two halves. Chapters 1–7 are written in a mix of Hebrew and Aramaic (Chaldean). Its structure is like a tree (see Figure 1). The second half, chapters 8–12, are in Hebrew.

This latter half depicts the great controversy between good and evil just before the end of time. It is filled with special messages for Spiritual Israel. Gabriel said just before Jesus appeared to Daniel the third time, *"But thou, O Daniel, shut up the words, and seal the book, [even] to the time of the end [eth qets]: many shall run to and fro, and knowledge shall be increased"* (Daniel 12:4). What part was sealed? Many suggest the whole book. We will soon discover which *portion* of Daniel 8–12 was specifically closed till the very end of time. Notice that E. G. White includes chapter 7 in her broad understanding of this last-day setting: "Honored by men with the responsibilities of state and with the secrets of kingdoms bearing universal sway, Daniel was honored by God as His ambassador, and was given many revelations of the mysteries of ages to come. His wonderful prophecies, as recorded by him in chapters 7 to 12 of the book bearing his name, were not fully understood even by the prophet himself; but before his life labors closed, he was given the blessed assurance that 'at the end of the days'–in the closing period of this world's history– he would again be permitted to stand in his lot and place. It was not given him to understand all that God had revealed of the divine purpose. 'Shut up the words, and seal the book,' he was directed concerning his prophetic writings; these were to be sealed 'even to the time of the end.' 'Go thy way, Daniel,' the angel once more directed the faithful messenger of Jehovah; 'for the words are closed up and sealed till the time of the end.... Go thou thy way till the end be: for thou shalt rest, and stand in thy lot at the end of the days.' Daniel 12:4, 9, 13."[1]

---

[1] White, Ellen G.; *Prophets and Kings,* p. 547.

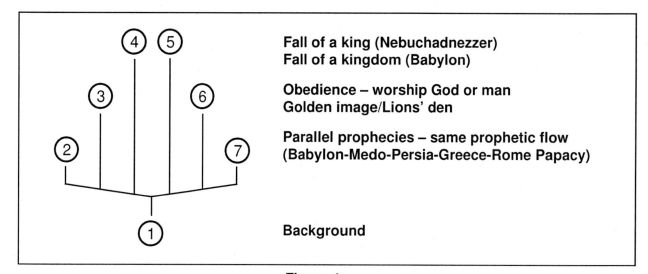

Figure 1

The *sealing* was symbolic of a barrier to understanding. The meaning of Daniel 8–12 would not be fully grasped until the "time of the end." As we shall see, the opening of this treasure house of prophetic knowledge would come progressively. This explains why there has been such divergence of opinion as to what these prophecies mean. God made it clear that those prophecies could not be understood until the time they were needed. No effort to know or solve the time periods of Daniel 12, as one example, would meet with success until the very end. It simply was not part of God's plan. There are "great and solemn events which we must know *as we stand* on the very threshold of their fulfillments."[1]

"These messages were given not for those who uttered the prophecies but for us who are living amid the scenes of their fulfillment."[2]

How do we know that it was only a **portion** of Daniel that was to be sealed? Hippolytus wrote a remarkable treatise on Daniel 1–7 in the third century. He understood those chapters much like we do today.[3]

Secondly, E. G. White affirms that only a part of that book was closed.

"In the Revelation all the books of the Bible meet and end. Here is the complement of the book of Daniel. One is a prophecy; the other a revelation. The book that was sealed is not the Revelation, but that *portion* of the prophecy of Daniel relating to the last days. The angel commanded, 'But thou, O Daniel, shut up the words, and seal the book, even to the time of the end.' Daniel 12:4."[4]

This is quite a revealing comment. Daniel was not instructed to seal prophetic understanding until the final Hebrew portion was presented. And then, as will be seen, only one of two visions of Daniel 8–12 was to be closed. It was the vision that, repeatedly, Gabriel, then Jesus, said related to the time of the end (*eth qets*).

"As the message of Christ's first advent announced the kingdom of His

---

[1] White, Ellen G.; *Manuscript Releases*, vol. 32, 1896.
[2] *Ibid.*

[3] White, Ellen G.; *The Prophetic Faith of Our Fathers*, vol. 1, p. 272.
[4] White, Ellen G.; *The Acts of the Apostles*, p. 585.

grace, so the message of His second advent announces the kingdom of His glory. And the second message, like the first, is based on the prophecies. The words of the angel to Daniel relating to the last days were to be understood in the time of the end. At that time, 'many shall run to and fro, and knowledge shall be increased.' 'The wicked shall do wickedly: and none of the wicked shall understand; but the wise shall understand.' Dan. 12:4,10."[5]

Another unique setting unfolds in these special chapters. They are sequenced, event-filled messages and are repeatedly set within a *time period.* Two of those messages were so important that heaven would not let Gabriel convey the details to Daniel. Jesus, the "man clothed in linen" (12:6) and the "certain saint" (8:13) personally appeared to the prophet to state those time periods. Fascinating and extremely important to grasp, most of the time periods were incomplete. One might reveal an ending but no beginning. Another a beginning and no clear ending. This revelatory technique was developed for a specific reason. Since the visions were presented in segments, partially due to Daniel's inability to receive them all at once, that prophetic unveiling helps the student to tie the right positions together. It also prevents spurious manipulation of the periods. Knowing this incredible way the messages were given, there is only one way the timing pieces can be linked to each other.

The expanse of time covered by these prophetic *time periods* spans from the decree to reestablish the theocracy of Israel in their homeland (9:25) to the deliverance of God's people and the special resurrection (12:2).

Many scholars have attempted to show that the *little horn* of Daniel 7 is the same period as the *little horn* of Daniel 8. This conclusion avoids several key *differences.* Parallels do not always mean the same timing. The differences must also be studied. As this is done, vast frontiers of new light open. In this case, *a second rise of the papacy.*

In contrast to the four sequenced kingdoms of Daniel 2 and 7 (Babylon, Medo-Persia, Greece and Rome), the vision of chapter 8 begins with a ram (vs 3), which refers to Medo-Persia (vs 20) in an end-time setting. Why isn't there a representation of Babylon to make a perfect recapitulation or repetition of Daniel 2 and 7? Some say it is because he was in Babylon and the vision looked *forward* – thus, Medo-Persia. Daniel was in Babylon for the other two visions also. This is not only a new vision, it introduces an entirely new message. In the previous visions the focus was on the *kingdoms.* Here, the focus is on the restoration of a covenant people. The kingdoms of Daniel 8 are timing markers for the prophecy. That, in turn, becomes an interpretative key.

The two animals presented – the ram and he-goat – are sanctuary atonement animals. The emphasis of the vision begins and is actually on Persia, the last and higher ram horn. Darius was the first Mede ruler and Cyrus the last, then four Persian kings followed: Cambyses (530-533 B.C.), False Smerdis (522-486 B.C.), the great King of Persia Xerxes I (Ahasuerus of Esther's time;[6] 485-465 B.C.) and Artaxerxes I (Artaxerxes Longimanus;[7] 464-424 B.C.)

Why is the focus on Persia? That is the time period when the visions of Daniel 8–12 *began.* The issues do not re-

---

[5] White, Ellen G.; *The Desire of Ages,* p. 234.

[6] White, Ellen G.; *Prophets and Kings,* p. 605.
[7] *Ibid.*

late to Babylon or the Medes. The 2300 atonement-year prophecy and the 490-year probationary prophecy for God's people began during the Persian Empire, specifically during the reign of Artaxerxes I.

The ram, the animal used as a trespass offering, represented the Ram of God. His people were challenged to become like Him, outlined in 9:24. They were to put away sin and transgression and be restored *fully* to heaven's favor. This is covenant completion imagery. The he-goat represents Satan, working through his agencies, especially the *little horn*, trying to thwart the covenant promise from being fulfilled.

Thus, the broad themes in Daniel 8–12 draw on deep spiritual issues for God's remnant people. The brush sweeps over the canvas of time and rests finally on the great final battle between Christ and His people and Satan and his. It is a miniature portrayal of the whole book of Revelation, yet filled with unique information as Revelation's introduction. God presents to His people details about events and time periods related to the very end of time.

CHAPTER 4

TWO VISIONS AND TWO RIVERS

The storyline of chapter 8 begins during King Belshazzar's third year of reign. He was the last King of Babylon and was the monarch who would see the terrifying handwriting on the wall: "Thou art weighed in the balances and found wanting." These words are a metaphor for the great judgment day at the end of time when spiritual Babylon falls – "The hour of His judgment has come" (Revelation 14:7-8). At this time Daniel had the initial part of two parallel visions that would eventually draw to a close the whole book (Daniel 8–12).

Daniel was likely in the capital city of Babylon at the time but experienced this vision as being in Susa or Shushan of the province of Elam. This city was nonexistent at that time, having been leveled to the ground by Assyria some years previously. The geographical imagery doesn't stop there. He is *specifically* along the bank of the Ulai River. Why such detail? Visions at rivers will be portrayed twice more before Daniel finishes writing to make sure we don't miss a special association being referenced! More on this a little further on. Together, these collective pictures develop a story that brings the reader right down to the end of time.

The rivers, the banks and the messages are association with Jesus drawing on His roles as High Priest, Judge and King – and His sovereign control over all the world. Though prophetic events given to Daniel will make it seem at times as though Jesus has forsaken His people, these images are reminders that He has not. *In addition*, within those unique settings, *timing prophecies* are given three times.

Putting everything in proper sequence, a beautiful panorama suddenly appears, which fulfills Habakkuk 2:3. *"For the vision is yet for an appointed time, but at the end it shall speak, and not lie: though it tarry, wait for it; because it will surely come, it will not tarry."* What vision? The final end of wickedness and the triumph of God's people (the incredible message given to Habakkuk just before the Babylonian captivity approximately 620 B.C.).

Daniel said that "a vision appeared to me" (8:1) and "I saw in vision" (8:2). The Hebrew word here for "vision" is *chazown*. This is one of several Hebrew words used for "vision" – but is very specific in its usage here by Daniel. In chapters 8–12 its connotation simply means a *revelation*. Daniel is very careful in using this word because it is different from another Hebrew word for *vision* that he will use, which has a very different application.

Next, we discover Daniel once again at the Ulai River (8:16) (a continuation of what occurred that day, which began in 8:1). Jesus' voice, "a man's voice," from between its banks commands (imperative) Gabriel to help Daniel understand what was just given to him in vision.

We now move to chapter 10 for another river scene. Daniel is now by the Hiddekel or Tigris River (10:4). In the beginning of that chapter Daniel said he "had understanding of the vision." The Hebrew word used there for vision is *mareh.* This word merits special attention and will be dealt with later.

Briefly, however, *mareh* portrays the imagery of a beautiful people ready for a wedding – at the end or culmination of something. Daniel (10:1) said he grasped the meaning of the *mareh.* But later we will see he could not understand the *chazown* vision.

He notes that suddenly he is alone because his friends fled as "a great quaking fell upon them" (10:7-8) with the Tigris River vision. What vision? The *mareh.* What was Daniel shown? An incredible picture of Jesus (10:5-6). This imagery is the *same* as John sees in Revelation 1. This is a segué to that very first chapter. This *ends* the four segments of the *mareh* vision.

Here is where each of these "vision" words are used:

Daniel	ch 8	ch 9	ch 10	ch 11	ch 12
Chazown	1-13	21	9-21	1-45	1-13
	15				
	17-27				
Mareh	14, 16	22-27	1-8		
	26				

Gabriel appears later to Daniel, after he was delayed by Satan (10:13). Since the *mareh* ended in 10:9, the word for vision now (10:14) is back to *chazown.* From this point to the end of the book only the *chazown* will be referred to. In fact, this is so important that Gabriel told Daniel, "I'm not here to talk about the *mareh* any longer but to address the *chazown*" (10:14). Thus, in our study of these chapters a distinction of *great importance* is made between the two. This will, in turn, open up great understanding to the book of Revelation.

Finally, in Daniel 12 he is once again by a river (10:5) (likely the Hiddekel since that is the last one mentioned). He sees two beings – one on either side of the river (12:5). Here Jesus appears again and personally continues Gabriel's expose' of the *chazown* vision and brings it to a close. Three times Jesus comes to Daniel. Why did He do that? Two times He presents *timing prophecies.* He does not leave those specifics to Gabriel. In garb that illustrates His activities, Jesus opens future periods of earth's history for the last generation who live on this earth. These appearances finally show His future role as the great controversy comes to an end.

Here are the three times rivers are mentioned with their respective visions:

Vision	*River*
Chazown vision begins ch 8	Ulai – 8:2
Mareh vision is *added* to ch's 8, 9, 10	Hiddekel – 10:4
Chazown restarts in ch's 10:14 by Gabriel, then	Hiddekel – 12:5
Jesus finishes it in ch 12	

These are the *only* places where the two rivers are mentioned in the whole book of Daniel. What can we learn from this? And why is this so important?

"The light that Daniel received *direct* from God was given especially for these last days. The visions he saw by the banks of the Ulai and the Hiddekel, the great rivers of Shinar, *are now in process of fulfillment, and all the events foretold will soon have come to pass* [1896]."[1]

Note the word "visions" here is plural. There is recognition of more than one presentation to Daniel that is given especially for the end-time. In 1896 they were in the process of fulfillment. A very crucial question must be addressed. What por-

---

[1] White, Ellen G.; *Manuscript Releases,* vol. 16, p. 334 (1896) (emphasis added).

tion of these visions was not yet fulfilled? Daniel began to stand in his place in 1798 at the end of "time times and dividing of time" (7:25). However, as we shall see, that understanding would not be *completed* till later. The seal (singular) that's blocking understanding must first be *fully* removed from the *chazown* vision.

Why are these details so important to grasp? The *mareh* vision outlines the major events related to the completion of a covenant people. It addresses legal issues that will be resolved in a perfected people who vindicate God's character. The *chazown* vision is the story of how Satan and his agents will try to thwart what God is trying to do through His people.

Each is in event-driven settings, often during specific periods of time. Each message templates over the book of Revelation, where incredible details expand. This is the story of how the great controversy scene finishes.

But what about the rivers? Why are visions and rivers associated together in the last half of this book? Each time a river is mentioned, Jesus either appears or is already there! At the Persian Ulai River comes the scene of the great controversy between good and evil (Daniel 8). Jesus appears and promises that spiritual deliverance will come to God's people (8:14). It specifically says that He is between the banks of the Ulai River. Water in prophecy (rivers are no exception) means people, multitudes, nations and tongues (Revelation 17:15). Jesus' *location* shows He is sovereign over all of these, and in that setting, assures us that the great conflict with sin will end.

But – why two rivers? If water symbolizes people in general, why is another river mentioned? Persia symbolizes deliverance to God's people, and the Ulai River is most fitting to assure us that His omnipotent plan to restore His people *will happen.*

Daniel is on the banks of the Hiddekel or Tigris River of Babylon in chapter 10. The Euphrates River, which feeds and supports the city of Babylon, is avoided in Daniel (the book of Revelation deals with that in chapter 16). By the Hiddekel Jesus appears in the majesty and splendor of **all** the imagery the Bible represents Him as. What He says to Daniel is not recorded. Jesus stands there and wants us to look, think and not miss one detail. He typifies a Priest, a Judge, an Advocate and a King above the waters, controlling all! At the Ulai Daniel didn't see Jesus but heard where His voice came from. Now he sees Jesus without the voice. The imagery shouts: "Daniel – people of all ages – it is I, God, your Friend, your Deliverer! I'm an Advocate and King for you!"

Amazing as it may seem, what Daniel sees of Him in chapter 10 is how John is introduced to the visionary scenes of Revelation (chapter 1). Except that when Jesus comes to John, He first speaks; then John makes an effort to turn and get a full view of Jesus. That symbolizes our Christian walk. We first hear His voice speaking to us. Then as we seek Him with all our hearts, He comes into full view, and Oh, how lovely is our Lord!

Finally, Daniel sees Jesus as High Priest and advocate above general waters where He gives the most awesome timing prophecy in the whole Bible. He has promised deliverance (chapter 8), He assures us who He is (chapter 10) and now (chapter 12) He tells us when that deliverance will come! God cares! If you have any question about that, study Daniel 8–12. He is leaving no room for doubt – if we study and know these astounding truths.

Next we will look at what the "time of the end" or "the end" means in these visions.

CHAPTER 5

THE "END-TIME" DECLARATIONS

Gabriel told Daniel in the twelfth chapter, *"But thou, O Daniel, shut up the words, and seal the book, even to the time of the end:"* (vs 4). How close is the "time of the end" to the end? If it is more than one generation, it's far. Jesus said that all the signs He presented (including Daniel 8, 11 and 12 and Matthew 24:15) would occur within one generation (Matthew 24:34). That seems to be a good place to begin.

Shutting up the words and sealing the book simply meant it wouldn't be *understood* until that *end-time*. Gabriel had just completed giving Daniel the *chazown* vision when he made the above statement (12:4).

Additional timing messages for that vision would yet be given (12:5-13) – by Jesus Himself. Yet, they too would be sealed. That barrier to understanding encompassed Daniel and all of God's people for the next 2500 years! This unique and crucial fact helps frame chapters 8–12. Repetitive allusions to the *chazown* vision messages occur in Revelation, but they also were not to be open to comprehension until the "time of the end."

When does this "time" refer to? Are we close enough to the end to be part of that increase in knowledge? The Bible explains itself if we look carefully. The Hebrew for the words "the end" is *eth qets*. This relates to an *extremity of time.* Its Old Testament use, however, is very special, *conveying a message related to a time of judgment.* It also draws upon a *period when* a people will be waiting for a wedding. The contextual imagery por-trays a time when the great controversy between good and evil is closing. It represents a time when punishment of the wicked occurs and God's people are ready for the marriage to the Lamb. It is a time of *finality*. This terminus is illustrated when the "end" of all flesh occurred at the flood (Genesis 6:13) or when the "end" of Israel came (Ezekiel 7:2-6). It is also used in the context where the *results* of the wedding ceremony will "know no *end*" in God's kingdom (Isaiah 9:7).

"The words of the angel to Daniel relating to the *last days* were to be understood *in the time of the end*. At that time, 'many shall run to and fro, and knowledge shall be increased.' 'The wicked shall do wickedly: and none of the wicked shall understand; but the wise shall understand.' Dan. 12:4, 10."[1]

If we believe we are in the time of the end, and most readers will, the time has arrived to fully grasp what the *eth qets* means. Incredible clues have already been given to us, telling that it would be during the time of judgment and when God's people are preparing in a special way to live with Jesus throughout eternity. We will discuss later in greater detail the timing of the judgment. However, to help us now, *that time* of final legal activity would occur *after* the end of the 2300 atonement evenings and mornings of Daniel 8:14.

"The message itself [Revelation 14:6-7] sheds light as to the time when this movement is to take place. It is declared

---

[1] White, Ellen G.; *The Desire of Ages*, p. 234.

to be a part of the 'everlasting gospel;' and it announces the opening of the judgment. The message of salvation has been preached in all ages; but this message is a part of the gospel which could be proclaimed only in the last days, for only then would it be true that the hour of judgment had come. The prophecies present a succession of events leading down to the opening of the judgment. This is especially true of the book of Daniel. **But** *that part of his prophecy which related to the last days* [*eth qets*], *Daniel was bidden to close up and seal 'to the time of the end.'*"[2] **After** the judgment was opened at the end of the 2300 evenings and mornings (atonement years), **another** time period would occur that, for Daniel and all others, was shut to understanding until that time came.

Let's now look at some of the *eth qets* insights Gabriel shared with Daniel. The remarkable *chazown* vision began in 8:1-12. Then Gabriel, on behalf of Daniel, asked Jesus, who was right there with them at the Ulai River, "How long shall be the vision?" (8:13). Jesus answered by not really answering. He gave that popular 2300-evening-and-morning prophecy in 8:14 (again, we'll deal with that later). Daniel was not satisfied (8:15). Jesus requested that Gabriel explain the "2300" *mareh* prophecy further – "make him understand!" But, amazingly, Gabriel began to explain verses 1-12, the *chazown* prophecy. Why? Because that was foundational to understanding the "2300" prophecy, which finally continued in chapter 9.

The reason the above paragraph is introduced here is to give a very brief background to something Gabriel now says in the middle of his *explanation* of

the *chazown* vision. There he helps us understand the *eth qets.* There are two crucial things he observed.

First, "Understand O son of man [speaking of Daniel – an honorable way to address Daniel – he was favored of God]: for at the time of the end [*eth qets*] shall be the vision [*chazown*]" (Daniel 8:17).

Did you catch that? At the *eth qets* (the end) will be the *chazown* vision. So *everything* that Daniel hears regarding that vision (which intermittently goes to the end of chapter 12) will be after the "2300" prophecy. In addition, the words "son of man," though here addressed to Daniel, draw upon its only use in the Old Testament of a divine personage found in Daniel 7:12. That imagery refers to the glorified Son of Man in the *executive judgment scene.*

Gabriel goes on with the second amazing revelation: "*And he said, Behold, I will make thee know what shall be in the last end* [future] *of the indignation* [God's wrath]*: for at the time appointed the end shall be*" (8:19). That's powerful. Let's study it further.

The Hebrew word for "last end" is *acharyth* and refers here to the *prophetic future.* In this context Daniel would be given specifics of what would occur in the future around the time of the *zaam* – God's wrath. When is that? That is answered in the book of Revelation. It is well after the "2300" prophecy ends. It is talked about in several places, including within the third angel's message of Revelation 14 and in 16:18-20.

Now comes the most important information. "*At the **time appointed** the end shall be*" (8:19).

If we know when the time appointed is (that's specific), we will know when the *eth qets* is. Isn't that incredible? Little clues are being dropped by Jesus and

[2] White, Ellen G.; *The Great Controversy,* pp. 355-356.

Gabriel to make sure that we make no mistake as to when the end of time is. What is the word for *time appointed? Mowed.* If we can understand when the *mowed* is, we will know when the *eth qets* is!

Will we be able to figure that out — that is, when the *mowed* is? Remember what Gabriel said at the beginning of the verse. "I will make thee know." He promised. That answer does come in a most wonderful way, but not for many years. In fact, it is so important and sensitive and full of legal and great controversy themes, Jesus will *personally* tell Daniel. Because there is so much other information that we need to go over to understand Jesus' response, we will visit that story later. But to give a hint, it is carefully and thoroughly answered in chapter 12. In fact, Gabriel's questions of 8:13 waited years for the answers, which are found right in that same chapter. They, too, were *personally* answered by Jesus.

Let's go over what we have learned in little thought packages:

1. After the 2300 evening and morning prophecy ends there would be a special period of time called "a time appointed" (*mowed*).

2. That period was sealed from understanding until the end of time.

3. That time, at the end of time, was called *eth qets* or "the end" — at the time of judgment and when all is ready for the wedding.

4. Thus, a puzzle is opened up for us: If we can figure out when that "appointed time" (*mowed*) occurs, we will know when the *eth qets* or "the end" really is.

5. God told us exactly how we can time this in Daniel 12.

6. This period is when the everlasting covenant *begins* to be completed.

7. It comes when God's wrath *begins* to be poured out.

We must now begin, once again, with the first part of Daniel 8 as Gabriel starts to unfold the *chazown* vision. Recall that chapters 8–12 are a unit. Now that we've noted the end-time, everlasting covenant setting, we can study more deeply the prophetic messages. Though the great controversy theme will start and develop there as a preface to Revelation, it is crucial to grasp a great legal opus unfolding. This swells as a giant wave approaching the shore or the crescendoing sound of a beautiful orchestra till, finally, by the end of Revelation all charges brought by Satan against God will have been settled, all promises to God's people to escape his accusations will have been judicially resolved.

CHAPTER 6

STRANGE ANIMALS REPRESENT WORLD POWERS
AND – SOMETHING ELSE FAR MORE IMPORTANT

*"In the third year of the reign of king Belshazzar a vision appeared unto me, [even unto] me Daniel, after that which appeared unto me at the first. And I saw in a vision; and it came to pass, when I saw, that I [was] at Shushan [in] the palace, which [is] in the province of Elam; and I saw in a vision, and I was by the river of Ulai. Then I lifted up mine eyes, and saw, and, behold, there stood before the river a ram which had [two] horns: and the [two] horns [were] high; but one [was] higher than the other, and the higher came up last. I saw the ram pushing westward, and northward, and southward; so that no beasts might stand before him, neither [was there any] that could deliver out of his hand; but he did according to his will, and became great. And as I was considering, behold, an he goat came from the west on the face of the whole earth, and touched not the ground: and the goat [had] a notable horn between his eyes. And he came to the ram that had [two] horns, which I had seen standing before the river, and ran unto him in the fury of his power. And I saw him come close unto the ram, and he was moved with choler against him, and smote the ram, and brake his two horns: and there was no power in the ram to stand before him, but he cast him down to the ground, and stamped upon him: and there was none that could de-*liver *the ram out of his hand. Therefore the he goat waxed very great: and when he was strong, the great horn was broken; and for it came up four notable ones toward the four winds of heaven"* (Daniel 8:1-8).

Standing in vision by the beautiful Ulai River, perhaps even sensing being away from his pressing duties in Babylon, Daniel is now given details of this *chazown* vision (8:1-2). Supernatural revelations were not new to him, but this time it would be one of the most frightening experiences he would ever have. As he went into vision he was first aware of where he was, then he looked "up" and saw a ram (*ayil*). Let's see if we can discover why God began this amazing vision this way.

THE RAM (8:3)

This animal, a male sheep, has a rich history in the Old Testament. In the context of what is being introduced here, it is a sanctuary animal used to typify making everything *right with God or being in a binding covenant dedication to Him*. It was the sacrificial animal, symbolizing the Deliverer and Restorer. This was illustrated in many ways, such as:

1. One of the animals slain when God instituted His covenant with Abraham (Genesis 15:9)

2. A guilt offering (Leviticus 5:15, 19:21-22)

3. One of the animals used in burnt offerings (Numbers 28:11, I Chronicles 29:21)

4. On Mount Moriah when Abraham was about to slay Isaac, it was a ram that became his substitute (Genesis 22:13). It therefore **symbolized Jesus – the Deliverer.**

5. And, of special importance, a ram was part of the Day of Atonement services (Leviticus 16:3, 5), even being called the "ram of atonement" (Numbers 5:8).

6. This animal was further illustrated by those Israelites who took vows to become a *Nazarite*. They offered a ram as a peace and *purification* offering. They became "holy unto the Lord" through that ritual (Numbers 6:8).

Yet, in Daniel 8:20 we are told it represented Medo-Persia. Why? That nation would **deliver** God's people out of Babylon. This is so important for us to grasp! That *era* will also help set the timing for atonement prophecies, which occur far in the future! The ram's typology begins to open the door to an incredible mystery of *how and when the covenant promise will be completed.* Chapters 8–12 are all about *finishing* the everlasting covenant with God's holy people. How? Through deliverance and restoration. Those chapters also tell how Satan will fight to prevent that from ever happening. That *deliverance ram* was a perfect way to begin this amazing story.

On the Day of Atonement, the people became *holy unto the Lord.* The ram, on that Day, came to the altar (note this) *from the east*, moving towards the west, proleptically pointing to the second coming of Jesus from the east for His holy people!

Does this sound like something exciting is developing? We are beginning one of the most amazing prophecies in the Bible. Already we have seen imagery from Daniel's day all the way up to the second coming of Jesus. Before we go further, there is more to examine.

If this vision *begins* with Medo-Persia, something has already happened to Babylon (according to the sequence of the Daniel 2 image and beast vision of chapter 7) – *Babylon is fallen.* That information ties to prophecies in Revelation. Two immediately come to mind:

"Babylon is fallen, is fallen, that great city, because she made all nations drink of the wine of the wrath of her fornication" (Revelation 14:8).

"Babylon the great is fallen, is fallen, and is become the habitation of devils, and the hold of every foul spirit" (Revelation 18:2).

How did physical Babylon fall? Daniel 5 says King Belshazzar saw that bloodless hand write a message on the wall – that God's representative, Daniel, interpreted. Babylon was found wanting, numbered and finished. How? At that moment Cyrus, *who came from the east*, had dried up the Euphrates (which ties to the sixth plague) so the kings of the east might come and enter the city, causing Babylon to fall!

Was Cyrus an important figure in prophecy? He not only brought down Babylon (a great symbol of apostasy in the book of Revelation), but he prefigured the Messiah.

Cyrus	Jesus
My shepherd (Isaiah 44:28)	Good shepherd (John 10:11, Hebrews 13:20)
His anointed (Isaiah 45:1)	God anointed Him (Acts 10:38)
Came from the east (Isaiah 46:11)	Comes as lightning from the east (Matthew 24:27)
Set captives free (Isaiah 45:13)	Deliverance of captives (Luke 4:16)
Called righteous (Isaiah 45:13)	The Righteous (I John 2:1)[1]

Suddenly, we find ourselves right at the very beginning of this prophecy, looking into the face of a message with broad duality of meaning! Let's outline what has been discovered so far.

Daniel's Day	End-Time
Babylon fallen	Babylon fallen
Time period when Babylon falls	Time period when Babylon falls
Rise of Medo-Persian period when 2300-year prophecy begins	Time period after 2300-year prophecy ends
Ram – symbolic of deliverance	White horse – symbolic of those with deliverance message
Ram represents God's people becoming holy	144,000 represent God's people who are sealed
Cyrus comes from the the east	Jesus comes from east (Matthew 24:27)
Cyrus symbolizes Jesus	Jesus is coming
Ram introduces how the covenant promise will be completed	Story of the Everlasting covenant being finished

---

[1] Robertson, Patricia; "Cyrus – A Great Biblical Exemplar," *EndTime Issues…,* February 2003.

STRANGE BEHAVIOR (8:4)

Suddenly, Daniel sees the ram pushing towards the west, north and south. Where, then, is he coming from? As noted under the Day of Atonement imagery above, he is coming from the *east!*

Pushing (*nagach*) means to thrust with its horns. As it exercised its power, coming from the salvic east, it became great. This ram's kingdom was so strong no one was able to defeat him. His influence and power filled the earth.

Daniel was astonished and intrigued. The Bible says he was diligently meditating on or "considering" this message. The ram was now in control of the four directions of the earth. Its influence was worldwide. The ram was even able to accomplish exactly what he desired. That is, until something most unexpectedly happened. And here another dual application is introduced.

THE TERRIBLE HE-GOAT (8:5-8)

The second beast to appear to Daniel was this swift male goat, moving so quickly that its feet didn't touch the earth. Knowing the sequence of kingdoms from Daniel 2 and 7, we see that this goat was a symbol for Greece. That is exactly what Daniel 8:21-22 confirms.

It displayed violent action against the ram as described in verses 6-8. Historically, its initial great horn represented Alexander the Great, who conquered Medo-Persia; and the four horns that came up afterwards were the four succeeding generals – Lysimachus, Cassander, Seleucus and Ptolemy. But – that is where the similarities to the previous *kingdom* stories must end.

We've seen that there are no animals in this *chazown* vision to represent Babylon. Interestingly, there is no animal to represent what followed Greece – that is,

Rome. This goat was the last. Why? The great spiritual truths God is presenting didn't require rehashing something already given two times before. The Persia–Greece *time period* serves as a time marker to begin the 2300-year prophecy of Daniel 8:14. But wait! Gabriel said that this vision was for the time of the end (8:17) and for the time appointed at the time of the end (8:19). Something else of end-time importance must be introduced in this he-goat/Greece symbol. If the ram represented the powers that bring deliverance to God's people and Greece came to destroy Medo-Persia, this goat must be a power trying to thwart the deliverance and restoration of God's people!

The he-goat was also a sanctuary animal. Recall that this part of Daniel was written in Hebrew for "Israel." From now on whatever will unfold in the rest of this chapter and book is specifically for God's *chosen people* to grasp. Since the atonement deliverance ram is a sanctuary animal, *in this setting*, the he-goat must also relate to sanctuary imagery at atonement.

Let's look at this he-goat closer. Jesus made an interesting observation in the New Testament that when He, the Son of Man, came in His glory at the great harvest, the *sheep* and the *goats* would be divided. The sheep would be on His right hand, the goats on His left. Then He explained: The sheep were blessed and were invited to inherit the Kingdom. The goats were cursed and ordered to depart to the everlasting fire prepared for the devil and his angels (Matthew 25:32-34, 41). The sheep and goats – God's people versus Satan's. Is that the message of Daniel 8? Let's look.

On the Day of Atonement two goats were chosen. One to represent Jesus and His blood that cleanses from sin (Hebrews 10:4); the other, Satan. The sins of all repentant Israel that were cleansed by Jesus' blood, were transferred to the goat, *symbolizing Satan*. That goat was led into the wilderness to die with those sins (Leviticus 16:21). Satan will bear the "goat" sin curse of all the righteous during the millennium. During that time the earth will be *desolate* – an issue addressed shortly in *this* prophecy.

Something is starting to fall into place. The "atonement ram" is contrasted with the "sin goat" Jesus versus Satan – God's people versus Satan's. This must be the *time* when Jesus is delivering God's people in an atonement process and Satan's people or agents will fight them or persecute them, trying to prevent that from ever happening. That is *exactly* what this vision is all about.

Ancient Time	**End of Time**
He-goat – "Greece"	Satan – time short
Harms ram – people at time of Babylon's fall	Makes war with saints
Delivered by the "anointed" Cyrus	Delivered by the anointed Jesus

"I saw Satan would work more powerfully now than ever he has before. He knows that his time is short and that the sealing of the saints will place them beyond his power; he will now work in every way that he can and will try his every insinuation to get the saints off from their guard and get them asleep on the present truth or doubting it, so as to prevent their being sealed with the seal of the living God.—Ms 7, 1850, pp. 2, 3. ('A Vision God Gave Me at Brother Harris',' August 24, 1850.)"[2]

Note what the he-goat did to the ram:

---

[2] White, Ellen G.; *Manuscript Releases,* vol. 8, p. 220.

1. Ran into the ram with the fury of its power (vs 6)

2. Smote (*nakah*) the ram – meaning strikes it, might even kill it (Jesus, martyrs)

3. Cast him to the ground

4. Stomps (*ramac*) on him. In this setting, ram not killed but persecuted.

What does all this mean? Christ and Gabriel will continue to lay out the beautiful meaning of this. It is going to unfold like an orchestra playing its musical scores. For now, let's simply look briefly at this foundational imagery to help us in our subsequent study.

Ram	He-goat
Atonement ram	Guilt/sin bearer
Jesus	Satan
God's people	Satan's people
Ancient and Spiritual Israel	Apostates
Deliverance	Bondage, death
Love, liberty	Hate, persecution

Everyone represented by the he-goat hates all those represented by the ram. They are in controversy, in fact, *the great controversy* between good and evil, right and wrong, sin and righteousness. And that is what the rest of the chapter is all about. As previously noted, the Persian empire begins the *timeframe* when the 2300 atonement evenings and mornings begin. It also heralds the onset of the final cleansing *period* allotted to God's people, the 70 weeks of years (Daniel 9). That, too, as we will discover, has a dual application.

The "ram of atonement," the ram of "peace/purification offering of the Naze-rite," focuses on the time *when* God's people will become holy unto Him and be delivered. We will discover that this is when they become legally and morally perfect. Chapters 8–12 are filled with legal language. Most of this prophecy relates to the time *after* the 2300 atonement years end. Then the antitypical Day of Atonement will begin. This will come to *focused* significance when the *mowed* or "appointed time," first mentioned in 8:19, arrives. "For at the *time appointed* the end shall be." (Reviewed in the previous chapter.)

Two great time periods are opening up to us. One represented by the fall of Babylon (Persian Empire setting), the other *after* the 2300 years are completed when another Babylon falls. From now on to the end of the book, both will be addressed. The progressive focus, however, is on the *end*. Remember the *eth qets* from the last chapter!

The imagery of the ram and the he-goat shows that at the time God's people become "holy," a power with "fury" or "choler" will smite or persecute them. When does this happen? At the sealing (Revelation 7) and the fifth Seal (Revelation 6) they will have no fighting power (*koach*); which means, though weak, they or what they represent still endures. The ram might even *appear* as dead, like the two witnesses of Revelation 11. All this implies that though God's holy ones, His remnant, will be stomped upon, cast down and made "helpless," they still have the capacity to *endure*.

A very important piece of information must be emphasized. Satan and his agents do come to their end. This is part of the incredible message in chapters 8–12. The he-goat power will soon be *represented* by the *little horn power* which shortly thereafter will become the *king of the north*, which comes to its end.

Now, let's look at that *little horn* power. That is the next story in this astonishing saga. Gabriel put it right here in the *chazown* vision. There are two *little* *horn* time periods introduced in Daniel. We will now discover which one this *little horn* represents.

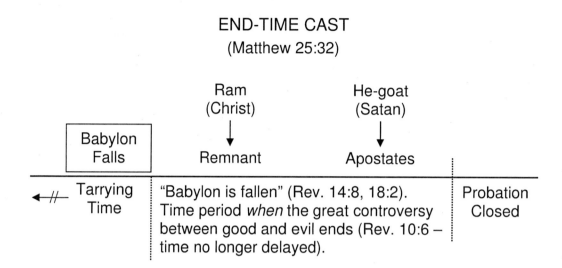

 END-TIME CAST
(Matthew 25:32)

	Ram (Christ) → Remnant	He-goat (Satan) → Apostates	
Babylon Falls			
←—//— Tarrying Time	"Babylon is fallen" (Rev. 14:8, 18:2). Time period *when* the great controversy between good and evil ends (Rev. 10:6 – time no longer delayed).		Probation Closed

CHAPTER 7

THE EVIL LITTLE HORN – WHENCE DOES IT COME?

"And out of one of them came forth a little horn, which waxed exceeding great, toward the south, and toward the east, and toward the pleasant [land]" (Daniel 8:9).

The study of the ram and he-goat opens up exciting information of a *restoration atonement typology*. In fact, soon we will see that it is a Jubilee Atonement. But what about that *little horn*? One immediately is tempted to go back and review the *little horn* of Daniel 7:8, 20-21 and 24-26 that had a face, mouth and power to subdue kings and hurt the saints. In fact, the parallels are so close, many scholars have said they are exactly the same in repeated prophecy, called *recapitulation*.

Before we're tempted to go down that path, there are two other issues, 104 often overlooked, that need addressing. One, there are significant *differences* between the two horns. Two, the timing clues reflect an altogether different period of history. Keeping those in mind, let's see how the *little horn* is introduced.

"Therefore the he-goat waxed very great: and when he was strong, the great horn was broken; and for it came up four notable ones toward the four winds of heaven. And out of one of them came forth a little horn, which waxed exceeding great." Daniel 8:8-9a.

The *little horn* arises out of "one" of "them" and becomes exceedingly important and powerful (*gadal*) just like the he-goat did. What does the *little horn* arise from? Is it from "one" of the four horns or Grecian kings of the he-goat? (In chapter 7 the *little horn* came out of the Rome beast.) The preceding noun is "winds" (the word "heaven" explains "winds"). Then, grammatically, it has to be from "one" of the "winds" of heaven, meaning one of the *directions* – north, south, east or west. The prophetic statement is *directional* and totally unrelated to empires or political origins. This can be shown through Hebrew studies.

The *little horn* waxed exceedingly great and (*here it comes*) "towards the south and towards the east and towards the pleasant *land* [or west]" ("land" is not in the original text) (Daniel 8:9b). Where did the *little horn* come from? It came from the "winds" of the *north*. By coming from the north, its power spreads throughout the world.

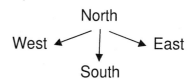

Why did it come from the north?

Psalm 48:2 says God's throne is in the north. But this is an evil power, as we shall see. We then look to a surprising text in Isaiah.

"For thou hast said in thine heart, I will ascend into heaven, I will exalt my throne above the stars of God: I will sit also upon the mount of the congregation, in the sides of the north: I will ascend above

the heights of the clouds; I will be like the most High" (Isaiah 14:13-14).

Satan wanted to be like God and have His ruling and controlling power. *So do his agents*, such as the *little horn*. Winds represent strife and conflict. The *little horn* is an emissary of Satan, pretending to be God.

We are told in Daniel 8:23-25 that that *little horn*:

1. Harms God's holy people

2. Magnifies himself in his heart and

3. Stands up against the Prince of princes (Michael – God)

This *little horn* is anti-God and represents the papacy just like the *little horn* power of Daniel 7, which uprooted three kingdoms and ruled 1260 years. The latter came to its end (7:11) by force in 1798 via Napoleon's army. The *little horn* of Daniel 8 has power over the whole world and will come to its end "without hands" (8:25). The first rules until just before the judgment "sits" (7:26), and his rule is "taken away." The second, *as we will see*, comes *during* the judgment, after the 2300 atonement evenings and mornings. These are the first clues that it is a second rise of the papacy after the wound is healed, being vastly different from Daniel 7.

Putting this in perspective, there is a major time gap between the Grecian empire and this second rise of the papacy. The four he-goat horns rise toward the four winds (directional, over all the world). The *little horn*, in "the latter times" when the "transgressions are full" (8:23), arises from *somewhere* in the four directional corners of the earth. This time it will become a Biblically defined global power. When it comes to its end, it will be without hands. God controls its final destiny. Imagine if we tried to make the papacy come up at the time the Greek empire ended. It just wouldn't fit. Some expositors quickly rush in to claim the *little horn* represents two things: First, pagan Rome – then, papal Rome. That is an uninvited attempt to add to the Bible. There is no animal or beast in Daniel 8 as the bearer of the "little horn" or an associated symbol.

This chapter presents a second rise of the papacy, which is so important that Gabriel later gave Daniel 11 as a special reinforcement message. There, he presented two rises of the papacy to make this very clear!

In the next two chapters other clues of its last-day timing will begin to emerge. Next we look at how that evil horn misuses its power.

CHAPTER 8

THE LITTLE HORN ABUSES ITS POWER

"And it waxed great, [even] to the host of heaven; and it cast down [some] of the host and of the stars to the ground, and stamped upon them. Yea, he magnified [himself] even to the prince of the host, and by him the daily [sacrifice] was taken away, and the place of his sanctuary was cast down. And an host was given [him] against the daily [sacrifice] by reason of transgression, and it cast down the truth to the ground; and it practiced, and prospered" (Daniel 8:10-11).

Just like the *little horn* power of Daniel 7, the end of time *little horn* defies God and hates His people. Satan dreamed of exalting himself above the clouds and stars, ascending right into heaven to the side of the north and trying to sit right on God's throne, even appearing like Him (Isaiah 14:13-14). Revelation 13 shows the fulfillment of his dreams through kingdoms and people, acting out his wishes. This *little horn* is the *first introduction* as to how that will play out at the end of time. It personifies Satan so closely one could almost say it is he. Here the papacy is his perfect ambassador. Let's discover why.

Daniel 8:10-11: The *little horn* "waxed great." This comes from the Hebrew word *gadal*, meaning it increased in power and authority. This didn't come suddenly but developed and crescendoed. In fact, its greatness was exerted against the "host of heaven." Host (*tsaba*) means a carefully regimented group of people, *God's army.* It implies that they are totally dedicated. Though

the sun, moon and stars are called "host of heaven" (Genesis 2:1), which is always recorded as a singular word, here in figurative Hebrew language, "host" is plural.

Heaven (*shamayim*) means either the physical heavens or the abode of God. The stars (*kowkab*) are personified as God's people, especially His leaders (cf. 12:3). The immediate context relates here to the physical heaven. Therefore, the very first things that Gabriel notes about the *little horn* are:

1. It would have increasing power and authority.

2. It would extend that power to or over God's loyal people.

Like an unexpected storm, the *little horn* imagery turns violent against the "host" and "stars." They are cast (*naphal*) fiercely to the earth. If that weren't enough, the *little horn* stomps (*ramac*) on them. This immediately brings to mind the "Gentiles" *treading underfoot* God's church (Revelation 11:2) and satanic powers *warring* against God's people (Revelation 12:17; 13:7), all in an end-time setting.

Now we can begin to understand the *little horn*'s mission:

1. Neutralize God's people, His loyal army and their leaders

2. Persecute them

3. War against them

This is a description of spiritual warfare at the highest level. A battle is now underway. God's people, for a while, become its victims.

Why would the papacy or *little horn* do these terrible things? Like the leaders of Christ's day, truth undermines the credibility and authority of falsehood. God's remnant people threaten the very foundation of that horribly false antichrist system.

That *little horn* doesn't stop there. Now the real *anti-God* spirit of this power is portrayed. It "waxes great" to heaven and to the "prince of the host" (vs 11). The same word (*gadal* – "waxed great" or "magnified" himself) is used. It exhibits a growing defiance against God, the head or *Prince* (*sar*) of His army. What else is this wonderful *Prince* called? Michael – "the great prince" (Daniel 10:13, 20-21, 12:1). He is also the "Prince of Peace" (*sar-shalom*) (Isaiah 9:5).

God is so intent that everyone understand what this *little horn* power represents, He embellishes many of these thoughts again! (Daniel 8:25 and 11:36-37). With these texts collectively, we discover:

1. Craft and deceit is his policy

2. He arrogantly magnifies himself

3. By peace he destroys (others do his evil work)

4. Does whatever he wants

5. Exalts himself above every god

6. Speaks against God

7. Doesn't honor the God of the early Christian church

8. Undermines the very dignity of women

Already we've seen how he persecutes God's people, those who repre-

sent Him. A picture now of unprecedented haughtiness and disdain for God is painted. It is so bad, the actions of the *little horn* are so ghastly, shocking and horrendous, it is repeated several times to convince any doubter how terrible the papacy is.

This is what God said through that mighty angel (8:11b). *Here it is*: "by him [the *little horn* – papacy] the daily [sacrifice not in original] was taken away, and the place of his [*Prince* of the host] sanctuary [God's dwelling place] was cast down." First, we saw arrogant actions against God by harming His people; now, it attempts to destroy two important things *directly related* to Him (Messiah the Prince):

1. The "daily"

2. The "*place* of his sanctuary"

We can assume right here that these two things must be very important to God and threaten the papacy so much that it must get rid of them!

Let's first look at the "daily" or *tamiyd*, meaning *continual – perpetual.* This is used as a descriptive adjective in most places in the Old Testament, referring to the morning and evening burnt offering. That's why so many translators wrongly add the word "sacrifice" after the word "daily." But here *it is a noun* – the *tamiyd* is "taken away." A similar message is noted in 11:31 and 12:11!

Let's pause and simply catch our breath. What has been happening in these two verses? The *little horn* is:

1. Against God's people

2. Against God

He persecutes and now takes away two very special things that belong only to God. To make sure we don't forget, E. G.

White had an insightful reminder: "Then I saw in relation to the 'daily' (Dan. 8, 11, 12) that the word 'sacrifice' was supplied by man's wisdom, and does not belong to the text."[1]

Where in the Bible is *tamiyd* used in relation to the "sanctuary?" The sanctuary is where God resides or tabernacles. His dwelling place or sanctuary is cast (*shalak*) down, abandoned or destroyed. The Hebrew word for "place" used in this verse is *makown*. This is a little-used word in the Old Testament and usually refers to God's *dwelling place*.

Those expressions mean a false or deceptive power (*little horn*) enters God's place of dwelling (our hearts, God's church, His throne room in heaven). It sets aside or abandons something that is *perpetual* or *ongoing*. What is perpetual or ongoing in the "sanctuary?" If the sanctuary is God's dwelling place (that is the reason it exists), His continual presence must be replaced with the presence of something evil! Isn't that what Satan has been trying to do (Isaiah 14:13-14)? Isn't that what the papacy is all about – trying to be like God? They ever claim to be God and to change His laws!

Then where is *tamiyd* used, showing that it represents God's continual presence in the sanctuary? *This is one key to understand the "daily." Here are the places*:

- *Tamiyd* is used for the shewbread of continuity or continual presence of God.

  "And thou shalt set upon the table shewbread before me always [tamiyd]" (Exodus 25:31).

  "Every Sabbath he shall set it in order before the Lord continually

[tamiyd] *... by an everlasting covenant." Leviticus 24:8. It is called the "continual (tamiyd) shewbread"* (II Chronicles 2:4, Numbers 4:7).

- *Tamiyd* is used to indicate the perpetual light from the golden candlesticks.

  "Without the veil of the testimony, in the tabernacle of the congregation, shall Aaron order it from the evening unto the morning before the LORD continually [tamiyd]: [it shall be] a statute for ever in your generations. He shall order the lamps upon the pure candlestick before the LORD continually [tamiyd]" [Leviticus 24:3-4 (cf. Exodus 27:20-21)]. *"He shall order the lamps upon the pure candlesticks before the Lord continually [tamiyd]."*

- *Tamiyd* is used to represent the continual burning of incense at the altar of incense.

  "And Aaron shall burn thereon sweet incense every morning: when he dresseth the lamps, he shall burn incense upon it. And when Aaron lighteth the lamps at even, he shall burn incense upon it, a perpetual [tamiyd] incense before the Lord throughout your generations" (Exodus 30:7-8).

- *Tamiyd* is associated with the continual presence of God in the cloud and fire above the tabernacle: *"So it was alway [tamiyd]: the cloud covered it by day, and the appearance of fire by night"* (Numbers 9:16).

In the golden candlestick we see God's perpetual presence through His Spirit (symbolizing spiritual power). In the shewbread was God's presence, continually on His throne at the side of the north, as the

---

[1] White, Ellen G.; *Early Writings*, p. 74.

33

staff of life. This was renewed each Sabbath, drawing on the imagery of renewal, the Creator and His sovereign Lordship. In the altar of incense we see represented the mediatorial work of Jesus and His atoning blood ever pleading for man.

What does the *little horn* do to take away or remove the heavenly presence from the tabernacle?

There is an astonishing parallel in II Thessalonians 2. Just before Jesus comes, the man of sin will be "revealed" (*apokalupto* – unveiled to the world). Paul said, "Let no man deceive you" (vs 3). What does it say about that man of sin?

- He opposeth and exalteth himself above all that is called God

- He is as God

- Functions as if he is sitting in the *temple* of God

- He has deceivableness of unrighteousness

- His followers don't receive the love of truth

- Then he and the wicked will be revealed

- The mystery of iniquity will be taken out of the way

- Then Jesus comes

Paul outlined exactly what we have been studying here in Daniel! This *little horn* is the end-time rise of the "man of sin."

God's work of providing light, intercession and life is taken away. Jesus' work on man's behalf, His righteousness in the incense, His cleansing blood is blocked from working on men's hearts.

The Sabbath renewal in the life of the shewbread is gone. We are given beautiful discernment relative to this in Numbers 4:7. God is instructing what goes on the table of shewbread. Of the many things, the last and most important is the "bread of continuity" – *lechem tamiyd.* That's our next key to understanding the "daily!" This bread was refreshed every Sabbath morning (Leviticus 24:5-8). The Sabbath renewal was represented each week by replenishing the bread.

The twelve loaves, representing each of the twelve tribes, symbolized God's continual presence among them. They depicted a holy, unbroken relationship with them. The Sabbath became a symbol of *when* His presence was refreshed. The bread of life (John 6:37-38) came to them in a special way that day. The *little horn* does something to take that refreshing presence of God away! God's authority is somehow defied and His unbroken presence ceases.

The holy Sabbath renewal is a revival of man's relationship with God and He with them. This shewbread was often referred to as the "bread of His presence." The *little horn* takes the place of God. We shall see shortly that he does this by blocking God's law from being written in the heart (Jeremiah 31:33, Hebrews 8:10).

In place of the lifesaving presence of God, man's presence and power are appealed to through artificial standards and claims. He is "sitting in the temple of God," trying to be "as God!" The *little horn*'s agents try to forgive sins, crucify Jesus over and over in the eucharist and claim salvation through an earthly organization.

The *little horn* promotes, as we will see shortly, a terrible sin against God. This breaks the covenant relationship with heaven, and it leads to a barrier to God's dwelling in or tabernacling *with us*. In that sin, claims of redemption are transferred to man. *In this, only Satan's presence can now be with man (little horn imagery).*

In the final "key" that God has tucked into the wonders of the Old Testament, this Sabbath renewal is part of the everlasting covenant! What is man's *continual* reminder of God's promise to restore man?

"Wherefore the children of Israel shall keep the sabbath, to observe the sabbath throughout their generations, [for] a perpetual covenant" (Exodus 31:16).

The "daily" refers specifically to the Sabbath as God's perpetual refreshing presence. It is a continual reminder of His power and promise to complete the everlasting covenant! That's what it said in Leviticus 24:8 – it was a reminder of the covenant.

We are told that a "transgression" that becomes an "abomination" leads to that "daily" being taken away.

- Sin – transgression – becomes a

- Barrier to God's presence. In turn,

- The covenant relationship is broken

- His indwelling presence in man ceases.

- Satan's power is now in control.

- The Sabbath – a reminder of creation's power (the power of creation is forgotten) is thwarted.

The crucial question that we must now answer: "What mysterious sin could do this terrible thing and throw truth to the ground?" It is so vital for us to discover the answer to this question that Gabriel will be very specific. It is related to the *tamiyd.* That's what the next chapter is all about!

CHAPTER 9

THE LITTLE HORN'S SIN

"And an host was given [him] against the daily [sacrifice] by reason of transgression, and it cast down the truth to the ground; and it practiced, and prospered" (Daniel 8:12).

Previously, we saw the papacy exercising power against God's people, persecuting them, arrogantly speaking and acting against God and causing the refreshing *Sabbath bread of His presence* to be abandoned from the heart. That corrupt organization changed so many of God's laws by *tradition* (much of it with pagan roots) that God could no longer dwell in the sanctuary (church or heart).

If this all seems overwhelming to you, we want to stop briefly, just for you – Gabriel is describing the most terrible persecution that God's people will ever experience. He is presenting Satan and his agents at their most powerful and devilish hour with overt hatred towards man and God. But – as a good counselor and adviser always does, Gabriel says, Hope is coming. And what beautiful hope it is. Let's continue our study together. Wonderful and encouraging things will soon be shared.

We've seen so far this anti-God force impeding the atonement process, opposing the covenant relationship and, with resistance, trying to create a schism between God and His people. In what we have already learned, we can conclude that the papal *little horn* has become *exceedingly* powerful. He is doing something to take away the divine Sabbath presence from the sanctuary of man's heart and His people.

The ram represents Jesus and His sacrificing people who are seeking to become a pure covenant host. The he-goat symbolizes Satan and his people coming against them – just like Greece came against Persia. *The little horn is Satan's last-day representative who is out to hurt the final stages of the redemptive process.*

We have seen what this papal power will do, but what is the great "sin" or transgression that *causes* all these terrible things to come about? The pivotal text in this message is verse 12: *"And an host was given [him] [little horn] against the daily sacrifice by reason [here it is] of [transgression], and it cast down the [truth] to the ground; and it practiced, and prospered"* (Daniel 8:12).

Previously, the Hebrew word for host (*tsaba*) related to the heavenly Prince's people. Now, using the very same word, Gabriel says the *little horn* also has a "host" against the "daily" or God's restorative presence, especially His *divine Sabbath presence.* This imagery of support ties with Revelation 13:3 where there is loyalty to the *beast* (another symbol of the papacy) from the *whole world.*

The basis for all the actions of the *little horn* is a *transgression* (*pesha*). This word symbolizes those who reject God's *authority, laws and covenant.*

1. Authority – as Creator

2. Laws – standards of God's kingdom

3. Covenant – restoration agreement

In the context of the ram and the he-goat, we see the conflict between good and evil. In the abandonment of the "daily" we find a rebellion against God's presence and His Sabbath rest. In the challenge against God's dwelling place in the sanctuary we see a man-produced barrier impeding the convicting work of God in man's heart. This is rebellion against the very atonement covenant process. God had previously inspired David to write: *"Thy way, O God, is in the sanctuary: who is so great a God as our God?"* (Psalm 77:13). The word for "sanctuary" is *qodesh.* We will see that again in verse 14. *Qodesh* means a holy or a sacred place. It is wherever God's presence resides – His *temple.* That could be any place from our own hearts to His church to the sanctuary of heaven.

Here in Daniel the papacy and its supporters sin against God's covenant, His law and His authority. This transgression drives away God's presence. The power of His transforming grace is replaced by a man-made institution.

God's authority, the great objective of man's restoration (law) and His promise of rest (covenant), are *all embodied in the Sabbath commandment.* The *little horn*, the papacy, uses its power to undermine God's holy Sabbath day. *All the symbology seen in the previous few verses comes to this focal point.* The *pesha* is against the law that God wrote on stone and told us to "Remember." To actively war against God's people, appealing to laws that promote falsehood (a transgression), the *little horn* or papacy promotes a false Sabbath!

Amazing is the clarity of Scripture. The message defines the issue further by saying that truth is cast to the earth. Truth is *the* defining attribute of God. For man it depicts salvation and the way of life. This apostate power tears at that

foundation. To make this blasphemous power more hideous, Daniel said it *practiced* and *prospered.* The linguistics here means it *fashioned its own standards and prospered.*

How does the *little horn* sin?

1. It makes its own moral standards ("practiced" – *asah*)

2. It abandons truth

3. It blasphemes God – defies His authority

4. It takes away the Sabbath presence

5. It creates a barrier for the completion of the everlasting covenant

6. It impedes the Spirit working in the sanctuary of man's heart

7. It sets up a false sabbath against the fourth commandment

"In the last days those who are opposed to God shall prosper for a time through cunning and deceit (Daniel 8:12, 24f). But their success will be only temporary for God is preparing a time of judgment against all evil to accomplish His indignation (Daniel 11:36). It must be clearly affirmed that transgression of God's law will never finally succeed (Numbers 14:41)."[1]

Some of you may want to go back and restudy the last two chapters. In special language the terrible antics of the papacy are outlined. When each is studied, an amazing picture is painted. It is not unlike the fearful activity of the sea and earth beasts of Revelation 13 working together. Imagery is being developed

---

[1] Harris, R. Laird; *Theological Wordbook of the Old Testament,* vol. II, p. 819. Brown, Colin, General Editor; *New International Dictionary of New testament Theology,* vol. 2, p. 766.

that portrays the Babylon of Revelation, Jeremiah and Isaiah.

Next we will begin laying the groundwork to see when all this will happen.

Jesus told us when that appointed time would be. Of all things – when the *pesha* is matured! Exciting surprises and wonderful messages are just ahead.

CHAPTER 10

GABRIEL QUESTIONS JESUS

"Then I heard one saint speaking, and another saint said unto that certain saint which spake, How long shall be the vision concerning the daily sacrifice, and the transgression of desolation, to give both the sanctuary and the host to be trodden under foot?" (Daniel 8:13).

Two years previously, when encountering another vision (Daniel 7), Daniel struggled emotionally over what he was shown: "As for me Daniel, my cogitations much troubled me, and my countenance changed in me" (Daniel 7:28). "And the visions of my head troubled me" (Daniel 4:5).

In this vision he had just seen violence between the ram and the he-goat. Then the *little horn* hurt God and His people. Now he was once again filled with questions and concerns. "What is Gabriel trying to get across?," he thought. Daniel remained silent until *after* the 2300 prophecy (8:14) when he couldn't hold back any longer and asked "the meaning" (8:15) of this vision. In fact, things became so stressful he actually fainted (8:27). Because of this, both the *mareh* and *chazown* visions would have to be finished at other settings – years later!

Gabriel and Jesus knew what was going on. They came to help Daniel and all the students of his book. On Daniel's behalf, Gabriel is about to ask Jesus four questions that relate to the *chazown* vision. The answers wouldn't be finished for at least seven more years. BUT – Daniel never forgot those questions;

neither should we. This is how they unfolded.

"Then I heard one saint speaking and another saint said unto that certain saint which spake ..." (vs 13).

Don't be overwhelmed – this verse is really straightforward. That "certain saint" is Jesus and the saint speaking is the one which has been speaking all along – Gabriel. He prepares to ask those questions. Some margins call the "certain saint" the "wonderful numberer," but that is a Jewish scribe's suggestion which is not in the original. Yet, it fits in beautifully. The literal meaning, however, is "whoever it may be." This suggests Gabriel is about to ask a superior – the Holy One – the "nondescript," the "whoever it may be" – those questions.

That "certain saint" will appear to Daniel personally two more times before this book is finished! This is what each of those visits means:

1. Jesus as a "Certain saint" (8:13), a "man's voice" (8:16) – presenting the timing framework for the *mareh* and the *chazown* visions (they were different visions)

2. Jesus as King, Judge, Priest (10:5-6) – the defining imagery of Jesus as deliverer – and a beautiful segué into the book of Revelation

3. Jesus as High Priest – fully dressed in linen – final Day of Atonement imagery when the world will be divided into two groups (12:5-13)

Now the questions begin. Carefully look at each word. They are important to the last group of God's people – who are represented by the 144,000. Each question is packed with amazing revelation to us – right now.

"How long shall be the vision concerning the daily sacrifice, and the transgression of desolation, to give both the sanctuary and the host to be trodden under foot?" (vs 13).

Do you see something incredible? They are all *timing questions*. Gabriel is referring right back to the vision that has been unfolding. This question will come up again in Daniel and repeatedly in Revelation.

"How long" – or, more accurately, "till when" is the *chazown* vision? In essence, "When will this all happen?" "In what period of time in the future will this occur?" The answer begins in the next verse. Gabriel summarizes the key points of the vision *for Daniel* (and us) in this four-part question. We know Daniel is listening because he says, "then I heard." Here are those four key points:

When will the:

1. *Tamiyd* – continual *presence* of God be abandoned, especially related to the Sabbath?

2. *Pesha* – rebellion against God's authority, laws and covenant lead to desolation?

3. *Qodesh* – God's church be persecuted?

4. *Tsaba* – saints be persecuted?

How is Jesus going to answer? I'm sure Daniel is wide-eyed, leaning forward and concentrating very hard. Jesus is about to speak. He won't give us all the answers because Daniel simply can't get past the first part before fainting. Here is how those answers will play out:

1. Daniel 8:14 – Jesus tells us when spiritual deliverance occurs

2. Daniel 12:5-13 – Jesus tells us when physical deliverance occurs

Remarkable as it may seem, those responses are given in *legal* language. Why that way? Because Jesus is going to tell how the great controversy will end – legally – forever. When that happens God is *vindicated* and so are His people. Those answers have to be in legal language! He is also talking to the universe.

Before we begin to unfold one of the great Biblical mysteries, let's look at two Hebrew words we just mentioned. They're going to come up again.

The Hebrew word for "transgression" is *pesha*, which means sin or rebellion against God's *law*, *covenant* and *authority*. The word for "desolation," *shamen*, is associated with divine judgment or disaster. Later, we will find that this occurs when God expresses His indignation (*zaam*) or wrath (8:19) at the very end of time.

What is this all saying? The papacy or *little horn* will sin (*pesha*) against God's law, covenant and authority. This will lead to divine judgment recognized as God's wrath [which relates to the first four Trumpets and the Seven Last Plagues (Revelation 8, 16)]. Jesus, however, is going to get far more specific than that!

Let's listen now to His answer related to spiritual deliverance. Oh yes, the sanctuary will be cleansed – but that means far more than we've ever imagined!

CHAPTER 11

JESUS BEGINS TO ANSWER GABRIEL

"And he said unto me, Unto two thousand and three hundred days; then shall the sanctuary be cleansed" (Daniel 8:14).

Jesus is speaking here. We presume that Gabriel already knows the answer to all the questions he just asked the "Whoever it may be." Why? Jesus responds to Daniel: "He said unto me."

Remember that the four questions asked in 8:13 were all in the context of "How long," "Until when" or "When are all these things going to happen?" Jesus, in His great wisdom, chooses not to deal at first with the physical distress, persecution and hate against His people. "Daniel, your people will be spiritually delivered." We will have to wait until Daniel 12 for details related to the physical deliverance. We'll begin to analyze that in chapter 12 of this book.

Before we go on, you might be aware that many Bible translations, including the KJV, have wording errors. Daniel 8 and 9 are no exception. That is one reason there are so many strong and conflicting opinions relative to this particular verse.

The word "days" is not in the original. Neither is "sanctuary cleansed." The actual wording in Hebrew is: "Till evening–morning two thousand three hundred holy adjudicated."

Let's look step by step at these incredible words of Jesus.

Evening and morning is *Ereb boqer* – "dusk–morning" – each being a *time unit*. But together they convey a very powerful message. The very first use of this sequence came in Genesis 1:5, 8, 13, 19, 23 and 31. This is extremely important to grasp! – because many scholars try to make Daniel 8:14 represent only half days. In that Genesis account it means "there was an evening and there was a morning," delimiting the six days of divine creative activity. A Jewish day did begin with the morning and this was *the* ancient system for *computing time.* But there is a major *exception* in the Torah:

1. For festivals and sacred appointed times, the day began the evening *before* – more specifically:

2. The "night of the preceding day" became holy.

3. Examples:

   a. The Passover began on the evening before the fourteenth day of the first month (Exodus 12:6, 18).

   b. The exact same application is made for the Day of Atonement (Leviticus 23:28-32). That is where this text becomes so important – it refers to a *solemn appointed time.*

There is a "Sabbath of rest" built into this prophecy. What appointed evening–morning time or festival would tie to it? Since this *chazown* vision opened, the atonement ram of God's people and the evil he-goat (scapegoat – Satan) have been presented. They are associated with "God's dwelling place" or sanctuary imagery, which the *little horn* is trying to destroy (vs 11).

This chapter (Daniel 8) is referring to the final conflict right after Babylon falls. It is *when* God's people become holy. It is couched in *Day of Atonement* language!

The message Jesus gives here states that the things regarding Gabriel's questions will not occur until *after* 2300 atonement *evenings and mornings* are completed. Suddenly we know that it is 2300 years because the Day of Atonement was an *annual* feast! That is simply amazing information that has been tucked into that verse, waiting to be drawn out! Within the sacred *appointed time* setting, the "proof texts" that represent a day for a year or year for a day are *not* needed.

There is more. In this setting, a *restoration message* is being presented for a holy people. The *little horn* is out to thwart that from ever happening. The final controversy between good and evil is being described in ever-growing detail (which won't end until the completion of the book of Revelation). The 2300 Yom Kippur's, if you please, must pass before the *final atonement* or completion of judgment occurs. That's what the Day of Atonement was all about. It was when all the congregation of Israel was divided into two groups – those who repented and those who did not. That means that sometime after the 2300 years a judgment will be made that will be irrevocable! – a judgment with an atonement for some, a restoration before the Lord (Leviticus 23:28), and an eternal curse for others.

Remember, this verse (8:14) is Jesus' "general answer" to Gabriel's questions. Gabriel wanted to know when all the horrible little-horn activity would occur. Jesus says *after the 2300 years, but then im-mediately* talks about His people – those who will vindicate His name. What is He trying to convey?

Simply this: *Both* the *little horn*'s abusive behavior and the judgment occur *after* the 2300 atonement evening and mornings are ended. We'll learn more, far more, about the latter when we get to Daniel 9. But first, there is much more that Jesus put within that 8:14 *context* that we must concentrate on and understand.

Let's look at it further.

The final phrase, "then will the sanctuary be cleansed," is really made up of only two Hebrew words, *qodesh tsadaq. Qodesh* was used in the previous verse as "sanctuary," but *in a setting* that meant everything holy – God, His church and His holy people. God's people (church) and His name will become holy after the 2300 years. But He adds a very special word – *tsadaq.* What does that mean?

Tsadaq in this setting is a legal, ethical and theocratic expression denoting adjudication or vindication. The whole framework is couched in a Jubilee Day of Atonement (Leviticus 15, 25-26) setting where *full* restoration of holiness occurs. Taken together, *qodesh tsadaq* gives us a beautiful message of promise that after the 2300 years God's name, His church and His people will be holy and adjudicated – God will be vindicated and, together, an eternal, holy union will exist. All legal issues will be resolved. This is moral restoration of the kingdom of God. It is the completion of the everlasting covenant. To accomplish this, the sins in the soul temple *and* the heavenly sanctuary will all be removed or cleansed away by a legal act often referred to as "judgment."

Do you grasp what has been happening here in Daniel 8?

- This chapter is about the time when spiritual Babylon falls.

- The players in the conflict are God's people (His host) and Satan's representatives (the papacy and her host)

- God's law, covenant and authority will be tarnished and His people persecuted *after* the 2300 evening–morning atonement years.

- God's people and His church will be finally adjudicated sometime *after* the 2300 evening–morning atonement years, thereby vindicating God.

- They will be His eternal witnesses to His beautiful character. His righteousness will be seen in them. They will be holy. The 144,000 of Revelation are the living witnesses, bringing supreme honor to God.

Leviticus 19:2, 20 talks of God's ideal for man. It is holiness. I Peter 1:15-16 carries this on in New Testament imagery. Ellen G. White noted, "Moral perfection is required of all."[1] A condition will be reached of "sinlessness in which Adam lived before his transgression."[2]

Daniel 8:14 unfolds an incredible promise stemming from very pointed questions by Gabriel. God has much more to say about His standards of righteousness (9:24) and "when" this is to occur. Not only will the *little horn* persecute, but during this same period, God's people will become perfect – sealed – ready for translation. The exact "appointed time" for this is yet to be laid out *at some period in time* **after** the 2300 atonement evenings and mornings. We've alluded to it in the Preface. Even the three timing prophecies of Daniel 12 are all part of this amazing specific end-time message.

It is interesting to note that in Daniel 9, 490 years were given to ancient Israel to become holy. God knew before that vision was given that they would fail. That is why Daniel 8:14 was given *before* Daniel 9 – so we would *know* He knew! More on that later. This verse (8:14) is a remarkable message that He will someday still have a holy people – right at the end of time.

First, let's *revisit* Gabriel's follow-up to what Jesus just said. He uses words that will help us in the rest of our study.

---

[1] White, Ellen G.; *Christ's Object Lessons,* p. 330.
[2] White, Ellen G.; *Maranatha,* p. 224.

GABRIEL INTRODUCES END-TIME LANGUAGE

"Understand, O son of man: for at the time of the end shall be the vision.... And he said, Behold, I will make thee know what shall be in the last end of the indignation: for at the time appointed the end shall be." Daniel 8:17, 19.

Before we listen in on the third appearance of Jesus with Daniel in chapter 12, it would be very helpful to review once again Chapter 4 to refresh your thinking on the Hebrew words related to the "end of time."

Here is an outline of a few key points:

1. *"At the time [eth] of the end [qets] shall be the [chazown] vision (8:17)."*

   - Some of the older Strong's concordances incorrectly call this the *mareh* vision.

   - *Qets* refers to the end of time in the context of final preparations for a wedding.

   - *Qets* is also used to denote a time of final judgment.

   - From this verse alone we note the *chazown* vision is *end-of-time.*

   - In the next two chapters we will discover that it was the *chazown* vision that was sealed – not the *mareh.*

2. *"At the time appointed [mowed] the end [qets] shall be (8:19)."*

   - This is a very important timing statement. It tells us that if we discover when the *mowed* is, we will know when the end of time (*qets*) is.

   - That is exactly what Chapter 12 is all about.

   - Arguing further for the end-time setting in the first part of this verse, it shows that all these things relate to the indignation (*zaam*). That refers contextually to the time when God's wrath begins to be poured out right at the end.

If God painted on a canvas earthly events detailing the scenes of the last experiences of His people immediately preceding His return, it would be the subject of endless opinion, sensationalism and recycled hope – unless – there were timing clues to tell when it would happen. God is step by step developing very important thoughts about when the events of Daniel 8–12 will occur. Collectively, they create a timeframe into which the last half of Daniel and the book of Revelation fit.

Remember Gabriel's questions? They all related to *when* events would *occur.* Now we're going to tune into Daniel, who also has timing questions. He is going to personally address Jesus with questions as to *when* the events will *end.*

CHAPTER 13

DANIEL ASKS JESUS TIMING QUESTIONS

"And [one] said to the man clothed in linen, which [was] upon the waters of the river, How long [shall it be to] the end of these wonders? ... And I heard, but I understood not: then said I, O my Lord, what [shall be] the end of these [things]?" Daniel 12:6, 8.

This study begins the most important timing prophecies in the whole Bible! We have learned that *after* the 2300 atonement evening and morning prophecy several things would occur:

1. Babylon would fall.

2. The end (*eth qets*) would come.

3. It would be a time of judgment and wrath.

4. God would be vindicated.

5. The *little horn* or papacy would defy God and persecute His people.

6. The *little horn* would come to its end.

7. God's people would become holy.

8. At the "appointed time" (*mowed*) the end would be.

Gabriel's questions, asked over seven years previously about the papacy, remain unanswered (8:13). Jesus will answer those shortly. First, Daniel wants to know more about the future hope of God's people and their deliverance. What Jesus is about to say develops a timing framework that will show when the papal transgressions and the restoration of

God's people will occur during an "appointed time." Jesus will also tell us what begins the "appointed time," how long it will last and how it will end.

Just before Daniel reopens the timing concerns, he is introduced to Jesus once again. There, He is seen above the waters of the river. That river is unnamed but appears to be the Hiddekel or Tigris, last described in 10:4, whose waters represent God's people.

In the book of Revelation we repeatedly find the papacy trying to copy what Jesus did or does. One scene (Revelation 17) shows the harlot (apostate woman – the false church) sitting on waters – these represent her apostate people. Here we see Jesus above the waters of the river. Babylon was by the Euphrates River. The Hiddekel River was eastward, the direction of deliverance. Those were two of four Edenic rivers that watered the *eastward* Garden of Eden.

Here, Jesus, above the waters of the river, is described as being totally clothed in linen (*bad*). He was also in linen exactly the same way in Chapter 10 (vs 5). But there He displayed other exhibitions of His power as judge and king. Here He is seen as a High Priest on the Day of Atonement (Leviticus 16:4).

Holy linen coat Linen breeches Linen girdle Linen mitre	Collectively, they are called "Holy garments"

It is imagery of intercession and judgment. It symbolizes the great day of reckoning when eternal decisions are made. In that setting He can answer those questions of Gabriel and the queries of Daniel. As Priest and Judge He can tell God's people when things will come to an end. He is the arbiter of all destinies. This dress draws on the *final Jubilee Day of Atonement.*

Daniel is at the river noticing two individuals – one on either bank (12:5). In Jewish law legal matters can move forward in the presence of two witnesses (Deuteronomy 19:30-31). We are beginning to observe legal proceedings. Gabriel had posed questions of the defendant, advocate and judge. Now Daniel is about to start. The *chazown* vision was saturated with violence and hatred against God's people and against God Himself. All questions are focused on *one* thing: "*When* will justice come?" This proleptically echoes the cry of the martyrs of the fifth Seal of Revelation (6:10). What Jesus is about to say will answer all "How long?" questions for all time. This relates to the time of the end (*eth qets*), the appointed time (*mowed*).

Daniel's first question is at the end of verse 6, "How long *shall it be to* the **end** of these wonders?" Note specifically what he just asked. Gabriel, in 8:13, wanted to know when the *chazown* vision would *occur* or *begin*. Here Daniel wanted to know when the "wonders" of the *chazown* vision would *end!* Since Jesus has not answered either set of questions, we can now expect them both to be answered. But first – what does Daniel mean by "wonders?"

The Hebrew word for "wonders" is *pele* or *pelaot* and relates to the works and words of God. The *chazown* vision finally ended in 12:2. Several specific things came to their completion in rapid sequence there:

- End of papacy and evil agencies (11:40-45)
- Michael the great Prince stands up (vs 1)
- Time of trouble – worst in history (vs 1)
- God's people delivered – those written in the book (vs 1)
- Special resurrection (vs 2)

Those are the final "wonders" or things that finished up the *chazown* vision. Daniel wants to know when all these will end. He uses that special word we learned previously – *qets* for "end." "At what point in time, during judgment, will those things finally end?"

Daniel's question is so important. Many scholars feel that he is wanting to know when the evil career of the antichrist would come to an end. It's much broader than that alone. It is the timing of the last conflict between good and evil. Daniel wants to know when all this will finally be finished. After receiving a partial answer he repeats the question in verse 8, using different words: "What shall be the end of these things?" E. G. White put it this way: "Twice Daniel inquired, How long shall it be to the end of time?"[1]

Now Jesus – "the man clothed in linen" – lifts up His right *and* left hands to heaven and swears by Him that liveth forever (vs 7a). The right hand is lifted to assure truth, just as it is done in the courts of today. But the left hand – why did He raise that? Hebrew custom declared that when the left hand was raised, it was an oath against that person's blood – his life! In this incredible scene Jesus not only seals His words against the very authority of God but

---

[1] White, Ellen G.; *Testimonies to Ministers,* pp. 114-115.

50

places what He is about to say *regarding time* against His very life! He did shed.

Every reader should pause to think about what He is doing. There are three timing messages He is about to unveil. There is no other place in all the Bible where this legal gesture is used by a divine being! And, of all things, Jesus does it regarding *three timed prophecies.* What we are about to hear, Jesus placed His very life against! That makes them as important as His Word is! Those prophe-

His blood. The cross is our assurance that these prophecies will come true! cies tell exactly when evil will end, God will be vindicated and His people finally become holy. In the Daniel 8–12 theme, God and man are brought back into an eternal covenant relationship.

Now we will hear some of the most awesome prophecies in the whole Bible – directly from Jesus' lips – as to when, in the "appointed time," all things march to an end!

CHAPTER 14

THE THREE TIMED PROPHECIES OF DANIEL 12

"And I heard the man clothed in linen, which [was] upon the waters of the river, when he held up his right hand and his left hand unto heaven, and sware by him that liveth for ever that it [shall] be for a time, times, and an half; and when he shall have accomplished to scatter the power of the holy people, all these [things] shall be finished.... And from the time [that] the daily [sacrifice] shall be taken away, and the abomination that maketh desolate set up, [there shall be] a thousand two hundred and ninety days. Blessed is he that waiteth, and cometh to the thousand three hundred and five and thirty days" (Daniel 12:7, 11-12).

Few chapters in the Bible have created more opinion and conflict than this one. People like (with a little speculation mixed in) time predictions because they are "objective" and have an element of excitement. Jesus gives, however, very specific clues that make all speculation unnecessary. We have already been given very clear timing words, issues and events.

Remember, all the questions were associated with the *chazown* vision – that repetitive story of hostile events against God's people right at the end. Daniel just asked when that would all end. Here's the answer:

"It [the hostility] *shall be for a time, times and a half; when he* [king of the north – 11:40-45] *shall have accomplished* [finished] *to scatter* [persecute] *the power of the holy people* [remnant],

all these things [wonders of verses 1-2] *will be finished"* (Daniel 12:7b).

These remarkable thoughts tell us:

1. The hostility will last time, times and a half

2. Then the persecution ends and

3. The wonders will be finished

In review, what were those "wonders" that Daniel alluded to as to when the end of the *chazown* vision would be? (Daniel 11:40-45; 12:1-2):

1. King of North comes to an end (11:40-45)

2. Michael stand up (12:1)

3. Great tribulation (12:1)

4. Deliverance of God's people (12:1)

5. Special resurrection (12:2)

The Hebrew word for time here is *mowed*. Back in Daniel 8:19 we learned that if we could discover **when** this "appointed time" (*mowed*) or season was, we would know when the very end (*qets*) would be. Most scholars agree that in this setting *mowed* means a year. Thus, year (1), years (2) and half (6 months) equal three and a half years. Jesus is telling us that at the end of a three and a half year period the wonders of the *chazown* vision would be ended. All hostility against

God's people will end. The beauty of *deliverance* and the *resurrection* will occur at the end of that 1260-day period.

Many try to tie this to the 1260 years of papal power and suppression of the Dark Ages. That application lifts the whole Biblical setting out of context. The Dark Ages was a metaphor for what happens in literal time with these wonders right at the very end. Remember what we already discovered in 8:13 and 8:14. All these things must happen *after* the 2300 atonement evenings and mornings end.

At the end of time (*eth qets*), during judgment, is the "appointed time" (*mowed*). Now we know that the appointed time is 1260 days or three and a half years. Now we know what Habakkuk meant when he said that **at** the "appointed time" (*mowed*) the *tarrying* will no longer tarry! Note: This verse tells us when that period *ends.*

If we can discover when the appointed time begins, we will have a deeper understanding of that "appointed time." Jesus will tell us very closely when it does. Shortly after the appointed time ends is the *parousia* – the coming of Jesus. Will we know when that occurs? Only when He announces it. But we will know when it is near – "even at the doors" (Matthew 24:33). These great prophecies make it precision-clear as to *when* the tarrying time ends and the "appointed time" begins. We will discuss in later chapters how all this ties to Daniel 9, Revelation 11, 12 and 13. *This "appointed time" is the period that virtually the whole book of Revelation sits within.*

Mowed has even deeper implications. It's not only an "appointed time" but a time of religious assembly, a time to "meet the Lord" – the "tent of meeting" and a time to receive revelation. This is the time when God's people will be morally purified (*qodesh am*) and assembled

as His – forever. It is the time of the Loud Cry – the Trumpet's last call.

That is exactly what 8:14 said. After the 2300-"day" prophecy all God's people and His name would become holy and legally adjudicated! It all happens *when* the "tarrying time ends" and the "appointed time" begins.

"When Satan shall have accomplished his work of ensnaring all who will subject themselves to his deceptive influence, when he shall have finished his work of scattering abroad, Christ will rise up and bring deliverance to every one whose name is found written in the book of life. Satan and his followers will be destroyed. Then 'they that be wise shall shine as the brightness of the firmament; and they that turn many to righteousness as the stars for ever and ever.' [Daniel 12:3] –Letter 268, Dec. 17, 1903."[1]

This is how verse 7 looks graphically:

Deliverance of God's People
(vs 1)

1260 Days
(vs 7)

End *chazown* Vision

Special Resurrection (vs 2)

There is something *missing* in this timed prophecy – and that was done on purpose. We have an ending but no beginning. That comes in the next few verses.

Daniel is distraught because he simply doesn't understand (vs 8). Again, as we've already noted, he asks what that "future final end" means. Jesus tells him (just like Gabriel did in 8:26b) that the meaning would be kept from him and sealed until the time it would be fulfilled

---

[1] White, Ellen G.; *The Upper Look,* p. 365.

(vs 9) – at the very end of time (*qets*). But this still doesn't end what Jesus has to say.

In verse 10 Jesus clarifies that time as the point when there would be two classes of people in the world. We know that comes right at the end (Revelation 14). Again, that shows that the *chazown* ends during the last three and a half years of earth's history.

The words "the wise shall understand" are used in both Daniel and Revelation contextually to refer to the time Jesus will come again.

"*And he said, Go thy way, Daniel: for the words are closed up and sealed till the time of the end. Many shall be purified, and made white, and tried; but the wicked shall do wickedly: and none of the wicked shall understand; but the wise shall understand*" (Daniel 12:9-10).

"As the dew and the rain are given first to cause the seed to germinate, and then to ripen the harvest, so the Holy Spirit is given to carry forward, from one stage to another, the process of spiritual growth. The ripening of the grain represents the completion of the work of God's grace in the soul. By the power of the Holy Spirit the moral image of God is to be perfected in the character. We are to be wholly transformed into the likeness of Christ."[2]

Now comes another series of wonders for us today. Jesus is going to explain the 1260-day prophecy further by answering Gabriel's questions of 8:13. Many years have gone by. Daniel – and we – have had to learn more background information to get to this point. Let's listen in: "*And from the time [that] the daily [sacrifice] shall be taken away, and the abomination that maketh desolate set up,*

---

[2] White, Ellen G.; *Testimonies to Ministers and Gospel Workers,* p. 506.

[there shall be] a thousand two hundred and ninety days" (Daniel 12:11).

"From the time" means we are given a beginning. Intriguingly, *this* timed period doesn't have an ending. The 1290 days begins with the two main concerns that Gabriel had years ago (8:13): (1) The daily and (2) the abomination/transgression that leads to desolation.

The *little horn* – the papacy – takes away the continual presence of God by a transgression that removes God's authority, His law and covenant. He sits in the temple as if he were God. The Hebrew word here for abomination is *shigguwts.* This noun is always used to refer to idols that are abhorrent and detestable to God. Idols are an abomination (Jeremiah 16:18; Ezekiel 5:11, 7:20; II Chronicles 15:8). Now we have further insight into the *little horn*'s transgression (*pesha*) that removes the daily (*tamiyd*). An idolatrous standard is set up by the papacy, which begins the 1290 days. This takes away the presence of God. It is none other than the false Sabbath! It is the promotion of Sunday worship – a change of the Ten Commandments, which hold His character, law, authority and the keys to His everlasting covenant (see Chapter 8).

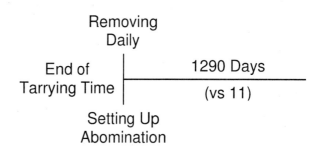

The word for days here is *yowm*. Daniel has been using this word for *literal days* elsewhere (1:14-15). In this context there is no reason to suddenly take this Hebrew word and make its meaning a year when there is no permission given. When *yowm* is used in the Old Testament and is used with a *number*, it *always* means literal days. Thus, we have:

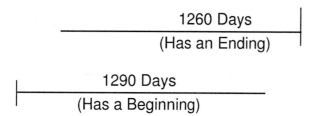

1260 Days
(Has an Ending)

1290 Days
(Has a Beginning)

At this point there is no beginning for the 1260 days nor ending to the 1290 days. Through verse 11, other than the lengths of time, it is unknown as to how far apart or close together these periods are.

The 1260 days ends with the deliverance of God's people and the special resurrection. The 1290 days begins with the Sunday laws.

Jesus now "fills in the gap." Verse 12 is a beatitude with promise. Yet the blessing is tied to a time period that has *neither* beginning nor ending. Those who wait for all these events and remain faithful through them, covering 1335 days, will be blessed. There it is – the beginning of the 1290 and the ending of the 1260 are 1335 days apart.

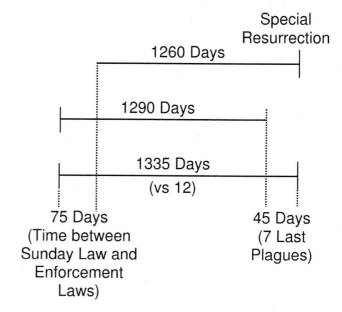

Special
Resurrection

1260 Days

1290 Days

1335 Days
(vs 12)

75 Days
(Time between
Sunday Law and
Enforcement
Laws)

45 Days
(7 Last
Plagues)

You protest – We are not to know when Jesus is coming! This is date setting!

1. What date? We haven't a clue from this when He is coming!

2. What coming? Daniel hasn't mentioned it. Jesus' coming is not at the deliverance of His people. That is when the day and hour are announced.[3] Jesus said we wouldn't know the day or the hour.

---

[3] White, Ellen G.; *Early Writings*, p. 15.

Let's listen to what He says. He tells us we will know when it is near, even at the doors (Matthew 24:33). Paul admonishes us to be children of the light so Jesus would *not* come as a thief (I Thessalonians 5:4-6).

We're now seeing the beginning and the ending of the *chazown* vision – the "appointed time" period, which encompasses issues that will occur during the last short period of earth's history.

There is a vast set of timing messages still tucked within Daniel 8–12. Type is to meet antitype! It transcends purely events. It drills deeply into the very bedrock of time. When God created this earth He introduced time. When He invoked prophecy, He placed it within segments of that time. They are His appointments for us to strengthen our faith and to *make clear the gospel message*! Remember what we discovered some time back? These timed prophecies will be part of the Loud Cry! They are to be enmeshed in the final gospel message. They give urgency to prepare for His coming.

Now we must go back to look at the *mareh* vision in more detail. This is the incredible story of how a holy people will be restored. It has far deeper meaning than we've ever discussed.

"We have no time for dwelling on matters that are of no importance. Our time should be given to proclaiming the last message of mercy to a guilty world. Men are needed who move under the inspiration of the Spirit of God. The sermons preached by some of our ministers will have to be much more powerful than they are now, or many backsliders will carry a tame, pointless message, which lulls people to sleep. Every discourse should be given under a sense of the awful judgments soon to fall on the world. The message of truth is to be proclaimed by lips touched with a live coal from the divine altar."[4]

---

[4] White, Ellen G.; *Testimonies*, vol. 8, pp. 36-37.

CHAPTER 15

DANIEL FAINTS –
THEN RECOGNIZES HIS MISTAKE

"And the vision of the evening and the morning which was told is true: wherefore shut thou up the vision; for it shall be for many days. I Daniel fainted" (Daniel 8:26-27a).

HE DIDN'T UNDERSTAND

When Daniel heard the 1260-year prophecy [time, times and dividing of times (7:25)] he was troubled, not fully grasping its significance. "But I kept the matter in my heart" (Daniel 7:28). Its content did not seem of urgent concern to inquire further.

Two years later another timing message came. This time a *time period* was imbedded in sanctuary imagery. A new theme within an atonement framework was presented. He was told when God's dwelling place and His people were to be cleansed and made holy. Right in the middle of that message another *little horn* arose intent on blocking that atonement.

That is why Gabriel asked the "whoever it is" (Jesus) those timing questions (8:13). When is all this going to happen? When Daniel heard that 2300 evening and morning atonement cycles had to pass, he was unable to separate the time of the Babylonian captivity (Jeremiah 25:11-12) from this lengthy period. Was Israel's punishment now going to be extended over two millenniums?

For now neither Jesus nor Gabriel would respond to the painful concerns of God's servant. They did convey five very important bits of information, however, to help Daniel put it into context.

1. Everything shown in the vision would be in the future (*achariyth*) *after* the 2300 evenings and mornings (8:17, 19).

2. That would occur in the time of the end (*eth qets*) when God's judgment and wrath occur (8:19).

3. That time or season would be called an "appointed time." It was distinct and set apart (8:19).

4. Then in 8:26 he finally made a very important distinction. The *chazown* vision was going to be sealed, not even understood, till the time of the end (12:4).

5. The evening and morning *mareh* vision was confirmed – it's really going to happen. (With that, everything abruptly comes to an end.)

All this information overwhelmed Daniel. For now it was more than Daniel could emotionally handle. *"And I Daniel fainted, and was sick [certain] days; afterward I rose up, and did the king's business; and I was astonished at the vision, but none understood [it]"* (Daniel 8:27). For a man gifted in understanding visions, this was indeed most troubling.

Daniel was told the *chazown* vision wouldn't be understood. But Gabriel never said the *mareh* vision was sealed!

He was so focused on the apparent delay in releasing God's people from Babylon, he failed to catch the positive clues.

But to Daniel's credit he began to study the prophecies related to the captivity.

"Still burdened in behalf of Israel, Daniel studied anew the prophecies of Jeremiah. They were very plain – so plain that he understood by these testimonies recorded in books 'the number of the years, whereof the word of the Lord came to Jeremiah the prophet, that He would accomplish seventy years in the desolations of Jerusalem.' Daniel 9:2."[1]

1. He was convicted and finally understood and, in faith, knew the captivity was only for seventy literal years (9:2).

2. He saw that Babylon had fallen in the vision, perceiving now that that literally had been fulfilled.

This typologically is the same restoration setting we see in the book of Revelation. Shortly after spiritual Babylon falls Jesus comes to free His people from bondage. The messages in Daniel 8–12 play out the final events in that restoration, which occur right at the end.

The issues Daniel finally understood are vital for us to grasp with great precision: Why were the children of Israel in bondage for seventy years? In the Chronicles of ancient Israel we find:

To fulfil the word of the LORD by the mouth of Jeremiah, until the land had enjoyed her sabbaths: for as long as she lay desolate she kept sabbath, to fulfil threescore and ten years" (II Chronicles 36:21).

The Sabbath land rest was every seven years (Leviticus 25:1-7). For 490 years those people rebelled against and defied God. For every Sabbath year of rest they missed (one out of seven), they were to be in captivity. Their homeland lay desolate for seventy years because of that many Sabbaths missed. Thus, the duration of their captivity.

Remember, this statute was part of God's everlasting, perpetual (*tamiyd*) – covenant (Leviticus 26:3, 15, 42, 45). Daniel recognized this when he began to pray.

Two years later he said that the *time appointed,* when all those things in the vision would occur, was "long." He finally understood the timing issues and understood the *mareh* vision (10:1). The conflict would be long, but the 2300-year prophecy is now grasped. It is helpful to know that part of Gabriel's revelations to him was open for all to know. It was unsealed.

What does that mean? The prophecy tucked within 8:14 was given long before 1844. It was "open" for the Advent pioneers before 1844 when they rediscovered the meaning of its timing. Then shortly thereafter, in the light of the cleansing and restoration, a covenant fulfillment message became clear.

THE CODE, COVENANT AND RESTORATION

In the beautiful statutes that were outlined by Moses, many of which apply to us today, a deeply important Levitical code was given in Leviticus 25:1-7. The children of Israel were to sow their fields for six years, but in the seventh it was to rest. *That whole year was sacred.* It was a Sabbath. The crops would produce enough food during the sixth year to cover that year *and* the next two, so on the eighth year when crops were sown again, enough food would remain until the new harvest came (Leviticus 25:19-22).

---

[1] White, Ellen G.; *Prophets and Kings*, p. 554.

This was God's covenant plan:

Year	Activity
1-5	Work
6	Work and prepare
7	Rest
8	Restore

That is also God's restoration plan for this earth.

This was so important that just a few thoughts later God said, "If ye will not harken unto me," then He began to describe the consequences of rebellion and disobedience to the statutes. He summed that up by saying, "But if ye will not hearken unto me, and will not do all these commandments; And if ye shall despise my statutes, or if your soul abhor my judgments, so that ye will not do all my commandments, *but* that ye break my covenant" (Leviticus 26:14-15), punishment will follow.

The whole covenant was a *plan of restoration* from sin. It made provision for the cleansing of sin so thoroughly that man would become holy, cleared of any wrong and be eternally one with Him. This is what was alluded to in Daniel 8. Satan, through his agent – the *little horn* – was attempting to prevent a covenant from becoming a reality. Right in the middle of the horrendous war comes Daniel 8:14. God will have a holy people – cleansed of all sin. Jesus is personally speaking in that verse.

The centerpiece of God's great plan was the atonement. Those who persisted in rebellion against the atonement would experience the sword, be scattered among the heathen and have their homeland become desolate.

"Then shall the land enjoy her sabbaths, as long as it lieth desolate … even then shall the land rest, and enjoy her sabbaths" (Leviticus 26:34). That is one reason why we know that during the millennium of desolation, when Satan is bound to this earth (Revelation 20:1-3), it is a time the land rests because the world has been in rebellion. That millennium is a seventh – one of rest. The eighth is restoration – a new earth.

Israel turned against God, and a curse of seventy years of captivity was placed upon them and their land was to be a "perpetual desolation" (Jeremiah 25:12). Again, why the seventy years in Babylonian captivity? Daniel restudied that. With all he had gone through and now Gabriel leaving him with dangling issues, he was forced to look at the prophecies like he never had before.

In those prophecies he found a promise, one which reverberates down to this day, as we will see later.

"For thus saith the LORD, That after seventy years be accomplished at Babylon I will visit you, and perform my good word toward you, in causing you to return to this place. For I know the thoughts that I think toward you, saith the LORD, thoughts of peace, and not of evil, to give you an expected end. Then shall ye call upon me, and ye shall go and pray unto me, and I will hearken unto you. And ye shall seek me, and find *me*, when ye shall search for me with all your heart" (Jeremiah 29:10-13).

This is what happened: *"In the first year of Darius the son of Ahasuerus, of the seed of the Medes, which was made king over the realm of the Chaldeans; In the first year of his reign I Daniel understood by books the number of the years, whereof the word of the LORD came to Jeremiah the prophet, that he would accomplish seventy years in the desolations of Jerusalem"* (Daniel 9:1-2).

Restoration was just about to occur. Cyrus, a symbol of Jesus, would mediate their freedom to the land of promise. This model guides us as it did Daniel, with beautiful understanding as to what lies just ahead for God's people. Babylon falls, Christ comes, God's people return to the promised land.

CHAPTER 16

A MIGHTY PRAYER OF RESTORATION

"And I set my face unto the Lord God, to seek by prayer and supplications, with fasting, and sackcloth, and ashes: And I prayed unto the LORD my God, and made my confession, and said, O Lord, the great and dreadful God, keeping the covenant and mercy to them that love him, and to them that keep his commandments; We have sinned, and have committed iniquity, and have done wickedly, and have rebelled, even by departing from thy precepts and from thy judgments: Neither have we hearkened unto thy servants the prophets, which spake in thy name to our kings, our princes, and our fathers, and to all the people of the land" (Daniel 9:3-6).

DANIEL HONORS AND RESPECTS GOD IN PRAYER

This stands as one of the few great prayers recorded in the Bible. Jesus' prayer to His Father (John 17) is the wonder of them all.

"And I set my face unto the Lord God, to seek by prayer and supplications, with fasting, and sackcloth, and ashes" (Daniel 9:3).

Daniel now knows that the seventy years are within one or two years of completion. In this prayer he positions himself as Israel's spokesman to complete their part of the promise. Daniel, in essence, becomes the guarantor of Israel's restoration.

In great submission he:

1. Presented supplications – earnest pleading

2. Fasted – deprived himself of food

3. Dressed in sackcloth – coarse dark cloth, symbolizing sorrow and mourning (II Samuel 3:31, II Kings 19:1-2). It was also a sign of repentance (Matthew 11:21).

4. Ashes – This likely was put on his head or he might have sat on a bed of ashes. Either possibility was a sign of total humiliation and sorrow (II Samuel 13:19, Esther 4:3, Jeremiah 6:26) – in this case, for Israel's sins.

Symbolically, this introduces the experience of the 144,000 waiting for their restoration. This is a Feast-of-Trumpets experience that all must traverse before they are pronounced holy and totally free of sin.

"With faith founded on the sure word of prophecy, Daniel pleaded with the Lord for the speedy fulfillment of these promises. He pleaded for the honor of God to be preserved. In his petition he identified himself fully with those who had fallen short of the divine purpose, confessing their sins as his own."[1]

Is there a reason that this prayer is recorded right in the middle of the *mareh* prophecy? This may be one of the most important issues for God's people to consider. Remember – the *mareh* vision is all

---

[1] White, Ellen G.; *Prophets and Kings,* pp. 554-555.

about the development of a perfect covenant people. While Daniel was praying, more of that vision was given. So far, only Daniel 8:14 and 8:26 are related to it. He was assured that spiritual deliverance would happen and that that group would be adjudicated and purified. God's dream for a divine character-vindicating church *would be* realized.

Daniel is gripped with the time in which he was living and knows that restoration to that *glorious land* would come only if repentance, mourning and humiliation occurred. What we see him doing is a great metaphor for God's people just before the end of this world. This chapter begins one of the most intensive outlines of how to become holy! Repeatedly, Gabriel said that these things were for "thy people." That was clarified in 12:1. "Thy people" were all those "found written in the book" of life. Daniel 8–12 is for us.

There is another amazing lesson that Daniel, under inspiration, conveys to all those claiming to be His. God made it clear that when His people break *His* covenant, He will measure out penalties (Leviticus 26:14-33). Then He will at some point *remember His covenant.* If His people follow a *restoration plan*, the covenant promise will be reestablished. BUT – we will see there is a limit to His mercy. Daniel 9, in fact, places a specific time limit on God's forbearance – then judgment follows. There is then no other chance.

Recognizing this, Daniel begins in this remarkable intercessory prayer for the restoration of his people with utter humiliation and submission. Daniel prays for us as well as for ancient Israel. BUT – there is one significant caveat for everyone. When Gabriel comes during this intercession, he will make it clear that probationary time will soon close.

Many Christians have applied that probation to Daniel's people only. Dispensationalists have made unwarranted gaps in the last week, opening up additional second chance timing at the end. There is, however, a solemn, overlooked end-time application specifically for you and me. This prayer continues to reverberate in the echo chambers of the heavenly sanctuary right up until probation closes at the very end. How that applies to us means everything to our eternal security!

The adjudication process of 8:14 represents a legal action within a court setting – "The judgment was set, and the books were opened" (7:10b). God made provision that we might have representation. That only happens when restoration steps are taken by us to represent God's character. The covenant is beautiful. *Jesus will represent us if we demonstrate that we represent His Father.* If we fail in using that opportunity, we are alone, without representation, and our case will be rejected. Daniel understands this well and begins those steps.

COVENANT RESTORATION

God said He would "remember my covenant," "remember the covenant of the ancestors" (Leviticus 26:42, 45) if these steps were followed:

1. Return to the Lord (Deuteronomy 30:2; Daniel 9:13, 4)

2. Humble the heart (Leviticus 26:41, Daniel 9:5)

3. Accept/understand why punishment is given (Leviticus 26:41; Daniel 9:7,11-12)

4. Harken to His voice (Deuteronomy 30:10)

5. Confess thine iniquity (Leviticus 25:40; Daniel 9:4, 14-15)

6. Confess iniquity of forefathers (Leviticus 26:40, Daniel 9:4)

7. Obey commandments, statutes and judgments (Deuteronomy 30:2, 16)

8. Love the Lord (Deuteronomy 30:15, 20)

9. Walk in His ways (Deuteronomy 30:16)

Listen to Daniel:

"And I prayed unto the LORD my God, and made my confession, and said, O Lord, the great and dreadful God, keeping the covenant and mercy to them that love him, and to them that keep his commandments" (Daniel 9:4).

Note how Daniel petitioned God:

He returns, recognizes and confesses	He knew the result of rebellion against the covenant
God, you keep the covenant (9:4)	If you break my covenant (Lev. 26:15)
We have sinned and done wickedly, rebelled by departing from thy precepts and judgments (9:5)	Despise my statutes (Lev. 26:14-15) Abhor my judgments (Lev. 26:14-15)
We know you have mercy and love to those who keep the commandments (9:4).	Not do all my commandments (Lev. 26:14-15)
Not harkened unto prophets, princes and our fathers (9:6, 10)	Not harkened to me (Lev. 26:18)

O Lord, righteousness belongeth unto thee (9:7)

To us confusion of faces, we are far and near in countries whither you drove us (9:7-8)

The Lord shall scatter thee among all people, from one end of the earth unto the other (Deut. 28:64)

Because we have sinned against thee (9:8)

To the Lord our God belong mercies and forgiveness (though we have rebelled)

This is the dividing point in Daniel's prayer. He has gratefully acknowledged the mercy and justice of God's character. Confession is repetitively moving forward. Now he notes that Israel belongs to God – "We still are part of you. We still are your people. You are merciful and forgiving – don't forget us!"

This is remarkable. Daniel is including himself with Israel and their rebellion. The prayer continues:

Haven't obeyed your voice to walk in your laws (9:10)

Walk contrary to me (Lev. 26:21)

Israel transgressed the law
A curse is poured on us (9:11) that is written in the Law of Moses (9:11)
Bringing upon us great evil (9:12)

Daniel now introduces an important symbol (vs 12). He personifies Jerusalem as apostate Israel receiving punishment. Jerusalem in the Old and New Testaments often represents God's people, His church and even His bride. It is God's city and holy mountain (vs 16).

Daniel repeats his pleas in verses 13-15. By now he has acknowledged that God's part in the covenant hasn't failed. The rebellion of Israel with resulting judgments is acknowledged. And, he has confessed all of the major sins that broke the covenant relationship with Him. Now he begins a wonderful series of requests. Again, this outlines a cry that is to be taken in refrain by all of God's people as long as time lasts. It's for you and me.

- Turn away your anger and fury (9:16)

- Hear this servant's prayer (9:17)

- Shine your face on your desolate sanctuary (9:17)

- Incline your ear, open your eyes to the desolations (within us) (9:18)

- This request is not because of our righteousness but because of your mercy (9:18)

- Forgive and respond (9:19)

- For your own sake and name (9:19)

The restoration of a temple, city and homeland is part of this prayer. Central to all, however, is its symbolism of the restoration of a people who also have become desolate of His continual (*tamiyd*) presence. It is a plea for *spiritual deliverance*. We previously saw that *tamiyd* was taken away in an evening–morning sanctuary setting. It represented His Spirit (through the oil of the candlesticks) and His Sabbath presence (through the shewbread) (Leviticus 24:8).

Everything in Daniel's prayer builds on the purification ram typology begun in Daniel 8, with the theme of an eternally restored holy covenant people. It is His *presence*, the *tamiyd*, that He craves to have sealed in the minds and hearts of His people. That will finally happen with the 144,000 in Revelation 7 and 14. That's us – if we follow the very same *restoration steps*. His character, the very nature of the divine, is to be part of us. Christ in us – that is our hope of glory today!

CHAPTER 17

FASTER THAN THE SPEED OF LIGHT

"And whiles I [was] speaking, and praying, and confessing my sin and the sin of my people Israel, and presenting my supplication before the LORD my God for the holy mountain of my God; Yea, whiles I [was] speaking in prayer, even the man Gabriel, whom I had seen in the vision at the beginning, being caused to fly swiftly, touched me about the time of the evening oblation" (Daniel 9:20-21).

Daniel has been praying to God for "your people" (9:15-16, 19), and suddenly in his little commentary he notes that he was praying for "my people Israel." He said the supplication was "for the holy mountain of God." This refers to Mount Zion (Joel 3:17), the southeastern hill in Jerusalem where God dwells.

Was that focus on the city, the temple or the physical restoration of Mount Zion? So many commentators view this literally and see the decrees for restoration *solely* as a brick-and- mortar theme. Daniel's prayer has been mainly for a covenant restoration of Israel – God's people. The previous chapter began to project when a holy people would be made *eternally right with God*. Why would there be a sudden shift away from a salvation theme to buildings and streets? It's a path we should be careful not to overemphasize.

The "holy mountain" or "Mount Zion" can mean Jerusalem (Isaiah 66:20, Daniel 9:16) and God's presence within His chosen people (Joel 2:1, Zechariah 9:13). In the New Testament it can refer to the church of God (Hebrews 12:22).

It was spiritually the place where God dwells. It will someday be the place where the 144,000 stand with the Lamb in the heavenly mansions (Revelation 14:1) where He dwells. That's what Daniel has been praying for (for his people, Israel, and himself) – his passion, once again, to have God tabernacling with them. This is so vital to grasp. We will see in the rest of this chapter many concepts that will tempt us to view them literally and geographically. If we do, our study will have been in vain.

While the prayer was in progress, Gabriel came. Daniel references him as the "man" whom he saw in the *chazown* vision "at the beginning" (8:15-16).

He comes swiftly by heaven's request while Daniel was praying between 3:00 and 4:00 p.m. – the time of the evening sacrifice. We know immediately that Gabriel traveled to earth in response to Daniel's prayer. This greatly helps us to anticipate a *reinstatement* message.

"At the beginning of thy supplications the commandment came forth, and I am come to show thee; for thou art greatly beloved" (Daniel 9:23a).

Daniel's prayer was a type of preparation all Israel was to make preceding the Day of Atonement, when all relationships were ratified, based upon the covenant promises. Symbolically, Daniel blew the shofar. What follows outlines the great preparation steps to assure the legal rightness of God's people.

"And he informed [me], and talked with me, and said, O Daniel, I am now

come forth to give thee skill and understanding" (Daniel 9:22).

"Therefore understand the matter, and consider the vision" (Daniel 9:23b).

Isn't that remarkable? Right at the very beginning of his three- to four-minute prayer, Gabriel was coming with the answer! God knew what response was needed to Daniel's heart cry.

Gabriel's answer is not totally a matter of assuring Daniel of ending the seventy years' captivity when Israel will go back to Jerusalem. His answer is far broader and deeply spiritual. He came *with another vision.* It needs skill to understand, and Daniel is going to receive that gift. But note, he is *commanded* to "understand" (*biyn*) the matter and consider (*biyn*) the vision. It is now ready to be continued.

"I'm going to give you special wisdom. You are to discern the deep meaning of what will be said – and to grasp the supreme depths of the vision. Concentrate carefully. This requires divine revelation." What vision? Amazingly – the *mareh*
vision.

Why does Gabriel talk this way? What Daniel will see and hear was of solemn importance. Also, the last time they were together, Daniel didn't understand the first part of the *mareh* vision (8:14) and fainted. In essence he says, "*Daniel, this time I want you to look at this information through spiritual lenses – not literal!*"

What was the *mareh* vision all about? The restoration of God's people! The time of spiritual deliverance. That's what he has been praying for! We know Daniel listened – very carefully. We'll tell you why a few chapters from now. But it might be good to let you know that in this setting Daniel symbolizes all of us. We are to pay attention to what was said as carefully as Daniel did.

CHAPTER 18

AN APOCALYPTIC ALLUSION NOT TO BE MISSED

Before we listen to the rest of that incredible *mareh* vision by Gabriel, it is very important that we take a trip to the library of Revelation. John's book helps to explain Daniel's book, especially the sealed portion. In fact, what we have been talking about ever since we started looking at Daniel 8–12 is all noted in Revelation: The fall of Babylon, the development of a holy people, papal power, persecution, the fulfillment of the everlasting covenant and time prophecies – just like Daniel 12! When the two are put together, they actually complement each other – and a beautiful picture of what God wants us to understand is painted in our hearts. That's what we want to do before we go further into Daniel 9.

JESUS APPEARS TO JOHN

"And I saw another mighty angel come down from heaven, clothed with a cloud: and a rainbow was upon his head, and his face was as it were the sun, and his feet as pillars of fire: ... and he set his right foot upon the sea, and his left foot on the earth" (Revelation 10:1, 2b).

Daniel was honored to have Jesus personally come and visit with him three times. This is the second time for John. This "mighty angel" *comes down* from heaven itself. This message or vision is part of an *interlude* or *pause* within another vision to add special information. It refers back to the time of the first Seal – the white horse – when the Latter Rain begins to be poured out.

Remember the pictures Daniel had of Jesus. It was different each time.

- Daniel 8:14-16 – Just a "man's voice" – he didn't actually see Him as far as we know.

- Daniel 10:5-6 – A dazzling picture, symbolizing lordship, advocacy and judgment – very similar to Revelation 1:13-16.

- Daniel 12:6-7 – A "man" clothed in atonement garb above the waters.

John's vision is a combination of the latter two visions of Daniel's. "The mighty angel who instructed John was no less a personage than Jesus."[1] There were times in the Bible when a pending judgment of enormous proportions was about to occur. God Himself often came to give the warning. They represented the *last opportunity* given to repent or be saved.

- Christ and two angels visited Abraham before Sodom and Gomorrah were destroyed (Genesis 18).

- Ezekiel was carried to Jerusalem by a Being like fire or glowing amber just before Judah and Jerusalem were destroyed (Ezekiel 8).

- Ezekiel was shown the glory of the Lord and His throne just before that glory departed forever from the temple (Ezekiel 10).

---

[1] White, Ellen G.; *Manuscript Releases,* vol. 1, p. 99.

- Jesus came to this world as the Savior before Jerusalem was destroyed (A.D. 70). He finally pronounced the sentence, "Behold your house is left unto you desolate" (Matthew 23:28). At the cross, the Jewish people ceased to be His chosen people – forever.

John is here experiencing the exact same thing. Just before the destructive judgments of the Seven Vials, a final warning is to be given. Jesus personally comes down with characteristics of a judge (face and feet) but still mediating and guiding (rainbow and cloud).

In Daniel, Jesus was above the waters, symbolizing His sovereignty and atoning care over all people. Jesus' feet now stand on the sea and the land. This has very special meaning.

"Setting His right foot on the sea, and His left upon the dry land, shows the part which He is acting in the closing scenes of the great controversy with Satan. This position denotes His supreme power and authority over the whole earth. The controversy has waxed stronger and more determined from age to age, and will continue to do so, to the concluding scenes when the masterly working of the powers of darkness shall reach their height. Satan, united with evil men, will deceive the whole world and the churches who receive not the love of the truth. But the mighty Angel demands attention. He cries with a *loud voice*. He is to show the power and authority of His voice to those who have united with Satan to oppose the truth."[2]

We are seeing fulfilled in Revelation what was only a proleptic message in Daniel. Here begins the final battle between the claimed sovereignty of Satan and the sovereignty of Christ. Why is this so important in our study of Daniel? What Gabriel is about to share with Daniel in chapter 9 talks about that very battle. So we urgently need to know the outcome of that sealed book of Daniel as depicted in Revelation to finish our study of that book!

AN OPEN BOOK IN JESUS' HAND

"And he had in his hand a little book open" (Revelation 10:2a).

In the hand of Jesus is a "little book" (*biblaridion*), and amazingly, it is open. That means it is not sealed *and* is open to our understanding. This scroll or book is not the same one noted in Revelation 5. That scroll will not be opened until the saints are enroute to heaven with Jesus. It is opened by Jesus and is a final timing Seal – when there is silence in the courts above. The little open book in Revelation 10 is already open and about to be eaten by John. What is the meaning of this "little book?"

"The book that was sealed was not the book of Revelation, but that *portion* of the prophecy of Daniel which related to the *last days*. The Scripture says, 'But thou, O Daniel, shut up the words, and seal the book, even to the time of the end: many shall run to and fro, and knowledge shall be increased' (Dan. 12:4). When the book was opened, the proclamation was made, 'Time shall be no longer' (see Revelation 10:6). The book of Daniel is now unsealed, and the revelation made by Christ to *John is to come to all the inhabitants of the earth.* By the increase of knowledge a people is to be prepared to stand in the latter days."[3]

---

[2] *Ibid.,* vol. 18, pp. 318-319 (1900) (emphasis added).

[3] White, Ellen G.; *Selected Messages,* vol. 2, p. 105 (emphasis added).

Isn't that astonishing news! Everything we have been studying in Daniel's sealed *chazown* vision is now open to us – including chapter 12, with those three timing prophecies! In Revelation the Book of Daniel becomes *Present Truth*. And it is to go to all the world!

Recall if you will the *mareh* vision that Gabriel is so anxious to continue there in Daniel 9. That was never sealed. But to understand it fully, we need to know the greater picture of the part that was sealed. Why? One part describes Satan working through his agents (the sealed portion). The other (the *mareh* vision) describes God working through His agents, the 144,000. When they are both revealed, we can see the final events of the great controversy that is unfolded in miniature, in a Daniel look-alike in Revelation 11.

"As we near *the close of this world's history*, the prophecies recorded by Daniel demand our special attention, as they relate to *the very time in which we are living*. With them should be linked the teachings of the last book of the New Testament Scriptures. Satan has led many to believe that the prophetic portions of the writings of Daniel and of John the revelator cannot be understood. But the promise is plain that special blessing will accompany the study of these prophecies. 'The wise shall understand' (verse 10), was spoken of the visions of Daniel that were to be unsealed in the latter days; and of the revelation that Christ gave to His servant John for the guidance of God's people all through the centuries, the promise is, 'Blessed is he that readeth, and they that hear the words of this prophecy, and keep those things which are written therein.' Revelation 1:3."[4]

---

[4] White, Ellen G.; *Prophets and Kings,* pp. 547-548.

We don't know when that book was opened, but it relates to what Jesus promised Daniel (12:13): "But go thy way till the end be: for thou shalt rest, and stand in thy lot at the end of the days." Yes, the Hebrew word for end is once again *qets* – the very end of time at the time of judgment when God's people are waiting for the wedding. Expositor White presents in her writings a *progressive* message of Daniel "standing in his lot" – which extends from 1798 to 1906. Little by little that sealed "little book" was to be open to our understanding.

But we can be even more precise as to the timing. There is a "little message" about the "little book" that keeps getting denied.

WHEN IS THE "LITTLE BOOK" FULLY OPENED?

"When the books of Daniel and Revelation are better understood, believers will have an entirely different religious experience. They will be given such glimpses of the open gates of heaven that heart and mind will be impressed with the character that all must develop in order to realize the blessedness which is to be the reward of the pure in heart....

"A wonderful connection is seen between the universe of heaven and this world. The things revealed to Daniel were afterward complemented by the revelation made to John on the Isle of Patmos. These two books should be carefully studied. Twice Daniel inquired, How long shall it be to the end of time?

"'And I heard, but I understood not: then said I, O my Lord, what shall be the end of these things? And He said, Go thy way, Daniel: for the words are closed up and sealed till the time of the end. Many shall be purified, and made white, and tried; but the wicked shall do wickedly: and none of the wicked shall understand;

but the wise shall understand. And from the time that the daily sacrifice shall be taken away, and the abomination that maketh desolate set up, there shall be a thousand two hundred and ninety days. Blessed is he that waiteth, and cometh to the thousand three hundred and five and thirty days. But go thou thy way till the end be: for thou shalt rest, and stand in thy lot at the end of the days.'

"It was the Lion of the tribe of Judah who unsealed the book and gave to John the revelation of what should be in these last days....

"The book of Daniel is unsealed in the revelation to John, and carries us forward to the last scenes of this earth's history."[5]

Revelation 10 shows that book already open. This and chapter 11 open the final scenes of the gospel call to the world. Thus we know that Daniel, tied to that chapter specifically, refers to:

- A time of revival

- The end of time and the last days

- Interestingly, the previous quotes were written in 1896 – thus they apply to then or afterwards.

"And the angel which I saw stand upon the sea and upon the earth lifted up his hand to heaven" (Revelation 10:5).

In a gesture reminiscent of Daniel 12, Jesus raised His hand to heaven to make another oath. In Daniel 12 He raised both hands, here one hand. Why the difference? The right hand is a covenant against the Almighty Father that this promise will come true. The left hand is from a Jewish court scene and seals the promise with the blood of the one making the guarantee. Here Jesus only needs to raise His right hand because Daniel's

timing prophecies are *now* coming true and the shedding of the blood of the covenant has already happened. The Messiah is now the Redeemer.

But – He does raise His hand with another oath. Why? Jesus is going to give another time declaration. This time it is specifically for the last generation. This is so important that the rest of the book can't be fully understood without knowing what is happening here.

"And sware by him that liveth for ever and ever, who created heaven, and the things that therein are, and the earth, and the things that therein are, and the sea, and the things which are therein, that there should be time no longer" (Revelation 10:6).

His right hand (by Jewish and Biblical custom) is raised, and He *swears* by the Creator of all creation. This ties to the incredible declaration of Exodus 20:11. Three times the words "things that are therein" or "all that in them is" are used in this verse. This compels us to acknowledge this oath of Jesus acting as a covenant angel, tying this timing message to the fourth commandment. Wonder of wonders – that is exactly what we saw in Daniel 12 – timing messages tied directly to the onset of the abomination of desolation when the fourth commandment was broken!

	Exodus 20:11	Revelation 10:6
Heaven	All that in them is	And the things that therein are
Earth	All that in them is	And the things that therein are
Sea	All that in them is	And the things which are therein

Are you beginning to see why all of this is so important? Both Daniel and

---

[5] White, Ellen G.; *Testimonies to Ministers,* pp. 114-115.

Revelation tie end-of-time prophecies to the Sabbath issue!

"Daniel shall stand in his lot at the end of the days. John sees the little book unsealed. Then Daniel's prophecies have their proper place in the first, second, and third angels' messages to be given to the world. The unsealing of the little book was *the message in relation to time.*"[6]

There it is. God is extremely interested in *time.* He has very important timing messages in Revelation that we *must* understand if we will successfully traverse the events at the very end.

Did you notice in the previous thought from E. G. White what else those timing messages were to be tied to? The three angels' messages. Part of those messages must include a message regarding *time.* Why? It will be the last call with a Loud Cry, and we will know how soon it will be before the deliverance of God's people and approximately when the Plagues will begin. Will we be setting a time for Jesus' return? Absolutely not – never! God Himself will reveal that. Those timing messages are specifically to couch the final message to the world in every urgent appeal possible – probation is about to close. To the 144,000 is given a message of moral consequences. The eternal destiny of the world hangs now on those last entreaties.

What does Jesus swear? "That there should be time no longer" (*hoti ouketi estai chronos*). In *context* this means "that there should no longer be a *delay* in time." Delay of what? Daniel 8–12!

This is exactly what Habakkuk was talking about years ago: *"For the vision* [chazown] *is yet for an appointed time* [like Daniel 8:19], *but at the end* [qets] *it shall speak, and not lie: though it tarry, wait for it* [where we are now]*; because it*

will surely come [Jesus' two oaths], *it will* [then] *not tarry"* (Habakkuk 2:3). Jesus is declaring to John that it's now time for it to "not tarry." The vision is no longer to be delayed.

"Revelation 10:6-7 speaks of the end of this period [where Christ is ready to come], which is the end of history. Daniel 'could not understand' this prophecy fully (cf. Dan. 12:7-8). He asked the angel *how long* it would be until the prophecy would be fulfilled (Dan. 12:6) and *how* it would be fulfilled (Dan. 12:8 – its 'outcome'). The angel told Daniel that he would not be able to understand these things because the full meaning of the prophecy was to be 'concealed and sealed up until the end time,' when finally it would be fulfilled and all would be revealed to the 'wise' *(maskilim)* living then (Dan. 12:9).

"In contrast to Daniel 12, the angel's oath in Revelation 10 begins an emphasis on *when* and *how* the prophecy will be completed, which is amplified in ch. 11. When the seventh angel sounds his trumpet, the prophecy of Daniel 11:29–12:13 will be fulfilled, and history will come to an end; that is, God's purposes in history will be completed, so that no more time is needed in this historical epoch for him to execute such purposes (in this sense 'time will be no longer')."[7]

JESUS DOESN'T WANT ANY MISUNDERSTANDING

"And there was given me a reed like unto a rod: and the angel stood, saying, Rise, and measure the temple of God, and the altar, and them that worship therein. But the court which is without the

---

[6] White, Ellen G.; *Manuscript Releases,* vol. 19, p. 320.

[7] Beale, G. K.; *The New International Greek Testament Commentary; The Book of Revelation* (William B. Eerdman's Publishing Company, Grand Rapids, Michigan, 1999), pp. 539-540.

temple leave out, and measure it not; for it is given unto the Gentiles: and the holy city shall they tread under foot forty [and] two months. And I will give [power] unto my two witnesses, and they shall prophesy a thousand two hundred [and] three-score days, clothed in sackcloth" (Revelation 11:1-3).

John, representing the 144,000, ate (at God's command) the "little book" of Daniel. It was sweet because it became an exciting message for God's people. But it turned bitter. Why? That final message brought persecution. At the time all those claiming to be God's are being judged (the living), persecution ("tread under foot") occurs.

Now notice how long the persecution is to last – 42 months – 1260 days. Amazing – the same period of persecution as in Daniel 12:7.

But there is a beautiful message in Revelation 11:3. The saints will prophesy for 1260 days. The same period. This is when, under the Latter Rain, the final message goes to all the world, often called the *Loud Cry*.

Now let's go back to Revelation 10, verse 7. *"But in the days of the voice of the seventh angel, when he shall begin to sound, the mystery of God should be finished, as he hath declared to his servants the prophets"* (Revelation 10:7).

What does this mean? When the seventh Trumpet angel sounds – the last trump – the mystery of God is finished. Do you grasp this incredible picture that is suddenly before us?! Daniel 12 tells us when the Mystery of Iniquity will end. Revelation 10 and 11 tell us when the Mystery of God will end. They are both exactly the same time! That is why Daniel and Revelation need to be studied together. They unfold each other with dramatic information that we all will need to know if we want to be among the 144,000.

TIME TO VISIT DANIEL 9 AGAIN

Now that we know the two mysteries are being worked out in these books, we can resume our study of what Gabriel is about to tell Daniel. We will shortly find that the incredible message he is going to tell us more about shows how those *two mysteries* finish.

Some of you might be wondering, "What happened to the 1844 era applications?" It is not the purpose of this book to deal with those historical, incomplete applications. They were a great metaphor for what is to happen at the very end of time. God hid the meaning of many of the timed prophecies so the Advent movement would occur. Now that we are at the end and the appointed time is about to begin, a full and precise understanding is vital to the last generation.

CHAPTER 19

TIMING OF THE RESTORATION

"Seventy weeks are determined upon thy people and upon thy holy city, to finish the transgression, and to make an end of sins, and to make reconciliation for iniquity, and to bring in everlasting righteousness, and to seal up the vision and prophecy, and to anoint the most Holy" (Daniel 9:24).

The most important prophecy in Daniel now begins. God wants to eternally establish His everlasting covenant with a group of loyal subjects – "thy people." The *little horn* is trying to thwart that through a specific sin, removing God's presence, defying Him and persecuting the saints (Daniel 8:9-12). In response to this, Gabriel asked Jesus when all this would occur (8:13). Jesus answered that question, as we have seen, in Daniel's last chapter (12:11-12). But He did give another very special bit of information. He gave a personal message to Gabriel (for Daniel's sake) that *after* the 2300 atonement evenings and mornings there would be a holy group of people who would be legally and eternally made right with God. Remember those very important Hebrew words, *qodesh tsadaq,* "holy, justified or adjudicated" (8:14). That refers to the final Jubilee Atonement. When God's people (collectively) are vindicated and, in turn, vindicate the character of God. That is the culmination of the mystery of Godliness. In Daniel 9:24 God gives "thy people" seventy weeks (of years) to accomplish that objective!

The 2300-"day" prophecy indicated when the *mareh* vision was to be accom-

plished. That vision wasn't sealed (8:26). And now comes this amazing, urgent, quick response to Daniel's prayer. Gabriel comes to share more information with him about – yes, that's right – the *mareh* vision. "I am come to show *thee* [understanding] ... consider the vision [*mareh*] (9:23).

GABRIEL BEGINS AN AWESOME DISCOURSE

"Seventy weeks are determined upon thy people and upon thy holy city" (9:24a).

"Weeks" comes from the Hebrew word *shebuah* or *shabua.* It literally means "sevened." It was used in various ways in the religious life of Israel. It could even refer to an oath since it represented the sacred or perfect number. If something was "sevened," it was declared of truth. This verse is commonly translated as "weeks" in the Old Testament, referring to a "period of seven." This can be seen as early as Jacob working for seven (*shabua*) for Rachel (after he completed his time for Leah – Genesis 29:27). It always refers to "seven" the twenty times it is used in the Old Testament.

There is another connotation that bears notice. God appointed *Shabua* of the harvest (Jeremiah 5:24). Between Passover and the celebration of the Feast of Weeks were seven *shabuas* (weeks) or 49 days. The next day began the Feast of Weeks, which later was called Pentecost. This was a time to present the firstfruits of the wheat harvest (Deuteronomy 16:9). During those *shabuas* several things occurred:

1. It *began* at the first fruits of the barley harvest (Leviticus 23:15-16).

2. That was the Feast of Unleavened Bread – celebration without sin.

3. The latter rain (March–April) fell early in this time.

4. The harvest of *wheat* ripened.

5. Everyone was ready for the harvest.

6. At the festival (Pentecost) firstfruits of the *wheat* were presented to God.

7. It was called the "Feast of Fifty Days," occurring at the end of May.

"Seventy weeks" or *shibim shabuas* are given to God's people. Why given in this language? It is more than a numeric probation. It is a time to receive power from heaven, prepare one's heart and be ready as an acceptable gift unto God. That is what Gabriel is about to tell Daniel – his people needed to be *restored.* Wheat represents God's people ready for the harvest. They were to be collectively ready! Remember the phrase, "thy people."

Seventy weeks – *shibim shabuas* – is 490 years. This is remarkable and prophetically provocative.

Daniel and his people had been in captivity for 70 years, one year for each sabbatical year of rest missed (II Chronicles 36:21, Jeremiah 25:12). That was a total of 490 calendar years that ancient Israel didn't observe the sabbatical years. In answer to Daniel's prayer, Gabriel informs him that Israel's *restoration* will not be complete until she goes through *another* 70 periods-of-seven (*shibim shabua*) or 490 years! That sabbatical

year (*shemitah*) is often called the Sabbath of Release (Leviticus 25:4-5).

Those Sabbath years were sacred and, as the land rested, it was a time to rest in the Lord. *Shenat Shabbaton* ("Year of Restfulness"). The symbolism for the Feast of Weeks (*Hag Hashavout*) is within the spiritual ministry of this time. It is sometimes called the *Hag Habikkurim* or the Feast of Firstfruits (Numbers 28:26) (that is a rabbinic name). It has also been called by the Jewish people *Hag Atzeret* or the closing festival because it ended the cycle for the spring feasts.

There is a profound message in this for the 144,000. They will be the firstfruits (Revelation 14:4). This group has a very special preparation and sealing experience to be able to ready the world, the great multitude, for His coming, which occurs at the fall festivals.[1]

What does this mean to us today? The ministry of the Spirit had its beginning at the Feast of Pentecost, the Feast of Weeks. Paul said, "For by one Spirit are we all baptized into [and this is key] one body, whether *we be* Jews or Gentiles (I Corinthians 12:13). That is exactly what Jesus said would happen after the 2300 atonement years. That is exactly what Gabriel is about to tell Daniel – what Israel must do to be holy and fully restored.

Israel had missed 490 Feasts of "Pentecost." Pentecost represented the completion of the wheat harvest that is tied to salvation in the gospels and relates to the Latter Rain. God sent His Son, made of a woman, made under the law, to redeem or restore us. How? By adopting us now as His sons and daughters. God sends the "Spirit of His Son" right into our hearts and we, too, as did Jesus, can call God

---

[1] White, Ellen G.; *The Great Controversy,* pp. 399-400.

our Father! (Galatians 4:1-7). That is the completion of the everlasting covenant. That is what Daniel 8–12 is all about. That is a Pentecostal experience. That is what Israel is about to be told they *must* experience to be *restored.*

Long ago God said that failure to keep all the statutes, judgments and commandments would result in the "breaking of my covenant" (Leviticus 26:15). Daniel understood that – that is why he prayed the way he did. Thus we find the whole *mareh context* relates to a broken covenant and now its *restoration.* Daniel also grasped the 490 years. In the next chapter he said, "The appointed time was 'long:' and he understood the things, and had understanding of the vision (*mareh*)" (10:1). Daniel also understood the dual meaning of all these prophecies! One related to the appointed time or warfare at the *eth qets*, the other right then – his people needed to be *restored.*

What did Gabriel mean by "are determined" for his people? The word "determined" (*chathak*) is unique in that this is the only place in the Bible it is used. Its root comes from a word meaning "cut." In this context it is best seen as "marked out" or "decreed" for thy people and the holy city.

Who are "thy people" noted here? The immediate context is Daniel's people – ancient Israel – still in captivity. *It also refers to spiritual Israel "still in captivity,"* waiting to be called out of Babylon. Several years from now Gabriel explains this further: "At that time *thy people* shall be delivered" (after Michael stands up and during a great time of trouble). What does all this mean? Everyone that "shall be found written in the book" (12:1) are called "thy people." Once again, this whole issue of finishing the everlasting covenant of *restoration* has a dual application. One for ca. 550 B.C., the second

for the remnant at the final "appointed time" (*mowed*) right at the end.

What about the meaning of the holy city? The word "holy" or *qodesh* we have seen several times before. God longs for His people to become holy (8:14). He wants the same for the "city" (*ir* or *Iyr*). This is an unusual use of this word in relation to God's people. It suggests in a literal application a walled city or a fortified city. It's allusions are distinctly to Jerusalem. But – Jerusalem's walls were destroyed at Nebuchadnezzar's invasion. What could this intimate? Is a "probation" being put on a walled city? That would be out of context.

Jerusalem is a metaphor for God's people, especially as a corporate body. There is grave danger in interpreting prophecy through literalism. It tends to draw away from covenant language, promises and spiritual restoration themes. The issue of the holy city is visited again in Revelation. This represents God's church, His corporate body, which symbolizes all those who will be citizens of the promised New Jerusalem.

This is why we've already seen "the holy place and the host are to be trampled" (8:13; cf. Isaiah 63:18, Zechariah 12:3, Revelation 11:1-2 – "And the holy city shall they tread under foot forty and two months"). The temple, Mt. Zion, Jerusalem and "thy city" all refer to Israel, God's people. It is part of the beautiful language we even saw in Daniel's prayer, indicating: Daniel, your nation, your people, those God still calls "My people" have 490 years to become holy. God's people are *all* those written in the Book of Life. Remember the Danielic thought – this message refers to us also.

We've just dealt with the *timing of the restoration.* Next we'll look at the *conditions of the restoration.* Could that refer to us too?

CHAPTER 20

WHAT HEAVEN REQUIRES

"… to finish the transgression, and to make an end of sins, and to make reconciliation for iniquity, and to bring in everlasting righteousness, and to seal up the vision and prophecy, and to anoint the most Holy" (Daniel 9:24b).

Daniel and his people are in captivity. They've been there for a long time, nearly two generations. Prophecy has decreed that they are soon to be released. In preparation for that, Gabriel is about to give some of the most solemn instruction heaven has ever presented to man. This advice, as with this whole visit, is for us too. Remember that breathtaking discovery: We are also "Daniel's people!" We have also been in captivity – for a long time – in a faltering world and slaves to sin. Prophecy has decreed that we are soon to be released. In preparation for that Gabriel presents a divine advisory. This is the next iteration of the Elijah message.

Daniel prayed a *covenant restoration prayer*. God has always done His part in that agreement. So, as a follow-up to that prayer, Gabriel outlines what God's people must do to complete their half of the contract. But, before we journey into that classroom, there is an observation we must make. This may come as a new thought: The issues of the covenant are spiritual – not bricks, mortar, walls and streets. It is true that there are promises of reinstatement of material blessings. As Jerusalem would become the center of Daniel's people again, the New Jerusalem will soon become ours – *if spiritual matters are properly ad-*dressed. This visit is concerned with the heart and soul of God's people. Amazingly, Gabriel isn't that concerned about the streets and walls. That must be understood. It all relates to completion of the everlasting covenant.

What must *Israel* do to be restored to God's favor? Again, this is what Gabriel said: *"… to finish the transgression, and to make an end of sins, and to make reconciliation for iniquity, and to bring in everlasting righteousness, and to seal up the vision and prophecy, and to anoint the most Holy"* (Daniel 9:24b).

These six steps reflect the Levitical transition from a sin offering through the atonement to the final cleansing of the sanctuary, followed by a tabernacle feast celebration. It is a reminder to Daniel's people, and an eschatological model for the generation who will live just before probation closes, of an antitypical Jubilee Day of Atonement.

God repetitively uses six in preparation for a seventh rest or solemn holy time. He took six days to create before a seventh rest. Moses had six preparation steps to complete the tabernacle (Exodus 25-31). There are here six issues to address *during* this unique 490-year period to be in covenant compliance. Does the 490-year time span also have anything to do with the final remnant people at the end? There are end-time parallels with every other part of this prophecy. This *whole* message has a dual application. That question will be studied a few chapters from now.

"TO FINISH TRANSGRESSION"

To finish (*kala*) means to interrupt what is in progress relative to transgression (*pesha*). *Pesha* means rejection of God's *authority* and *covenant*. By inference, their allegiance has been to themselves and to this world. They have rebelled against God's partnership agreement, and in turn, His *law*.

We saw this word, *pesha*, some time ago related to the *little horn*. One of the terrible things that Gabriel said the papacy was doing was *pesha*. That was considered so bad that it would lead to desolation or utter destruction (8:13). Imagine what is happening here! God's people have been guilty of the very sins that the papacy will have committed right at the end! No wonder it is mentioned first. We can hear God saying: "All you who claim to belong to Me, all you in Babylon who love the world – sever, interrupt those ties and make ME your first priority once again. Identify with My law, so you know what I stand for. Discover once again that I am above all. Remember, I'm your Creator. I'm the only sovereign being who rules over all."

Israel and its leaders had placed themselves in God's place, just as the papacy would do. Astonishing as it may be, that is exactly what John recorded the apostate Christian church would be like right at the end of time! Laodicea didn't feel it needed any God-input (Revelation 3:17). In fact, that church (Is anybody listening?) didn't even have Jesus – He was *outside, banging* on the door, hoping someone would let Him in (Revelation 3:20).

That's alarming. That means this first issue is also for you and me today. Laodicea is in denial – that's bad. It may talk and sing and pray *Jesus,* but He isn't even in the house. There are many defense mechanisms that man has.

Some help us to cope during crises. They can act as shields when there is danger. But sometimes they can lead to "desolation" and harm if reality is not addressed. This is one of those times. Gabriel is saying to all of God's people, "Interrupt, stop, cut off everything that might be a barrier to a restored relationship. In Laodicea that barrier is the door of self-satisfaction and what's piled against the door.

God continues: "Recognize your need and begin right now to look to Me – Jesus. Your attention has been on yourself and the gods of this world – I want first place in your life!" *Pesha* – that horrible word means one is 180° away from God. To sever ties with self, one has to turn 180° *towards* God.

"TO MAKE AN END OF SINS"

No – this is not double-talk with *pesha*. To make an end (*chatham*) means to *finish* or *terminate.* An ancient Hebrew scribe when translating this even said it might be best translated, "seal off" those sins (*chattaah*) – or anything done against God – "stop sinning."

Well, that's what Daniel confessed (9:5), "We have sinned." Israel *as a nation* must now cease sinning. This message was for a *people.* It is a great invitation theme for *God's church.* Though it applies to individuals, the central issue of this *mareh* vision is perfecting a *holy people.* It won't happen unless these steps are followed – including turning away from sin.

The book of Revelation once again comes up on our screen. It shows God reminding us today that the remnant will be looking to Jesus and giving up sin (Revelation 12:17 and 14:12) – that's amazing. Most wonderful of all, they do *exactly* that and become white (white horse of Revelation 6:2 – the 144,000) and are clothed with white garments (Revelation 7:13) – *they all give up sin.*

But I can hear a reader of this chapter mumble, "That was a different dispensation." I can't think of one reason – not even one the size of a grain of sand – as to why that makes any difference. The issue at stake is sin, not the sinner in some era of time. The cross put God's signature on the covenant – that is the *only* reason it is called "new." To finish the covenant, sin must be terminated.

How complete will that commitment be? "Those who come up to every point, and stand every test, and overcome, be the price what it may, have heeded the counsel of the True Witness, and they will receive the latter rain, and thus be fitted for translation."[1]

Did you catch that? Only those who deal with every test – sin – will receive the Latter Rain. Still skeptical? I hope not, but just in case:

"Not one of us will ever receive the seal of God while our characters have one spot or stain upon them. *It is left with us to remedy the defects in our characters, to cleanse the soul temple of every defilement. Then the latter rain will fall* upon us as the early rain fell upon the disciples on the Day of Pentecost."[2]

"Today you are to give yourself to God, that you may be emptied of self, emptied of envy, jealousy, evil surmising, strife, everything that shall be dishonoring to God. Today you are to have your vessel purified that it may be ready for the heavenly dew, ready for the showers of the latter rain; for the latter rain will come, and the blessing of God will fill every soul *that is purified from every defilement*. It is our work today to yield our souls to Christ, that we may be fitted for the time of refreshing from the presence of the Lord – fitted for the baptism of the Holy Spirit."[3]

"The heart must be emptied of every defilement, and cleansed for the indwelling of the Spirit. It was by the *confession and forsaking of sin*, by earnest prayer and consecration of themselves to God, that the early disciples prepared for the outpouring of the Holy Spirit on the day of Pentecost. *The same work, only in greater degree, must be done now.*"[4]

Thus – what we've seen so far applies to God's people in all ages beginning in 538 B.C. sin is to be put away.

"To make reconciliation for iniquity"

We're to finish transgression, make an end to sin and now *make* reconciliation (*kaphar*) for iniquity (*avon*). Doesn't that sound familiar? All throughout the New Testament we are advised to make amends for wrong by turning away from it and making things right.

In this setting, God's people *collectively* are to do this. That is the greater meaning of *avon*. Corporate guilt is to be addressed. As a people, atonement, restitution, turning away from wrong must occur. Repentance is to be made. All are to be reconciled back to God.

Inherent in this, and within those first two steps, is a crucial implication. If God's people are to do all this, there must be provision made to legally adjudicate those sins. Judicial punishment is the only alternative. Thus, in Gabriel's invitation, mercy is offered – take these steps and you will be judged as reconciled to God. He is going to make provision for your restoration. The promise is in the asking!

Holiness for His people is a singular objective of a holy God. He has no goals

[1] White, Ellen G.; *Testimonies,* vol. 1, p. 187.
[2] *Ibid.,* vol. 5, p. 214.
[3] White, Ellen G.; *God's Amazing Grace,* p. 205.
[4] White, Ellen G.; *The Review and Herald,* March 21, 1897.

shy of His own character. Everything designed in the plan of redemption works towards that goal through three mechanisms:

1. Substitution
2. Legal settlement
3. Re-creation

Daniel 8–12 covers all three. The process begins with the substitutionary ram atonement and ends with a holy people. That is exactly what is to be accomplished within the 70 weeks-of-years or 10 cycles of 49. The legal issues were prophesied in Daniel 8:14 – when God's people become holy, they are adjudicated and without sin.

In the 70 weeks there are ten Jubilee cycles given to Israel to complete restoration. There are ten Jubilees (*the whole period that can be allotted*) to complete the full re-creation process.

God is pleading, Give up your rebellious attachment to the world and fall in love with Me, stop sinning, turn away from sin by repenting and making restitution. All are parts of what we know as the "steps to Christ" – all parts of the salvic plan to bring mankind back to Eden restored.

Substitution, legal settlement and re-creation must occur within those 490 years. Yet Daniel 8:14 states that the legal issues won't be complete until *after* the 2300 evenings and mornings. Could part of that 490 years be finished at the very end? The prophecy anticipates *another* Israel when the covenant is completed!

"TO BRING IN EVERLASTING RIGHTEOUSNESS"

This now takes on maturing dimensions. The objective of the first three

was a never-ending righteousness. The word for "bring" (*bow*) means to cause to come – God's people have a part. That part we've just gone over.

Everlasting righteousness (*tsedeq*) is associated with the word "cleansed" in 8:14. There it is a verb, here a noun. There it is a prophecy – here it is a fact that must exist. *This is righteousness in a legal setting.* It implies that a forensic matter has been completed. What is that matter? God's people are eternally holy – sinless – something has happened to their sins, something has changed them – charges have been dropped.

A fascinating legal declaration will be made regarding these people who come to that point: *"... he that is righteous, let him be righteous still: and he that is holy, let him be holy still"* (Revelation 22:11).

In the ancient theocracy, *cyclic holiness* came through the yearly Day of Atonement. Every 49 years this was associated with a 50th or eighth year added to the final seven or Jubilee. *When everything* became legally right, *restoration had occurred.* Amazing are the words used above in Revelation where God puts two words back to back: *righteousness and holiness.* That is exactly the beautiful message that *tsedeq* conveys!

God's people, within the span of ten Jubilees, must reach the moral standard of God (Christ) and be legally right with all issues that sin brought against each person.

Do you catch a little glimpse of excitement as to what is happening? The steps God wants *everyone* to take who are recorded in that Book of Life are being unfolded right before our eyes! It sets the stage for understanding Christ our Righteousness in the New Testament, *and* it outlines how we are to understand the astounding truths about God's people in the book of Revelation.

The perpetuity of "everlasting" right-eousness prepares us to move forward into eschatological times!

"TO SEAL UP THE VISION"

At first it appears as though we have a translation error. The word here for vision is *chazown*. Gabriel said he was coming to deal with the *mareh* vision which talks about God's people becoming holy. Suddenly, we have another shift of thinking to the *chazown*. A mistake? No – it *is* correct.

What is Gabriel trying to say? The *chazown* vision is the unfolding of how satanic agencies will try to prevent that "holiness" in God's people – especially the *little horn*, the harlot "mother" (papacy) and her "daughters" (Revelation 17). But Gabriel is noting that the *chazown* vision is going to have to be *chatham*, a verb that means *to seal*. [Earlier in Daniel the king sealed the stone on the lions' den (Daniel 6:17-18). In Daniel 12 parts of the *chazown* vision were to be sealed from understanding (Daniel 12:4)]. What does *chatham* mean here in God's instruction?

In this context it means that everything prophesied about that vision must come to *an end*. That *chazown* vision, which involves the papacy and apostate Protestantism and all her sympathizers, must come to an end. Wonder of wonders! This brings us right back to the beginning of Daniel 8 where Babylon has already fallen (Revelation 14 and 18). The *little horn* competes with the objectives of the covenant message. That controversy must come to its end. All things related to the opposition must be completed.

Gabriel is saying, before these restoration matters can come to a close, Babylon must inevitably fall! Isn't that almost beyond words! Daniel and Revelation hold hands and talk about

lation hold hands and talk about exactly the same message! Remember – Daniel 8–12 is the preface to the book of Revelation. The last vestige of that wicked "city" ends in Revelation 18:19.

"TO ANOINT THE MOST HOLY"

Anoint (*mashach*) is to consecrate – a sacred setting aside. The most Holy (*qodesh qodashim*) usually refers to the tabernacle or something holy. It is the term for the Most Holy Place in Exodus 26:33-34. What does Gabriel mean?

Is the temple going to be built again in Jerusalem and will God's presence once more enter the Most Holy Place (either anciently or now?). That is out of context in what we have been looking at. Notice the incredible symbolism here implied:

Step One:

| Identify once again with God | Passover Feast |

Step Two:

| Cease sinning | Unleavened Bread |

Step Three:

| Atone for the past | Pentecost – Renewal (Latter Rain) |

Step Four:

| Cleansing of hearts | Day of Atonement |

Step Five:

| Satan assumes sin | Scapegoat |

Where is the final step or Feast of Tabernacles? At the end of the 490 years, the last festival of the sacred Jewish year is Tabernacles – that is when Jesus comes.

Here, in great typological language, we note the Levitical transition from the sin offering through the atonement with cleansing of the sanctuary – all in readiness for the land rest Jubilee and then the final Jubilee when everything is restored. *This verse is an eschatological model for the people who will live at the end of time when "The kingdoms of this world are become **the kingdoms** of our Lord, and of his Christ; and he shall reign for ever and ever"* [Revelation 11:15 (cf. Isaiah 27:13)].

"In that day shall the branch of the LORD be beautiful and glorious, and the fruit of the earth *shall be* excellent and comely for them that are escaped of Israel. And it shall come to pass, *that he that is* left in Zion, and *he that* remaineth in Jerusalem, shall be called holy, *even* every one that is written among the living in Jerusalem" (Isaiah 4:2-3).

We've now been presented with beautiful ties back to Daniel 8, forward to Revelation, of what must occur with this probationary time given to prepare for the end. It is *unequivocally* a predominantly eschatological message.

Why is God giving this to Daniel? Chapters 8–12 are mainly end-time. Since our study began, this message has come over and over. But what about Daniel's people? Don't they count here? God has brought a message to Daniel's people as to what they must do. But God *already knows* they are going to fail. How? The 2300 evening and morning prophecy was given several years ago. That projects way into the future. (Remember, that is why Daniel originally fainted.)

But in mercy the terms of probation are given for God's people from that time through all future ages. It is couched in the *mareh* and *chazown* vision messages and the cleansing of the heavenly sanctuary. This time, the language depicts a *task completed.*

Does Daniel grasp this? The words of Gabriel are quite firm and even stern when he begins. Daniel is not to become emotional over the message this time, and he is promised understanding. By the next chapter, which is two years later, Daniel says he now understands (10:1) the *mareh* vision.

When does the 490-year period begin? That will be discussed in the next chapter. If it begins in the B.C. era, it won't reach to the end of time. Is it a prophecy that is to be repeated? If so, there is no precedent elsewhere in Scripture for this. How can we reconcile the dual message within a fixed timing context? Stay tuned.

CHAPTER 21

GOD SETS A DATE THROUGH A CIVIL DECREE

"Know therefore and understand, that from the going forth of the commandment to restore and to build Jerusalem ..." (Daniel 9:25a).

One of the great fascinations of most prophetic books is the amazing number of time-related prophecies. A riveting study comes when examining the meaning of this time-driven verse.

In a dual command Daniel was asked to *know* and *understand. This was not to be a sealed message.* It was fully open, and each detail conveys a specific truth. When Gabriel arrived from heaven he said he came to give *skill* and *understanding* (vs 22) to the *mareh vision* (vs 23). Now he makes it clear – "Don't miss what I'm about to tell you." That includes us also: "Know therefore."

It is almost without precedence that God tells us what must be done to spiritually synchronize with heaven's timetable – that 490 years is mankind's *time period* to come into full compliance with heaven. A timeless God has given to man timed boundaries. God and man are to partner inside of those boundaries. The 70 weeks-of-years is God's final response period given to mankind. It is a time of probation set within ten Jubilee cycles. We will discover an amazing story of how this was temporarily put on hold for a time, called the *tarrying time,* and what starts the timeclock again at the *appointed time.*

WHAT WAS TO BE RESTORED?

This heaven-ordained block of time is to start at the *command* to "restore" and "build" Jerusalem. This all sounds easy and appears to be a history-driven point in time – but there are challenges. First, we need to understand several words – "restore," "build" and "Jerusalem." They are the object of the command or decree. In the immediate context Jerusalem (*Yeruwshalaim*) refers to the city that had been destroyed. This is the object of restore and build. Is this a reference to a physical restoration of Jerusalem?

Gabriel gave the 70-week probation to "your people and your holy city." Is a destroyed city going on probation? In prophecy the temple, sanctuary and Jerusalem are often used metaphorically to represent God's people and His church. Daniel's prayer has already alluded to this. Up to this point, Daniel 9 has been fully focused on spiritual restoration. Why would God tie a secular, asset-driven decree to the beginning of eternal issues? He wouldn't – and that is important to know and understand. *That decree must include a spiritual restoration command.* That is what the previous verse was all about.

The Hebrew word for "restore" is *shuwb*, used in many ways throughout the Old Testament. Its most important use relates to the restoration of a *covenant community.* It denotes a returning to the Lord in a sense of repentance, turning from evil and towards good. It also conveys a meaning of returning from exile. Isn't that amazing? God's people have been in bondage – in exile. The decree must show that they are released to return to the Lord. Again, that is exactly what the previous verse meant.

The Hebrew word for "build" (*banah*) usually means to construct a physical structure. But throughout the Old Testament it is repeatedly used as a metaphor for God building up His kingdom, His nation and Israel. Again, the decree that Gabriel talks about must include a spiritual restoration command.

Daniel knew that the 70 literal years of captivity were coming to a close. He had been earnestly studying Jeremiah, Isaiah and Chronicles. Something dramatic would soon occur in answer to his prayer regarding the end of that prophecy. Gabriel, however, is drawing his attention to a wider scene – one that encompasses moral issues. The eternal beauties of glory must be opened up to God's people. A wider spiritual scene is being unfolded upon their release from bondage. This must be grasped! A scene that transcends ancient Israel and her land to the time of the Messiah, even far beyond when a spiritual Israel looks forward to the heavenly promised land – when the New Jerusalem becomes His bride.

The decree to restore and build Jerusalem is a command to return to God and restore the everlasting covenant with God's people. Then they would become holy – and that is what Daniel and Revelation are ultimately all about.

CIVIL DECREES TO HELP ISRAEL

"*From the going forth of the commandment ...*" (Daniel 9:25). Much conflict occurs between Bible scholars as to which decree or commandment should be honored (there were many given). This word, "commandment" or *dabar*, must convincingly establish a date to prevent fracturing the 70 weeks-of-years prophecy.

Long before Daniel's time (590 B.C.) and the exile, the Lord revealed to Isaiah details of Israel's deliverance from Babylon.

"*Thus saith the LORD, thy redeemer, and he that formed thee from the womb, I am the LORD that maketh all things; that stretcheth forth the heavens alone; that spreadeth abroad the earth by myself; ... That confirmeth the word of his servant, and performeth the counsel of his messengers; that saith to Jerusalem, Thou shalt be inhabited; and to the cities of Judah, Ye shall be built, and I will raise up the decayed places thereof: ... That saith of Cyrus, He is my shepherd, and shall perform all my pleasure: even saying to Jerusalem, Thou shalt be built; and to the temple, Thy foundation shall be laid. Thus saith the LORD to his anointed, to Cyrus, whose right hand I have holden, to subdue nations before him; and I will loose the loins of kings, to open before him the two leaved gates; and the gates shall not be shut; ... I have raised him up in righteousness, and I will direct all his ways: he shall build my city, and he shall let go my captives, not for price nor reward, saith the LORD of hosts*" (Isaiah 44:24, 25, 28; 45:1, 13).

Isaiah's fascinating prophecy even *assumed* Jerusalem and the temple would be destroyed long before the exile. A rescuer whom God called His anointed (*mashiah*) or chosen one was a worshiper of the pagan God Marduk. Yet he, Cyrus, would be instrumental in having God's people "come out of Babylon."

Some time before the exile (627 B.C.) Jeremiah warned that out of the north an *evil* will break upon "the inhabitants of the land" (Jeremiah 1:14). Later (610 B.C.), he told Judah that they had broken the covenant with God and this evil would come upon them. Finally, around 605 B.C. he prophesied that Nebuchadnezzar

– "my servant" – would take them captive for 70 years, after which Babylon would be forever desolate.

It was noted in II Chronicles 36:21-23 that after the land "enjoyed her Sabbaths," at the end of the 70 years prophesied by Jeremiah, Cyrus, king of Persia, would make a proclamation (*qol*) in writing to build the temple in Jerusalem. That prophecy was written during a time when the Babylonian king had already started exploits against Jerusalem (approximately 609 B.C.). It refers to the same prophecy as Isaiah above.

Cyrus' *decree* was not made until 538 B.C, 71-72 years later. "Now in the first year of Cyrus king of Persia, that the word of the LORD by the mouth of Jeremiah might be fulfilled, the LORD stirred up the spirit of Cyrus king of Persia, that he made a proclamation throughout all his kingdom, and *put it* also in writing, saying, Thus saith Cyrus king of Persia, The LORD God of heaven hath given me all the kingdoms of the earth; and he hath charged me to build him an house at Jerusalem, which *is* in Judah. Who *is there* among you of all his people? his God be with him, and let him go up to Jerusalem, which *is* in Judah, and build the house of the LORD God of Israel, (he *is* the God,) which *is* in Jerusalem. And whosoever remaineth in any place where he sojourneth, let the men of his place help him with silver, and with gold, and with goods, and with beasts, beside the freewill offering for the house of God that *is* in Jerusalem" (Ezra 1:1-4).

In that decree the vessels of the "house of the Lord" were returned and the temple was to be built.

Could this be the *dabar* Gabriel was referring to? Since this related to the 70 years of Daniel's exile, it could not be the 490 years Gabriel was referring to. Neither would his message "from the Lord"

be apropos as the "commandment" for restoration.

That conclave that returned to Palestine at the end of the literal 70 years numbered 50,000, with Cyrus appointing Zerubbabal as head and Joshua as high priest. They had long been deprived of visible tokens of God's presence but now built an altar on the old site of the daily burnt offering. This brought deep conviction to the people of God's leadings. This *began* one period of *restoration*[1] – but was incomplete to the prophecy.

The fulfillment of this decree was so vital that Satan resisted the efforts so mightily that Gabriel was obstructed in dealing with the prejudiced mind of Cyrus until Jesus Himself came to change the course of the battle (Daniel 10:15). The 538 B.C. decree fulfilled prophecy for the exiles to return and begin rebuilding their homeland. The prophets Haggai and Zechariah were raised to help direct the minds and efforts of the people.

Because of the continued harassment from Judah's neighbors, especially the Samaritans, the Jewish leaders appealed to Darius Hystaspes, now ruler of the Medo-Persian Empire. He asked a question, "Who commanded you to build this house; and to make up these walls?" (Ezra 5:9). Darius I found and reviewed Cyrus' decree and issued another (approximately 515 B.C.) (Ezra 6:1, 6-12). The temple was finally completed in Darius I's sixth year (vs 15). Was this the decree (*dabar*) or judgment that Gabriel was referring to? Surely importance must be given to this decree because that temple would be where the Messiah would appear (Haggai 2:9, 7).

Around this time (515 B.C.), God, through Zechariah (2:1-5), again made it clear that Jerusalem was to be rebuilt.

---

[1] White, Ellen G.; *Prophets and Kings*, p. 567.

Then comes Xerxes (Ahasuerus), of the story of Esther's fame, and his successor Artaxerxes I (Artaxerxes Longimanus). Under very favorable influences, Ezra asked this king to permit him and his people to return to Jerusalem. Another decree (457 B.C.) was given to Ezra. This was very different from the previous two decrees. Ezra was given special powers, a system of government was to be established, everything was to be done "according to the law of thy God" (7:14, 26), and "the God of heaven" was acknowledged as supreme (vs 23). Was this the decree that Gabriel was referring to?

Another commandment presented itself from Artaxerxes I. Nehemiah received word (444 B.C.) that many of the Judean Jews were in great affliction and the walls in Jerusalem had not yet been built and the city gates had been burned. Nehemiah presented the problem to the king. In his request he made it clear that the city "lieth in waste" (*hareb*) – desolation and ruin (Nehemiah 2:17).

Through a series of letters from the king, Nehemiah was given safe passage. Also, he was provided a royal escort. Under his leadership the wall was rebuilt (Nehemiah 6:15). Nehemiah set up rulers over Jerusalem. Then the people fasted and repented, and a great revival took place, and the Levites were reestablished as spiritual leaders. Were the letters of 444 B.C. the commandment to restore Jerusalem?

WHICH DECREE SHOULD WE CHOOSE?

How were the Jews to know when the time was to begin? It would indicate when the Messiah would appear. Gabriel's initial challenge was for them to be fully cognizant of the commandment (*dabar*) – the authoritative word that would encompass the restoration (*shub*) or spiritual revival. That was when the covenant relationship was permanently developed with Jerusalem (*Yᵉruwshalaim*) – God's people. *Only one decree formally addressed the spiritual issues.* The others were clearly physical restorative commands. Artaxerxes I's decree went way beyond the physical restoration to include *the resumption of the theocratic rule with Israel.* They were *decreed* to be once again God's people.

At the time of Ezra's arrival with a large retinue of Jewish captives from Babylon, he was told that many leaders of Judah had intermarried with the heathen nations. With deep earnestness he confessed and repented of Israel's sins (Ezra 9). All the men of Judah and Benjamin gathered themselves in Jerusalem, confessed their sins and put away their strange wives and their children by them.

This brought to Israel a major revival. It reversed a behavior that had originally contributed to the Babylonian captivity over 70 years before.

"This was the beginning of a wonderful reformation.... Wherever Ezra labored, there sprang up a revival in the study of the Holy Scriptures."[2]

Of all four decrees, only the one given in 457 B.C. embodied *within the decree* the reestablishment of a theocratic form of government, the appointment of spiritual leaders and the requirement that all *must* obey God. This was even established upon threat of death if not followed.

Thus, no decree fits the declaration of Gabriel except that of Artaxerxes I in 457 B.C. It is a spiritual issue – *not* one of building assets!

In the next chapter we will begin to analyze why the 70 weeks-of-years was broken up into numerical divisions. That

---

[2] *Ibid.,* pp. 622-623.

had great spiritual meaning to God's people then, as it does to us today.

CHAPTER 22

THE SEVENTY-WEEK PROPHECY IS BROKEN UP

"Know therefore and understand, [that] from the going forth of the commandment to restore and to build Jerusalem unto the Messiah the Prince [shall be] seven weeks, and threescore and two weeks: the street shall be built again, and the wall, even in troublous times" (Daniel 9:25b).

It's been happening over and over again throughout this book. A heavenly message comes to Daniel. Then, sometime later it is repeated in another way to fill in the details. This time Gabriel didn't wait years before a thought was repeated or recapitulated. He only waited one and a half minutes. Let's listen in. This is deep – but really amazing.

Seventy weeks of years were set aside by heaven to develop a holy people and bring in everlasting righteousness. In a 490-year period the work of restoration and redemption was to be completed and God's kingdom established – forever. Centuries later in prophecy related to that time, John heard the heavenly host sing, "The Lord our God, the Almighty, reigns." That happened *right after* Babylon fell (Revelation 19:6). Daniel just witnessed the fall of Babylon. Could this time prophecy be a metaphor for the end of time? Is it possible that what John saw ties directly to these 490 years? If everlasting righteousness (9:24) comes to the universe only at the very end of time, there must be a link of vital importance.

THE FIRST DETAILS OF THE SEVENTY WEEKS

Daniel didn't have long to wait for the details to come in. From Artaxerxes I's restoration command (spiritual decree) to the Messiah the Prince was to be "seven weeks, and threescore and two weeks." Strange indeed. We have now a Messianic prophecy put *within* those seventy restoration weeks of years. But why the division of time: 7–62–[1]?

Let's back up and see where this is leading. Artaxerxes' decree was in 457 B.C. Four hundred and ninety years later, counting the transition year zero, brings us to 34 A.D. The first seven weeks equal 49 years, which would be 308 B.C. – a point in the early inter-testament times. Anything significant then? Historically – No. Spiritually – Yes.

The 49th year would end the first (of ten) cycles of seven times the land would rest (Leviticus 25:3-7). God's people would have enjoyed seven Sabbath years of rest. And – the fiftieth year would be a holy year of liberty – full restoration (Leviticus 25:8-55) – a Jubilee.

That first "seven" was the first of ten Jubilee cycles that was to be part of the restoration *theme* for Israel's journey to reconciliation, holiness and everlasting righteousness. The covenant had been broken. God said in promise that even if Israel would "pine away" in an enemy's land because of sin, He would still "remember my covenant ... for their sakes ... that I might be their God" (Leviticus 26:38-45).

The curse of a broken covenant was certainly anticipatory, having been given around 1450 B.C., 800 years before Nebuchadnezzar made good what God had warned. But now, *for the sake of the covenant*, that He might be their God once more, ten Jubilee restoration cycles are given. In prophecy "ten" means "a whole." Wonder of wonders – at the end of the sixty-ninth week, God would enter the scene as the Messiah that He might become the Deliverer and Restorer – God to them again! But this time so very personal – the Messiah God is to become man's Savior. What a Prince! That puts the *mashiyach* or "anointed deliverer" as *Prince* (*nagiyd*), 483 years after the secular decree, in 27 A.D. (counting year zero).

It is important to know that the Old Testament also uses *mashiyach* for Saul, Cyrus and David. Thus, it is a generic word for a king that is chosen or singled out and not a distinct appellation for God. However, the New Testament (Acts 13:32; Hebrews 1:5, 5:5), in referring to Christ's justice, salvation and kingdom rule, ties those thoughts back to Psalms 2:7, 45:6-7, 110:1-5 – the *mashiyach*. With the associated word "Prince" (*nagiyd*) the connotation is "the One on top" – the Messiah God – the Prince of princes (8:25) – God – will be anointed in 27 A.D.

WHY THE SIXTY-NINE YEARS?

The sixty-nine weeks of years does *not* fall on a Jubilee (34 A.D. does). 27 A.D. is at a *shabu'a* or sacred seventh year and is associated with *sheba* or "seven." In turn, a related word, *shaba*, means "to swear" or an oath. The Hebrews would *shaba* or "seven one's self" or "bind one's self" when making oaths.

Gabriel, in the sixty-nine weeks, gave sixty-nine cycles of land rest or sixty-nine sevens, which contextually conveyed a promise. "By sevens, I adjure, the Messiah will come and be the anointed deliverer." This concept is very important. He did *not* come on a Jubilee, making His role an automatic "restorer" *at the first coming*. He came *in promise* with all the *provisions* for a Jubilee restoration. Israel's probation was set on Jubilee cycles. The Messiah was sent *on promise* that all the provision for deliverance and restoration would come!

THE CITY'S ASSETS ARE ADDRESSED AGAIN

Gabriel said in essence, "You have seventy more sabbatical rest years and ten more Jubilee periods. At the sixty-ninth sabbatical rest, before probation ends forever, a Messiah will come. The anointed one will come to rescue your people. Every measure will be taken to bring holiness and deliverance to Israel."

Then he says something so very unusual right in the middle of this context: *"The street shall be built again, and the wall, even in troublous times"* (Daniel 9:25b). *At the time of the anointing* the streets will be built again and the wall in a time of trouble. What does that mean? We've noticed previously that the words "restore" and "build" really refer to the spiritual reclamation of God's people. Could a spiritual application pertain to the *street* and *wall*?

The Hebrew word for street (*r@chub*) is best translated "open area." It usually meant the city square – the center of activity for that town – the heart of the city. The public areas at the time of Israel's apostasy were places where idol shrines were built. Symbolically, the center – or heart – of God's people, His church, is to be "built up" – the same be "built up" – the same word we studied in the first half of this verse, *banah*, is again used. In the context of the *anointed Messiah,* the very center of God's people is to be restored, the pure woman symbol of Revelation 12 – God being the divine head and Israel His people. His kingdom was to be once again established.

But how can we address the "walls?" The Hebrew word really means a *moat* or a *trench* (*charuwts*). It refers to something sharply demarcated *that can never be changed*. In context, during troublous times God's people will be spiritually brought back to holiness by decisions that will never change. Like a moat around a city, it will be a protective barrier forever.

Why is it put right here in the middle of the messianic anointing? In a time of great distress and spiritual darkness the light of the Messiah will shine forth (Isaiah 8:22–9:2). Israel will be brought back to holiness. The objectives of this probation will be reached. Thus, within this prophecy is a great promise – a holy people/nation will come once again. Gabriel's prophecy will not come to naught. The outcome will be irrevocable. This is an announcement of the start of the Christian church!

IMPORTANT PROPHETIC CONCEPT!

Another dual application is set forth.

Christ's Day

- First Messianic prophecy fulfilled

- That *verified the promise of restoration.*

- Time of trouble for the Jewish nation – they failed their part in the covenant.

- The woman – God's true Christian church (Revelation 12) – again, *in promise*, would triumph.

End-Time

- During a time of great trouble

- God's people are made perfect and sealed (Revelation 7) – the church triumphs.

- Then the Messiah will come.

- The issues of Israel's restoration are completed.

That is amazing and so beautiful.

The application is incomplete for Daniel's day. That was *already known* because of the previous 2300 atonement evening and morning prophecy (8:14). Its antitypical fulfillment comes at the end of time, beginning with the 144,000. The greater *fulfillment* of the seventy-week prophecy, when Israel is spiritually restored, is at the end of time!

At that sixty-ninth week the "anointed one" was baptized. As He came out of the water the Spirit rested on Him in the form of a dove. He was anointed for His mission. It was then that John the Baptist with solemn import declared to the throng gathered that day at the Jordan River, "Behold the Lamb of God, which *taketh away the sin of the world*." The Messiah was to be sacrificed – "the Lamb." Restoration was to be complete. The world could become sinless.

The Bible says that John then bore record that He was the "Son of God" (John 1:34). What a Messiah. How precious the Lamb. What a Prince.

CHAPTER 23

VIOLENCE AGAINST THE MESSIAH

"And after threescore and two weeks shall Messiah be cut off, but not for himself:" (Daniel 9:26a).

The focus now moves towards Jesus. We know when that seventy weeks-of-years began (457 B.C.). It is made up of seventy seventh-sabbatical years. Within that timeframe there are ten Jubilee cycles – and we just learned that Messiah the Prince, Jesus Christ, the *anointed one* – would be baptized and anointed during the sixty-ninth Sabbatical year. That is when He began His ministry. That is when the foundation for the Christian church and era began to be laid.

Four hundred and ninety years were given to bring in everlasting righteousness. *The great controversy between good and evil must be completed within that time period.* Verse 24 has already made it clear that the issue Gabriel is addressing is an end-to-sin issue within a timed prophecy!

A step in that direction occurred at Jesus' baptism. John the Baptist resisted the task of baptizing Jesus. Firmly, Jesus said to him, *"Suffer it to be so now: For thus it becometh us to fulfill all righteousness"* (Matthew 3:15). That is, "Permit Me to be baptized of you, John, for it is necessary to demonstrate every aspect of righteousness."

In the requirements laid out by Gabriel to establish a holy people, three belonged to man and three were judicial acts of God. The first legal measure that God would exercise was to bring in everlasting righteousness. Thus, this seventy-week prophecy demanded that Messianic issues be addressed. At the Messiah's anointing He began the public demonstration, which would last three and a half years, showing what righteousness was like – a characteristic His church was to possess.

"Justice and judgment are the habitation of thy throne: mercy and truth shall go before thy face.... In thy name shall they rejoice all the day: and in thy righteousness shall they be exalted.... For the Lord is our defense; and the Holy One of Israel is our King" (Psalm 89:14, 16, 18).

The record says, "after threescore and two weeks" the Messiah would be cut off. Most scholars see this to mean sometime after the sixty-two weeks noted in the previous verse. That would include the previous seven weeks also. Thus, in general terms, at some point after the sixty-nine weeks are completed (after 27 A.D., the baptismal year), when Jesus was to be anointed, He would be cut off. We will be told quite precisely that that would occur in the middle of the following week.

Within this astounding prophecy Jesus is beginning to work out the divine plan to bring in everlasting righteousness. Do you grasp what this means? The everlasting covenant is about to get heaven's signature. Christ's death would ratify God's part of that phenomenal plan. His signature of blood would identify Him as a blood Brother to mankind, legally permitting Him to purchase back His kindred *even before the next Jubilee!*

"If thy brother be waxen poor, and hath sold away some of his possession,

and if any of his kin come to redeem it, then shall he redeem that which his brother sold.... After that he is sold he may be redeemed again; one of his brethren may redeem him: Either his uncle, or his uncle's son, may redeem him, or any that is nigh of kin unto him of his family may redeem him; or if he be able, he may redeem himself" (Leviticus 25:25, 48-49). Jesus became kin to us all, which paved the way to redeem or purchase us back!

The great theme of redemption, eradicating sin and fully restoring God's people, is in Daniel 8–12 and put distinctly within the seventy-weeks-of-years timeframe!

Its prophecy is for all time. It is not limited to a Jewish probation. Those 490 years encircle everyone everywhere who claims the name of Jesus. Relegating it to the past robs mankind of what will be finished in the whole book of Revelation as part of that timeframe. Putting the last week into a future dispensation mocks the very covenant of grace being worked out in this Messianic prophecy! Hermeneutic prejudice and linguistic minutia must be set aside. Contextual exposition is critical to grasp these celestial truths.

After the sixty-nine weeks the Messiah is "cut off" (*karath* or *karat*). This word has deep theological meaning. In a literal sense it is to cut something off or down, such as a tree, part of a body or even an idol. However, it is a metaphor in two important areas: (1) To eliminate or destroy by a violent act (Genesis 9:11, 41:36, etc.), (2) to "cut" or make a covenant (Deuteronomy 29:1, 12, 14, 25; 31:16, etc.).

The contextual implications encompass *both* figurative meanings. Jesus – Messiah the Prince – the "one on top" – is *violently eliminated*, completing His part in that covenant! That promise

needed blood, which flowed from His broken body. It was our kin brother who gave it! Remember Daniel 12, when Jesus raised both hands in an oath regarding those three time prophecies? His left hand was a blood oath or promise. Now that He is cut off, those three time prophecies, by the name of the God of heaven and the blood of Jesus Christ, will occur at the end of time! From the anointing all the way to the cross, legal and salvic issues are being worked out so righteousness could supervene. God's covenant provisions show that mercy and justice meet when the Messiah is *karath*. That violent death, in mercy, made legally accepable man's part of 9:24! That death satisfys the divine judgment of Genesis 2:17.

WHO JESUS DIES FOR

The record simply says, "not for himself" – or more literally, "there shall be nothing to him" [Hengstenberg].[1] His blood was shed for others. He died to save others. Self was given up in a selfless act. For our sins He died.

"Who hath believed our report? and to whom is the arm of the LORD revealed? ... He is despised and rejected of men; a man of sorrows, and acquainted with grief: and we hid as it were our faces from him; he was despised, and we esteemed him not.... But he was wounded for our transgressions, he was bruised for our iniquities: the chastisement of our peace was upon him; and with his stripes we are healed. All we like sheep have gone astray; we have turned every one to his own way; and the LORD hath laid on

---

[1] Hengstenberg, E. W.; *Christology of the Old Testament and a Commentary on the Messianic Predictions,* trans. Theod. Meyer and James Martin, 4 vols. (n.p., 1872-1878; repr., Grand Rapids, Mich.: Kregel Publications, 1956), vol. 3, pp. 114-115.

him the iniquity of us all…. Yet it pleased the LORD to bruise him; he hath put him to grief: when thou shalt make his soul an offering for sin, he shall see his seed, he shall prolong his days, and the pleasure of the LORD shall prosper in his hand" (Isaiah 53:1, 3, 5-6, 10).

"Who his own self bare our sins in his own body on the tree, that we, being dead to sins, should live unto righteousness: by whose stripes ye were healed" (I Peter 2:24).

CHAPTER 24

FOLLOWERS OF THE "PRINCE"

"... and the people of the prince that shall come shall destroy the city and the sanctuary;" (Daniel 9:26b).

Much debate surrounds the identity of this prince. We have previously noted destructive behavior by the he-goat, representing Satan the persecutor. Then the little horn (the papacy) followed, an agent of Satan, casting down God's dwelling place, the sanctuary, and persecuting God's people. This power stood up against the "Prince of princes" (8:25). Later we observe the "prince of Persia" was Satan (10:13-14).

But is the "prince" here Satan or the Messiah? The "prince" should be **P**rince. In verse 25 He was "Messiah the Prince." In the first part of this verse He is Messiah and now Prince. This represents a breakup of a word pair – Messiah the Prince.

Here we are introduced to a "prince" whose people destroy the city and its sanctuary. Nebuchadnezzar had done just that 70 years before. When this encounter from Gabriel occured, that temple and city were still in a desolate state. If this follows the death of the Messiah, however, which is the sequence in this verse, the city and temple would have to be rebuilt and destroyed once again. Who then represents this "prince" that will bring about another destruction? Who are the people?

The main theme within this prophecy has been *spiritual restoration* of God's people (Jerusalem) and His church (temple–sanctuary). Is a literal message suddenly being sandwiched between profound redemptive symbols?

Six hundred years later, just before Calvary, the Messiah Jesus said that the temple would be destroyed (Matthew 24:2 – it had been rebuilt). He also noted that "Jerusalem's house" would become desolate (Matthew 23:37, 24:15 – it would have had to have been restored). This history of Jerusalem's fall and destruction of the temple is well known to historians in the attack by Titus, the Roman general in 70 A.D.

Within *one generation* from the time of Jesus this occurred, fulfilling another prediction (Matthew 24:34). In another interesting application long before Jesus' death, He told sneering Jews that a sign of His Messiahship would be to destroy the temple, and in three days He would raise it up. But He spake of the temple of His body (John 2:19, 21). That "destruction" had a greater spiritual implication. The resurrection of the "Temple" had a future message of hope for spiritual Israel.

Daniel's people were given a probation of 490 years. In this part of that prophecy Gabriel is portraying through the destruction of Jerusalem and the temple that something terrible would occur to that people associated with *that probation*. Daniel would soon understand this from the 2300 evening–morning prophecy that *Israel would fail*. Daniel 9:26b is *directly* associated with the "cutting off" or death of the Messiah.

As Nebuchadnezzar fulfilled prophecy by taking into *captivity* the rebellious Israelites, here the Roman armies are the "people of the prince" who now *destroy* a nation that had passed their probation. God had warned them in many ways that the end would be desolation – destruction.

This verse reveals that Israel would have a spiritual fall through a literal prophetic destructive act.

JESUS ENVISIONS PROPHETIC FULFILLMENT

Jerusalem (His chosen people) and the temple (His church) were annihilated. Jesus said, "Behold, your house is left unto you desolate" (Matthew 23:38). "Therefore say I unto you, the kingdom of God shall be taken from you, and given to a nation bringing forth the fruits thereof" (Matthew 21:43). Christ's words warned Israel that Daniel's prophecies (9:26b) were just about to be fulfilled.

"The history of more than a thousand years of God's special favor and guardian care, manifested to the chosen people, was open to the eye of Jesus. There was Mount Moriah, where the son of promise, an unresisting victim, had been bound to the altar – emblem of the offering of the Son of God. There the covenant of blessing, the glorious Messianic promise, had been confirmed to the father of the faithful (Genesis 22:9, 16-18). There the flames of the sacrifice ascending to heaven from the threshing floor of Ornan had turned aside the sword of the destroying angel (1 Chronicles 21) – fitting symbol of the Saviour's sacrifice and mediation for guilty men. Jerusalem had been honored of God above all the earth. The Lord had 'chosen Zion,' He had 'desired it for His habitation.' Psalm 132:13. There, for ages, holy prophets had uttered their messages of warning. There priests had waved their censers, and the cloud of incense, with the prayers of the worshipers, had ascended before God. There daily the blood of slain lambs had been offered, pointing forward to the Lamb of God. There Jehovah had revealed His presence in the cloud of glory above the mercy seat. There rested the base of that mystic ladder connecting earth with heaven (Genesis 28:12; John 1:51) – that ladder upon which angels of God descended and ascended, and which opened to the world the way into the holiest of all. Had Israel as a nation preserved her allegiance to Heaven, Jerusalem would have stood forever, the elect of God. Jeremiah 17:21-25. But the history of that favored people was a record of backsliding and rebellion. They had resisted Heaven's grace, abused their privileges, and slighted their opportunities.

"Although Israel had 'mocked the messengers of God, and despised His words, and misused His prophets' (2 Chronicles 36:16), He had still manifested Himself to them, as 'the Lord God, merciful and gracious, long-suffering, and abundant in goodness and truth' (Exodus 34:6); notwithstanding repeated rejections, His mercy had continued its pleadings. With more than a father's pitying love for the son of his care, God had 'sent to them by His messengers, rising up betimes, and sending; because He had compassion on His people, and on His dwelling place.' 2 Chronicles 36:15. When remonstrance, entreaty, and rebuke had failed, He sent to them the best gift of heaven; nay, He poured out all heaven in that one Gift.

"The Son of God Himself was sent to plead with the impenitent city. It was Christ that had brought Israel as a goodly vine out of Egypt. Psalm 80:8. His own hand had cast out the heathen before it. He had planted it 'in a very fruitful hill.'

His guardian care had hedged it about. His servants had been sent to nurture it. 'What could have been done more to My vineyard,' He exclaims, 'that I have not done in it?' Isaiah 5:1-4. Though when He looked that it should bring forth grapes, it brought forth wild grapes, yet with a still yearning hope of fruitfulness He came in person to His vineyard, if haply it might be saved from destruction. He dug about His vine; He pruned and cherished it. He was unwearied in His efforts to save this vine of His own planting.

"For three years the Lord of light and glory had gone in and out among His people. He 'went about doing good, and healing all that were oppressed of the devil,' binding up the brokenhearted, setting at liberty them that were bound, restoring sight to the blind, causing the lame to walk and the deaf to hear, cleansing the lepers, raising the dead, and preaching the gospel to the poor. Acts 10:38; Luke 4:18; Matthew 11:5. To all classes alike was addressed the gracious call: 'Come unto Me, all ye that labor and are heavy-laden, and I will give you rest.' Matthew 11:28.

"Though rewarded with evil for good, and hatred for His love (Psalm 109:5), He had steadfastly pursued His mission of mercy. Never were those repelled that sought His grace. A homeless wanderer, reproach and penury His daily lot, He lived to minister to the needs and lighten the woes of men, to plead with them to accept the gift of life. The waves of mercy, beaten back by those stubborn hearts, returned in a stronger tide of pitying, inexpressible love. But Israel had turned from her best Friend and only Helper. The pleadings of His love had been despised, His counsels spurned, His warnings ridiculed.

"The hour of hope and pardon was fast passing; the cup of God's long-deferred wrath was almost full. The cloud that had been gathering through ages of apostasy and rebellion, now black with woe, was about to burst upon a guilty people; and He who alone could save them from their impending fate had been slighted, abused, rejected, and was soon to be crucified. *When Christ should hang upon the cross of Calvary, Israel's day as a nation favored and blessed of God would be ended.*"[1]

DEEPER SPIRITUAL ISSUES

Israel, as a nation, symbolized by Jerusalem, His people, ceased to be a favored people at Calvary – 31 A.D. Jesus told them that "favor" would be given to another people – another "nation."

Who were they? That wouldn't be clear until after the 2300 evenings and mornings! This whole message is part of the *mareh* vision. Daniel's literal people as the "chosen" would be destroyed. But Jesus has already given the very first bit of information about a beautiful restoration of another people. After 2300 atonement evenings and mornings a holy people will emerge that are forever legally right with the center of all – God's throne. The record in the sanctuary, the heavenly court, would be pure and holy.

The fulfillment to that covenant people is remarkably depicted in Revelation as the 144,000 – "the firstfruits unto God and to the Lamb." "They are without fault before the throne of God" (Revelation 14:4-5). They meet the requirements of Daniel 9:24. They "were redeemed from the earth" (Revelation 14:3) and entered into everlasting righteousness.

---

[1] White, Ellen G.; *The Great Controversy,* pp. 18-21.

WARNING

The prophecy of Jerusalem's fall and the destruction of the temple is a metaphor for the time of the end when Babylon falls.

In Revelation, Jerusalem (God's people) is depicted as Babylon (apostate people). That's why there is a **NEW** Jerusalem. Babylon is destroyed (Revelation 16:19).

God calls Babylon a "destroying mountain ... which destroyest all the earth" (Jeremiah 51:25). That imagery is one that goes beyond killing to *corruption*. Babylon is like a huge mountain (beyond human resistance) that *corrupts the earth.* This is clarified further in Isaiah 21:9 where Babylon falls, and with her demise goes the "graven images of her gods." The *transgression* and *abominations* that Daniel 8–12 allude to are false doctrines and idolatrous standards that corrupt the world. The same symbol holds for the wine in the harlot's cup in Revelation 17.

A remnant, the 144,000, triumph at the end. But the Christian church, so pure at its inception (Revelation 12:1) becomes corrupt. The same fate awaits those people, just as the Jews.

"The Saviour's prophecy concerning the visitation of judgments upon Jerusalem is to have *another fulfillment*, of which that terrible desolation was but a faint shadow. In the fate of the chosen city we may behold the doom of a world that has rejected God's mercy and trampled upon His law. Dark are the records of human misery that earth has witnessed during its long centuries of crime. The heart sickens, and the mind grows faint in contemplation. Terrible have been the results of rejecting the authority of Heaven. But a scene yet darker is presented in the revelations of the future. The records of the past,–the long procession of tumults, conflicts, and revolutions, the 'battle of the warrior ... with confused noise, and garments rolled in blood' (Isaiah 9:5),–what are these, in contrast with the terrors of that day when the restraining Spirit of God shall be wholly withdrawn from the wicked, no longer to hold in check the outburst of human passion and satanic wrath! The world will then behold, as never before, the results of Satan's rule.

"But in that day, as in the time of Jerusalem's destruction, God's people will be delivered, everyone that shall be found written among the living. Isaiah 4:3. Christ has declared that He will come the second time to gather His faithful ones to Himself: 'Then shall all the tribes of the earth mourn, and they shall see the Son of man coming in the clouds of heaven with power and great glory. And He shall send His angels with a great sound of a trumpet, and they shall gather together His elect from the four winds, from one end of heaven to the other.' Matthew 24:30, 31."[2]

---

[2] *Ibid.,* pp. 36-37.

CHAPTER 25

GOD'S WRATH EXPRESSED

"... and the end thereof [shall be] with a flood, and unto the end of the war desolations are determined" (Daniel 9:26c).

In Daniel 8:19 we noted the appointed time (*mowed*) heralded the very end of time (*eth qets*). To make clear what this was associated with, Gabriel said that it would be at the time of the indignation (*zaam*), which is God's wrath or time of God's final judgment.

From the 70-weeks-of-years prophecy it is clear that there is a direct application to the Jewish people and 70 A.D. But the greater and more important relevance comes at the end of this world's history. We know this by now because of the 2300-"day" prophecy (Daniel 8:14) and the meaning of *eth qets,* which directly relates to Michael standing up, tribulation, deliverance of God's people and the special resurrection (Daniel 12:1-2).

The verse being reviewed now (9:26c) reveals greater details of how all apostate people will come to an end (70 A.D. or very end of time).

The seven churches of Revelation represent seven types of corporate bodies that will exist at the very end of time. Amazing as it may seem, that book categorically notes that only two of those churches will be part of God's last-day people – Philadelphia and Smyrna – the 144,000 and the martyred groups, His two witnesses. Five have apostatized.

The "end" (*qets*) comes as a "flood" (*sheleph*). Though *sheleph* means a deluge of water, it alludes to a sudden end as quickly and unexpectedly as a flood. In this setting, it would be a "flood of wrath" (Naham 1:8) or judgment on the wicked.[1]

Though Satan, the *prince of this world,* has had controlling accesses at times to God's people and church through persecution and martyrdom, he and his agents will at the end be under the controlled wrath of God.

Qets is once again used. At that "end" will be the "*desolations*" of war. In 8:13 Gabriel said that a transgression would lead to "*desolation*" (*shamen*) – utter destruction. In 12:11 Jesus said the "abomination" would lead to desolation or destruction. That occurred literally in 70 A.D. when Titus sacked Jerusalem and the temple. The "city" and the "sanctuary" were destroyed. That will occur once again antitypically at the time of Armageddon (Revelation 16:16) just before "Babylon came in remembrance before God" (vs 19) (the "city"). Then the synagogue of Satan (Revelation 2:9) (the apostate "sanctuary") will be forever gone. Here, war is introduced as the immediate cause of its end. It is as if God is telling all His people, "Don't be concerned, ultimately apostasy, the *little horn*, those representing Satan and Babylon, will meet their fate in total annihilation."

We are reminded of apostasy in Isaiah's day. God's people were saying, "Prophesy not unto us right things, speak unto us smooth things, prophesy deceits"

---

[1] Harris, R. Laird, et al.; *Theological Wordbook of the Old Testament,* vol. II, p. 918.

(Isaiah 30:10). God bears with sin and deception only so long.

The verse ends with a most comforting word – *charats*. That destruction has already been *decided*. In fact, God *decreed* it. That is amazing and wonderful.

Again, what war (*milchamah*) will lead to this desolation? Revelation 14–20 opens the door to two wars – both called Armageddon. One is obviously a mortal conflict between men as the four winds are loosened, the other is the final battle between good and evil, principalities and powers, when the "wine of His wrath" is poured out without mixture.

Long before Babylon came onto the scene, Isaiah (chapter 21) and Jeremiah (chapters 50–51) said that it would come to its end – totally – never to rise again. Here, the papacy or *little horn*, which was part of Babylon, will come to its end – "he shall be broken without hand … he shall come to his end, and none shall help him" (Daniel 8:25, 9:45). The "he-goat" representatives will have a *measured period* of time to work (Daniel 12:7), but at the end will be the deliverance of God's people (Daniel 12:1) and destruction of wickedness. Here in Daniel we are seeing in miniature what the book of Revelation will unfold in greater detail for the world.

"But the cloud of judicial wrath hangs over them, containing the elements that destroyed Sodom. In his visions of things to come the prophet John beheld this scene. This demon worship was revealed to him, and it seemed to him as if the whole world were standing on the brink of perdition....

"When the storm of God's wrath breaks upon the world, it will be a terrible revelation for souls to find that their house is being swept away because it is built upon the sand."[2]

"'Behold, the Lord maketh the earth empty, and maketh it waste, and turneth it upside down, and scattereth abroad the inhabitants thereof.' 'The land shall be utterly emptied, and utterly spoiled: for the Lord hath spoken this word.' 'Because they have transgressed the laws, changed the ordinance, broken the everlasting covenant. Therefore hath the curse devoured the earth, and they that dwell therein are desolate: therefore the inhabitants of the earth are burned.' Isaiah 24:1, 3, 5, 6....

"The whole earth appears like a desolate wilderness. The ruins of cities and villages destroyed by the earthquake, uprooted trees, ragged rocks thrown out by the sea or torn out of the earth itself, are scattered over its surface, while vast caverns mark the spot where the mountains have been rent from their foundations."[3] Desolation will come!

We passed quickly through sixty-nine weeks of the seventy-week prophecy. The issues of Messiah the Prince unfolded. Then suddenly, the theme moved *away* from that time to the fall of literal Jerusalem, and even more relevant, to messages related to apostasy and corruption at the very end of time. Satan was successful in bringing all too many of God's people to turn against their very Savior. In these proleptic reflective messages Gabriel opens scenes that depict the final outcome of the *little horn*'s end-time work of Daniel 8. He lingers long enough to warn what lies ahead for God's church, then hurries back to the Messiah, only to return again to the end-of-time rebellion.

Remember, remember – in most prophecies there is often a literal mean-

---

[2] White, Ellen G.; *Testimonies,* vol. 6, pp. 14-15.
[3] White, Ellen G.; *Maranatha,* p. 305.

ing. But that is always a metaphor for a deeper spiritual message. Of *greater significance* is *always* the spiritual. In it the covenant restoration theme is forever appealed to at the great consummation.

CHAPTER 26

THAT LAST EVENTFUL WEEK

"And he shall confirm the covenant with many for one week:" (Daniel 9:27a).

This begins one of the most important and least understood verses in this series. Because of this, we are going to go carefully through its key words.

This verse refers to the *last* "seven" of the seventy of the sevens – "one week." Within its confines we will observe the *completion* of God's purposes for His people. Recall verse 24: Within the time period of 490 years – the seventy weeks of years – all sin would be put away, *everlasting* righteousness would be established, the *chazown* vision would be completed and everything would become holy once again. Time breaks *within* this seven-year period with the death of the Messiah and the sacrifice and oblations no longer being of any use. But "everlasting" (*olam*) – the most distant of times – eternity – is to begin at the week's end!

That may make some uncomfortable, having strictly historical views. What is God contextually saying? This prophecy sweeps history and terminates when the controversy with evil ends. It is when righteousness (*tsedeq*), the *legal resolution* of all spiritual conflict, ends with holiness in a people God can wed (Revelation 19). He has been trying to rivet that concept into our understanding since 8:14, when His people are made holy and righteous – when the *adjudication process begins.*

We're not eager to "toy with" or debate the *gap theory*; and that is exactly what it is, a theory with a terrible gap where the *last week* of the 490 years is artificially thrown into the future. We must analyze in context the meaning of the Hebrew words. The beauty of chapter 9 is *repeated* in the book of Revelation relative to the heavenly invitation. There, many promises associated with "he that overcometh" in the "144,000's victory" are given. Daniel 8–12 is a preface to that amazing book, including this verse.

"he shall confirm the covenant"

This presents an important challenge. Who will confirm the covenant? The Hebrew word for "confirm" is *gabar*. In Aramaic it suggests "rise or restore." But here in Hebrew its meaning is rich and affirming. In the verb tense (*hiphil*) used here it means confirms or validates the covenant.

Messiah the Prince ratifies what began in the Garden of Eden when Adam and Eve were promised a way of escape from the death penalty. The beauty of promise expanded and matured as God communicated His thoughts to His people.

"Now the God of peace, that brought again from the dead our Lord Jesus, that great shepherd of the sheep, through the blood of the everlasting covenant, Make you perfect in every good work to do his will, working in you that which is well-pleasing in his sight" (Hebrews 13:20-21a).

"And this is the covenant that I will make with the house of Israel; After those days, saith the Lord, I will put my laws in their inward parts, and write it in their hearts; and will be their God, and they

shall be my people" (Jeremiah 31:33). That is holiness restored.

A *covenant* implies a transaction between two sides. God has put man on a *timed probation.* Man's part of the contract must be completed within those *timelines.* Daniel acknowledged in his prayer that God kept His side of the covenant.

What if man doesn't keep his part of the agreement? God reveals a remarkable principle about His justice in Genesis 6:3, "My Spirit shall not always strive with man." Noah was then given 120 years of probation. In Daniel 9 the completion of the covenant was to be accomplished in 490 years. This time its termination would occur at the very *end of time.*

What would cause God to cease having a covenant of mercy toward mankind? There are many endpoints in the Scriptures. Examples include the end of the sixth millennium (Great Week of Time – Leviticus 25 setting), the gospel to all the world (Matthew 24:14), when God senses wickedness so deeply He wishes He hadn't created man (Genesis 5:5-6), when "the first heaven and the first earth were passed away" (Revelation 21:1).

The last week of the 70 is Messiah-driven. Heaven pulls all stops to give God's people a note of mercy and the sound of justice. The Rescuer comes and is anointed or set apart for His mission. He is killed by the people He came to save in the middle of this last week. In spite of this, before and after (3½ years and 3½ years) He continues to affirm His love, His promises and covenant of grace. That is the note of mercy.

An essential observation to focus on is the significance of this 490-year period – now in its last week. As the clock strikes the end of the 70th week, everlasting righteousness will have entered,

the opposition of Satan and his agents will have forever ceased and the heavenly courts will be cleansed of blood transactions. Daniel 9:24 is end-of-time restoration language. It goes way beyond 34 A.D.!

Before the cross He pleads His life of love and mercy. After the cross the disciples do the same as His representatives.

"For seven years after the Saviour entered on His ministry, the gospel was to be preached especially to the Jews; for three and a half years by Christ Himself; and afterward by the apostles."[1]

"Jesus Christ was a minister ... to confirm the promises made unto the fathers" (Romans 15:8).

"with many for one week"

"Many" (*rab*) is presumed to be an adjective referring back to the Princes' people – "many people." Confirming the covenant continues in a *special way* for one (*echad*) week. This refers to a cardinal number and implies unity of its individual timed parts (Exodus 26:6, 11; 36:13; Genesis 2:24, 34:16; Ezekiel 37:12; Malachi 2:5). That week is to be a unified whole in the context of restoration and redemption. "Week" here is once again *shabuwa* – a "seven-period." That is a perfect number. But we saw that imperfect, hellish Satan split that perfect whole into three and a half and three and a half. Three and a half is prophetically imperfect and associated with evil.

Satan or his agents will war against the covenant (*b@ryth*). Why? It *establishes* everlasting righteousness. It legally binds Satan and restores holiness to the universe. The covenant is destructive to Satan and any of his followers. He is doing everything to block its completion

---

[1] White, Ellen G.; *The Desire of Ages,* pp. 233-234.

and, in turn, keeping the seventy weeks probationary period from ending!

This is depicted in chapter 11 in an end-time setting:

- The *king of the north* "shall be against the holy *covenant*" (11:28).

- He shall "have indignation against the holy *covenant*" (11:30).

- Those that do "wickedly against the *covenant* shall be corrupt by flatteries" (11:32).

Satan or his agents war not only against the covenant but against the covenant Maker and covenant people for "one week" or a total of seven years. That is a prophetic unit of time. It will be split in two but **must** be put back together. *Echad shabuwa* is a whole. That *is why* there are several 1260-day (3½-year) prophecies in Daniel and Revelation. They *show* how the seven will be once again put back together. The last probationary week must be a whole because its last year is a Jubilee Atonement year when the covenant is complete and man's restoration occurs!

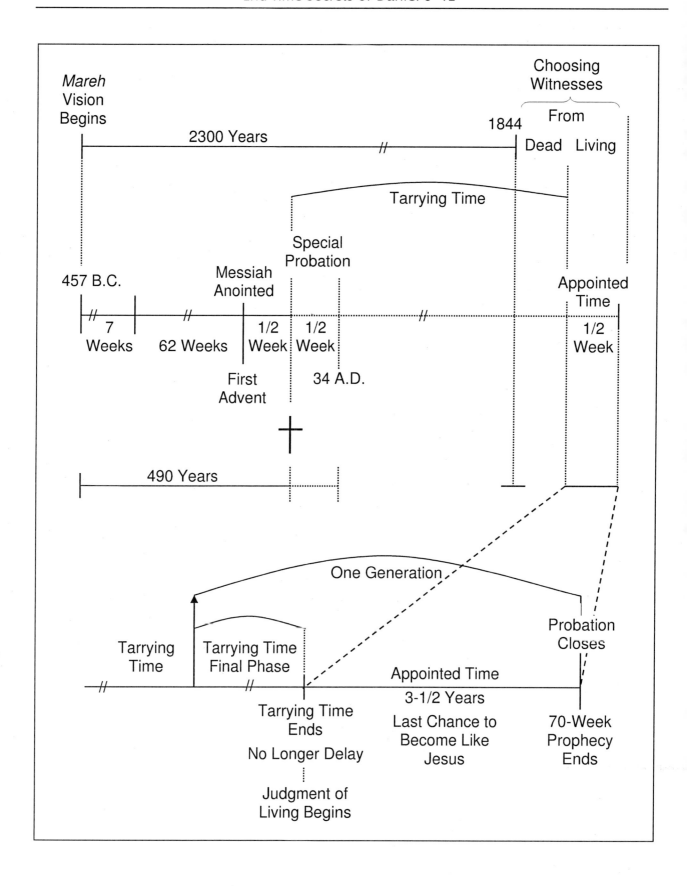

CHAPTER 27

SHORTENING THE WEEK
BUT NOT THE PROPHECY

"... and in the midst of the week he shall cause the sacrifice and the oblation to cease," (Daniel 9:27b).

In the last chapter we talked about the *sacred* last week of seven years of the seventy weeks of years. That last week ends ten Jubilee cycles. Therefore, that week will end when everything will be restored (outlined in verse 24). The covenant promises lead to destruction of Satan and his followers. If he can create a barrier to the restoration of a holy people, his claim as the "prince of this world" remains. That last "week" must be disrupted. If so, he is preserved from doom. The setting in Daniel 8–12 reveals that Satan proceeds under that premise.

Here in the midst of that week, "he" will cause something to end. The previous pronoun (vs 26) goes back to the people of the Prince (*nagid*) or those helping to fulfill God's plans.

In the "middle" or midpoint of the *shabuwa* the Messiah will cause the ceremonial Jewish system to cease. In the previous verse it said that *after* the sixty-nine weeks (nothing specific – a generic time declaration), the Messiah would meet a violent death. Here in the midst of this last week the theocracy of sacrificial ceremonies ceases. We know this was the point of Christ's death because the moment Jesus "yielded up the ghost" (Matthew 27:50) "the veil of the temple was rent in twain from top to bottom" (vs 51). The sacred divide between the Holy and Most Holy ceased for the Jewish people. Type had met antitype. Jesus became that veil – the portal to the Most Holy, God's throne. He became the confirmed way.

"The way into the holiest is laid open. A new and living way is prepared for all. No longer need sinful, sorrowing humanity await the coming of the high priest. Henceforth the Saviour was to officiate as priest and advocate in the heaven of heavens. It was as if a living voice had spoken to the worshipers: There is now an end to all sacrifices and offerings for sin. The Son of God is come according to His word, 'Lo, I come (in the volume of the Book it is written of Me,) to do Thy will, O God.' 'By His own blood' He entereth 'in once into the holy place, having obtained eternal redemption for us.' Heb. 10:7; 9:12."[1]

The "he shall cause" implies His death leads to *"the sacrifice and the oblation to cease."* At the three and a half year point ("midst of the week") the sacrifices, ceremonies and oblations ceased. The sacrificial lamb was supplanted by the Lamb of God. Type met antitype. There is no longer any need for the intricate ceremonial worship rituals.

"Little did the Jews realize the terrible responsibility involved in rejecting Christ. From the time when the first innocent blood was shed, when righteous Abel fell by the hand of Cain, the same history had been repeated, with increasing guilt.

---

[1] White, Ellen G.; *The Desire of Ages*, p. 757.

In every age prophets had lifted up their voices against the sins of kings, rulers, and people, speaking the words which God gave them, and obeying His will at the peril of their lives. From generation to generation there had been heaping up a terrible punishment for the rejecters of light and truth. This the enemies of Christ were now drawing down upon their own heads. The sin of the priests and rulers was greater than that of any preceding generation. By their rejection of the Saviour, they were making themselves responsible for the blood of all the righteous men slain from Abel to Christ. They were about to fill to overflowing their cup of iniquity. And soon it was to be poured upon their heads in retributive justice. Of this, Jesus warned them: 'That upon you may come all the righteous blood shed upon the earth, from the blood of righteous Abel unto the blood of Zacharias son of Barachias, whom ye slew between the temple and the altar. Verily I say unto you, All these things shall come upon this generation.' [Matthew 23:35] …

"Divine pity marked the countenance of the Son of God as He cast one lingering look upon the temple and then upon His hearers. In a voice choked by deep anguish of heart and bitter tears He exclaimed, 'O Jerusalem, Jerusalem, thou that killest the prophets, and stonest them which are sent unto thee, how often would I have gathered thy children together, even as a hen gathereth her chickens under her wings, and ye would not!' This is the separation struggle. In the lamentation of Christ the very heart of God is pouring itself forth. It is the mysterious farewell of the long-suffering love of the Deity….

"Israel as a nation had divorced herself from God. The natural branches of the olive tree were broken off. Looking for the last time upon the interior of the tem-ple, Jesus said with mournful pathos, 'Behold, your house is left unto you desolate. For I say unto you, Ye shall not see Me henceforth, till ye shall say, Blessed is He that cometh in the name of the Lord.' Hitherto He had called the temple His Father's house; but now, *as the Son of God should pass out from those walls, God's presence would be withdrawn forever* from the temple built to His glory. Henceforth its ceremonies would be meaningless, its services a mockery."[2]

We can grasp the rich meaning of this prophecy by looking at the gospels when Messiah the Prince came and was cut off. The gospels fill in the details of the *exact time* this final week would begin and this "midst" or midpoint would occur. It *began* at the anointing of the Messiah. At its *middle*, Jesus was crucified at Passover.

The leaders of the chosen nation of Israel and the rabble that followed brought Jesus to His death. They railed against the Messiah, bringing to an end the sacrifices and oblations that had grown ever more burdensome by tradition.

And that brings us to one of the most important and, unfortunately, opinion-filled issues. What did Jesus mean when He said:

1. The blood of the righteous will come against that generation in Jesus' day (Matthew 23:33-36) as part of a severance "woe" or curse?

2. "Behold, your house is left unto you desolate" (Matthew 23:38)?

3. "The kingdom of God shall be *taken from you*, and given to a nation bringing forth the fruits thereof" (Matthew 21:43)?

---

[2] *Ibid.,* pp. 618-620.

There is no other conclusion that one can come to – the Jewish nation would cease to be God's chosen people. When? When Messiah the Prince was "cut off" – the guilt of millenniums fell on that people. They were, as a nation, to bear an eternal curse.

Missing that point has brought in terrible misunderstanding and woe to the Protestant and virtually all of the evangelical world. Here's why. Gabriel told Daniel several minutes ago that 490 years were "determined" or decreed for "thy people" to become holy and have everything ready for a Jubilee restoration. Daniel's people "blew it." Their probation ended at the cross. That was 31 A.D. That was three and a half years short of the 490 years. And – that's a problem many expositors simply ignore or find fertile ground upon which to speculate.

"The once favored people of God were separating themselves from Him, and were fast becoming a people disowned by Jehovah. When Christ upon the cross cried out, 'It is finished' (John 19:30), and the veil of the temple was rent in twain, the Holy Watcher declared that the Jewish people had rejected Him who was the antitype of all their types, the substance of all their shadows. Israel was divorced from God. Well might Caiaphas then rend his official robes,

which signified that he claimed to be a representative of the great High Priest; for no longer had they any meaning for him or for the people. Well might the high priest rend his robes in horror for himself and for the nation."[3]

Before we can finish this verse, this issue must be explored in greater depth. The verse finishes with comments related to the end of the wicked people. The matter of perfecting a holy people and the completion of the covenant is *not* commented on further in chapters 8–12. But enough hints will be given from Gabriel and twice more by Jesus in person to tell us that the details of the last part of the three and a half years will be unfolded in the book of Revelation.

Recall – this is all part of the *mareh* vision, which was not sealed. Yet, its revelation was "cut short" at the "cutting off" of Jesus. There is simply no contextual gymnastics or linguistic exposition that can add to what is not. The nation of Israel ceased to be God's holy people *at the cross*. What do we do with the last three and a half years? It is *not* discussed in Daniel 9! Jesus personally returns to tell what will happen in the last three and a half years – the final time of the prince of this world – all in Daniel 12.

A probation is put on hold. That will be our study in the next chapter.

---

[3] *Ibid.,* p. 709.

A TIME GAP PREDICTED BEFORE THE 70-WEEK PROPHECY GIVEN

"... even until the consummation, and that determined shall be poured upon the desolate" (Daniel 9:27d).

SEQUENCE OF DANIEL 9:26 AND 27

The setting is 490 years of probation couched within seventy sevens. In sixty-nine weeks the Messiah would come. This is felt to be 27 A.D. at His baptism or anointing. Sometime *after* this sixty-nine weeks the Messiah is killed. That death causes the sacrifice and oblation to cease in the *midst* of the last week. This is when Jesus cried "It is finished," coinciding with the curtain in the temple being torn in two (Matthew 27:51).

Outside of the declaration that the Prince will validate the covenant with many for a week, the *end* of the seventy weeks is not defined. The completion of the everlasting covenant (Daniel 9:24) never occurred in that *immediate setting!*

The last half of verse 27 is a commentary insert:

"And for the overspreading of abominations he shall make it desolate, even until the consummation, and that determined shall be poured upon the desolate" (Daniel 9:27c,d).

We've seen the culmination of the messianic mission, now the end of all opposition. This important picture is developed to mesh with other abomination/transgression/desolation prophecies – especially in this book.

How? In verse 24 one of the covenant steps that had to occur was to "seal up

the vision and prophecy." That referred to the *chazown* vision. It was a prophetic sweep of opposing satanic agencies that would try to prevent the completion of the redemptive plan. Verse 27c declares that part of the agreement with "Israel" would occur *after the cross.* Then in 27d all opposition would cease.

Thus, associated with bringing in everlasting righteousness is the destruction of Satan's host. Satan's people (Babylon) nearly destroy the church and its form of worship, which leads us to the end of time, encompassing wrath and war. But desolation is promised (in prophecy) as the outcome. Because of those abominations it will become desolate, reaching to the great consummation ("even until the consummation") – it is all decreed (prophesied).

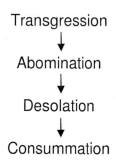

Transgression
↓
Abomination
↓
Desolation
↓
Consummation

Just as Jesus made the ties to Daniel in Matthew 24:15, the abomination leads to end-time devastation.

To further capture the exciting end-time meaning of Daniel's prophecies, we must move forward in time to crucial points conveyed by Jesus. It was on the

Mount of Olives that Jesus outlined the signs, events and prophetic links that would confirm the arrival of the last days. Within that awesome discourse were important sequences and, ignored by many, two ends of time.

"In his answer, Jesus did not take up separately the destruction of Jerusalem and the last great day of his coming. He mingled the description of these two events. When he spoke of the destruction of Jerusalem, his words referred also to the final destruction that will take place when the Lord rises out of his place to punish the world for its iniquity. The *entire chapter* [notice this insight] in which are recorded Christ's words regarding this, is a warning to all who shall live during *the last scenes* of this earth's history."[1]

This is an important concept that should settle many theological debates. There are two end-time messages within Scripture (outside the Flood). Matthew 24 outlines both. Verse 15 is pivotal in guiding us to *complementary information* in Daniel regarding each.

"When ye therefore shall see the abomination of desolation, spoken of by Daniel the prophet, stand in the holy place ... flee ..." Matthew 24:15 (cf. Mark 13:14).

Contextually, these thoughts are part of a sequence of events that introduces a terminus:

Jesus' day:

> Abomination
> Flee destruction – Jerusalem
> Tribulation
> End

[1] White, Ellen G.; *The Review and Herald*, December 13, 1898.

End of time:

> Abomination
> Flee destruction – Babylon
> Tribulation
> End

This *abomination* was to be a "sign" to God's people to "flee" away from the "city." As with most prophecy, Jesus inserted a useful timing element. When you see this abomination, flee so quickly you don't go back to the house to retrieve any belongings, not even an outer garment (coat) left at the edge of a field. That's urgent! The *abomination* is very bad and threatening – and a sign of the end! Daniel talks about the same abomination in several places!

Bdelugma is the Greek word used to express this abomination. *Toebah* is the Hebrew word Ezekiel chose (Ezekiel 8) to describe a similar abomination. *Siqqus* [shiqqowts] is the Hebrew rendition for abomination that Daniel used. The abomination will lead to desolation (utter destruction). Thus we now have this additional sequence:

Jesus' Day:

> Cross
> Time gap
> Abomination
> Flee destruction – Jerusalem
> Tribulation
> *Desolation – city*
> End

> 1260 Days

End of time:

> Cross
> Time gap
> Abomination
> Flee destruction – Babylon
> Tribulation
> *Desolation – world*
> End

> 1260 Days

Where do the 1260-day periods come from? Daniel 12 and Revelation 11 together put the last-day events within a three and a half year time period. (There are others, but they are outside the scope of this chapter.)

The fall of Jerusalem was over a three and a half year period also. Both periods depict a final probation. The 70 A.D. desolation is a metaphor of the final period of mercy before the world becomes desolate.

What was so detestable to God that it was called an abomination? The chief mythical Greek god Zeus was called "Lord of Heaven." The Jews developed a reactionary term against this designation – "an abomination that desolates." The abomination related to some false worship standard that took either the place of God or what He wanted. It related to an idolatrous substitute. It was an abhorrent practice in God's sight – something that took away honor from Him.

Jesus related this to a last-day sign of His nearness. He then specifically said that this abomination was the same one detailed by Daniel. *That means whenever he used it he was describing an end-time prophecy.* And that is exactly what Jesus wants us to conclude. He knew that rich and detailed information was already given to Daniel that would complement his end-time discourse. Thus he urged all – right in the middle of the chapter – to look at the signs that are also in Daniel. They would be transition signals, with warnings surrounding them, to know *when* the final end-time events would commence.

"DESOLATION" ADDS UNDERSTANDING TO CHRIST'S WORDS

Eremos (desolate) means an "area uninhabited" or one that has been laid waste and depopulated. Jesus warns that some abomination will lay Jerusalem waste. In a greater application it refers to the world and what will happen when it is laid waste by the Trumpets, Armageddon and the Plagues.

"Christ, upon the Mount of Olives, rehearsed the fearful judgments that were to precede His second coming: ... While these prophecies received a partial fulfillment at the destruction of Jerusalem, they have a more direct application to the last days."[2]

Daniel refers to desolations in chapters 8–12 several times. Except for Daniel lamenting Jerusalem's desolation in his prayer (9:18), they all relate to the final outcome of an abominable act. Four times in Daniel 8–12 the verb tense related to this suggests that someone has caused the sanctuary or altar (God's church and ministry) to be polluted, making it unfit for worship or the services to God. No wonder God permits the world to become desolate. Those texts relate to a power or being that *sins unto desolation:*

> 8:13:
> Transgression
> Little Horn
> Desolation

> 9:27:
> Abomination
> Prince
> Desolation

> 11:31:
> Abomination
> King of North
> Desolation

> 12:11:
> Abomination
> Final timing event (of Babylon)
> Desolation

---

[2] White, Ellen G.; *Testimonies,* vol. 5, p. 753.

Every one of these relates to either Jerusalem's destruction or the final destruction of the world. Many expositors have tried to bring in diverse historic events to account for this prophetic desolation outlined to the disciples. *We must revisit again and again the idea that Jesus defined two terminuses or end-time prophecies related to desolation –* future to His time!

It is vital to grasp another amazing concept. Jerusalem was destroyed or desolated *after the end* of the 490-year period during a three and a half year siege. There was a delay or gap of 40 years – but within a generation. It is precision-clear that false standards will lay siege to the world at the very end for three and a half years just before the world is desolated, following a time delay or gap called a *tarrying time.*

When the gap ends, the final probation period to gather the remnant and prepare for the tribulation begins and lasts three and a half years.

WHAT IS HAPPENING TO THE 70-WEEK PROPHECY?

Daniel 9 takes us to Christ's death and the termination of the sacrifice and oblation. It does not tell us what happens at the end – at least in that chapter. The only thing it states is that the Messiah will confirm the covenant for one week. Does that mean Jesus ceased his mediatorial work in 34 A.D.? Hardly. We must see Daniel 8–12 as a unit. Each part complements the other. The war goes to the *consummation* (9:27)!

Did Daniel's people reach perfection and bring in everlasting righteousness at the cross? Did Daniel's people reach perfection and bring in everlasting righteousness by 34 A.D.? To draw such conclusions circumvents what is in the prophecy.

Let's listen to what E. G. White resolves relative to this issue. The death knell of the Jewish nation sounds: "A divine voice had been appealing to them for three years and a half, but they hated it, and were plotting to silence it by death. 'God so loved the world, that he gave his only begotten Son, that whosoever believeth on him should not perish, but have everlasting life.' But the Jewish nation refused to accept the offering; and Christ took up the lamentation of unrequited love: 'O Jerusalem, Jerusalem, thou that killest the prophets, and stonest them which are sent unto thee, how often would I have gathered thy children together, even as a hen gathereth her chickens under her wings, and ye would not!' You have perverted my words, and wrested my entreaties."[3]

"The Kingdom of God shall be taken from you and given to a nation bringing forth the fruits thereof" (Matthew 21:43).

"Your house is left unto you desolate" (Matthew 23:38).

Probation for the Jewish people ended at the cross – the very time-period set aside for them to develop a holy character *was never completed.*

BRANCHES SEVERED FROM THE VINE

"What was Christ's grief to see the Jews fixing their own destiny beyond redemption! He alone could comprehend the significance of their rejection, betrayal, and condemnation of the Son of God. His last hope for the Jewish nation was gone. Nothing could avert her doom. By the representatives of the nation God was denied as their Ruler. By worlds unfallen, by the whole heavenly universe, the blasphemous utterance was heard, 'We have no king but Caesar.' The God of heaven heard their choice. He had

---

[3] White, Ellen G.; *The Review and Herald,* May 18, 1897.

given them opportunity to repent, and they would not. Forty years afterward Jerusalem was destroyed, and the Roman power ruled over the people. Then they had no deliverer. They had no king but Caesar. Henceforth the Jewish nation, as a nation, was as a branch severed from the vine – a dead, fruitless branch, to be gathered up and burned – from land to land throughout the world, from century to century, dead – dead in trespasses and sins – without a Saviour (YI Feb. 1, 1900)!"[4]

"But Israel as a nation had divorced herself from God. The natural branches of the olive tree were *broken off*. Looking for the last time upon the interior of the temple, Jesus said with mournful pathos, 'Behold, your house is left unto you desolate. For I say unto you, Ye shall not see Me henceforth, till ye shall say, Blessed is He that cometh in the name of the Lord.' Hitherto He had called the temple His Father's house; but now, as the Son of God should pass out from those walls, God's presence would be withdrawn *forever* from the temple built to His glory. Henceforth its ceremonies would be meaningless, its services a mockery."[5]

The cross – midst of the week – ended the Jewish nation's probation and favor.

"When Christ should hang upon the cross of Calvary, Israel's day as a nation favored and blessed would be ended."[6]

"When Christ upon the cross cried out, 'It is finished' (John 19:30), and the veil of the temple was rent in twain, the Holy watcher declared that the Jewish people had rejected Him who was the antitype of all their types, the substance of all their shadows. Israel was divorced from God."[7]

Many will protest that the Jewish probation ended in 34 A.D. There are numerous statements and allusions to this because that would have ended the 490 years. But – the *fulfillment* of the 70-week prophecy has not yet occurred. Daniel 9:24 awaits completion! The last three and a half years still tarries for a people to finally meet the divine ordered objective. The everlasting covenant is ratified but not completed.

"That which God purposed to do for the world through Israel, the chosen nation, He will finally accomplish through His church on earth today. He has 'let out His vineyard unto other husbandmen,' even to His covenant-keeping people, who faithfully 'render Him the fruits in their seasons.' Never has the Lord been without true representatives on this earth who have made His interests their own. These witnesses for God are numbered among the spiritual Israel, and to them will be fulfilled all the covenant promises made by Jehovah to His ancient people."[8]

That is plain and confirmatory. Spiritual Israel will be rewarded with the covenant promises. In the 144,000 will be seen the completion of 9:24.

WHAT DID HAPPEN BETWEEN THE CROSS AND 34 A.D.?

"Jesus was sitting in the midst of priests, rulers, lawyers, and Pharisees,– in the midst of men who had long been favored with the heavenly invitation, and who claimed to be guests for the feast of the Lord. But when the time came when they should have entered into the spiritual kingdom of heaven, when by believ-

---

[4] White, Ellen G.; *The Seventh-day Adventist Bible Commentary,* vol. 5, p. 1149.
[5] White, Ellen G.; *The Desire of Ages,* p. 620.
[6] White, Ellen G.; *The Great Controversy,* p. 21.
[7] White, Ellen G.; *The Desire of Ages,* p. 709.
[8] White, Ellen G.; *Patriarchs and Prophets,* p. 713-714.

ing on Christ they should have been partakers of his flesh and blood, when they should have received him whom their sacrificial offerings typified, they all with one consent began to make excuse. *Mercy was extended* to them, and *their probation was lengthened*, until three years and a half after the death of Christ [If it was already part of the 70 weeks, why "lengthen it?"], when the apostles declared: 'It was necessary that the word of God should first have been spoken to you; but seeing you put it from you, and judge yourselves unworthy of everlasting life, lo, we turn to the Gentiles.' The Lord gave the commission to go out into the highways and the hedges of the cities and villages, to go to the poor, the halt, the lame, and the blind, to minister to those who felt that they had need of a physician. Jesus had declared, 'I am not come to call the righteous, but sinners to repentance.' The wandering sheep must be hunted up. The Jews refused to accept the flesh and blood of the Son of God; they would not listen to his word, which he declared is spirit and life, and rejected the invitation to the gospel feast. Through their impenitence and stubbornness of heart in refusing the heavenly invitation, they themselves were rejected. The solemn words were spoken by lips that cannot lie, saying, 'None of those men that were bidden [and who have refused my invitation] shall taste of my supper.'"[9]

Once again the 1260-day prophecies of Daniel 12 and Revelation 11–13 unfold the time period of the last probation for God's people and the time when the prince of this world (Satan, beast) will attempt to thwart the completion of the covenant – finishing the last half of the last week of the covenant.

It is a baseless reason to reject any break in the 70-week continuity simply because others have created or accepted a *spurious seven-year* Jesuit gap theory relative to the 70-week prophecy. In fact, it is amazing that a gap isn't seen because of the 2300-year prophecy in 8:14! Before the 70 weeks began, God anticipated Israel's failure by giving that 2300-year prophecy. That in itself shows that Daniel 9:24 would never be completed by Israel of old and a gap was going to occur! It's incredible.

The seventy weeks of years has not been completed. Jesus said that would happen after the 2300 evenings and mornings (8:14). There would be a long *tarrying time. "Though it tarry, wait for it; because it will surely come, it will not tarry"* (Habakkuk 2:3). At the "appointed time" the final three and a half years of earth's history will resume. Then this great prophecy will see its termination at the deliverance of God's people.

The future understanding of this prophecy was noted by E. G. White: "As Daniel's prayer is going forth, the angel Gabriel comes sweeping down from the heavenly courts to tell him that his petitions are heard and answered. This mighty angel has been commissioned to give him skill and understanding – to open before him the *mysteries of future ages.* Thus, while earnestly seeking to know and understand the truth, Daniel was brought into communion with Heaven's delegated messenger.

"In answer to his petition, Daniel received not only the light and truth which he and his people most needed, but a view of the great *events of the future, even to the advent of the world's Redeemer.*"[10]

[9] White, Ellen G.; *The Review and Herald,* March 10, 1896.

[10] White, Ellen G.; *The Sanctified Life,* pp. 48-49.

CHAPTER 29

THE RAM OF GOD

– Daniel 10:1 –

When Daniel was given the ram and he-goat vision (Daniel 8), Belshazzar, Babylon's last king, was in his third and final year of reign. The *ram symbol* represented Jesus and those who claim to be His people – the remnant, His church[1] – at or shortly *after* the "fall of Babylon." Now in this chapter messages are continued that directly relate to that ram and this time was associated with the *mareh* vision. Following a pattern used previously to clarify a prophecy (e.g., Daniel 7 develops details of Daniel 2), this chapter, along with 11 and 12, brings greater meaning to Daniel 8 and 9.

The ram – Jesus, God's people, His Church – is persecuted by the he-goat. Daniel 8:14 comes in response to Gabriel's question as to when that would occur. There, Jesus promised it would be after **spiritual** *deliverance, when restoration* would come. In 9:24 He tells what must be done by the remnant to experience that deliverance. When **physical** *deliverance and restoration* occurs would be defined later in 12:7. God will not detail *that* deliverance until greater information is given to Daniel regarding the he-goat opposition and persecution in chapter 11.

In the swift and amazing 70-week prophecy Daniel's great prayer was partially answered relative to the *deliverance* and *spiritual restoration* of Israel. Gabriel had much more to share.[2] But Daniel had had enough for one sitting, noted in the Daniel 9:20-27 record.

It is now two years after the Daniel 9 contact. Cyrus, the Persian conqueror, has been in power for three years. And that is where our story begins.

Daniel ceased his administrative responsibilities in the first year of Cyrus' reign (Daniel 1:21). In that year, 538 B.C., Cyrus had decreed that the Israelites could go back and rebuild their temple in Jerusalem (Ezra 1:1-4, 6:3). Now, Daniel is two years "retired" and another revelation comes in response to earnest fasting and prayer.

HEAVEN'S RAPID RESPONSE – AGAIN

Daniel 10 begins with Daniel praying and craving for additional understanding of the prophecies. He was also pleading for help in the temple restoration, which now had begun. Discouragement had come upon the returned exiles, *and* Judah's enemies were seeking to thwart that work by God's people (Daniel 10:2-3 – discussed shortly). This opposition came from apostates – the he-goat "host" in symbolism introduced in Daniel 8.

Gabriel *later* told Daniel: *"Then said he unto me, Fear not, Daniel: for from the first day that thou didst set thine heart to understand, and to chasten thyself before thy God* [Daniel's prayer]*, thy words were*

---

[1] White, Ellen G.; *The Great Controversy*, p. 325.

[2] White, Ellen G.; *The Sanctified Life,* p. 49.

heard, and I am come for thy words" (Daniel 10:12).

This is another beautiful illustration of answered prayer. Though the fasting and praying lasted three weeks, the angel of God (Gabriel), came the "first day." Satan – the he-goat power – influenced Judah's enemies to write disparaging letters to Cyrus to resist the Jewish work. The battle between Satan (prince of the kingdom of Persia) and Gabriel was so intense that Michael (Prince of heaven) had to come and help him contain Satan. This influenced Cyrus and his successor, Darius, to work favorably for God's people. All this encompasses a remarkable prophetic metaphor related to the 144,000 at the very end of time. They will be praying and pleading for help and guidance. It will seem like their prayers are not heard. But God's "angel" will have been there all the time.

Spiritual restoration sought – prayers
(temple cleansing)

Antichrist – apostate people fight
(persecution)

Restoration promised
(everlasting covenant)

Deliverer strengthens
(Latter Rain)

Restoration comes (sealing)

Deliverance – God's people
(at midnight)

Desolation – of world

Then came beautiful words of hope to Daniel: *"I will show thee that which is noted in the scripture of truth"* (Daniel 10:21). His response?

"A thing was revealed ... and he understood the thing ..." (Daniel 10:1). This first verse is Daniel's response to what Gabriel shows in the rest of the chapter. His conclusions from what follows is given first.

How strange to begin this next vision in the third person (10:1) and in the next verse suddenly switch to the first person. So unexpected also was that the KJV twice says a "thing" was revealed to Daniel. But when we look at all this closer, the "thing" becomes utterly amazing.

"Thing" comes from a word that Daniel has used many times – *dabar*. It is translated more than eighty different ways in the Old Testament as a noun! When used here as a *substantive*, it represents a very important legal decree or word from God that explains something already presented.[3] What does this mean? In the midst of so much prophecy of persecution, the "thing" assures us that God's people will be given "due process." They will be protected from unfair and arbitrary rule. Though accused by Satan, God assures that His people will be given liberty, eternal life and inheritance of the earth made new. Isn't that incredible! The previous visions have a lot of doom and gloom. Now in beautiful legal language Daniel is assured that God's people will triumph! He said exactly the same thing in 8:14.

Daniel 10 Begins With a Conclusion

"In the third year of Cyrus king of Persia a thing was revealed unto Daniel, whose name was called Belteshazzar; and the thing [was] true, but the time appointed [was] long: and he understood

---

[3] Harris, R. Laird; Archer, Jr., Gleason L.; Waltke, Bruce K. *Theological Wordbook of the Old Testament,* vol. 1, pp. 178-179.

the thing, and had understanding of the vision" (Daniel 10:1).

In Cyrus' third year, in third person language, making it sound like he is a reporter of a dramatic message, "a *thing* was revealed to Daniel." Coming at a time when he had approximately two years to ponder the mysteries of recent visions, and following new visions and messages, he comes under such conviction that he blurts out: "They're true." "I understand the *mareh* vision" – that legal declaration of God that His people will be holy and adjudicated.

Verse 1 can be described as Daniel's breakthrough of understanding. He's excited and wants to share what happened with legal overtones! It continues the descriptive language begun in chapter 8. A legal finale' is being described, and Daniel *understands* that "thing."

Medo-Persia was symbolized by the ram (8:20), representing, as we have seen, God's people, His church and Jesus at the time Babylon falls. Also, the lesser horn of the ram is God's end-time people who are holy, having been adjudicated from sin, *proclaiming* the deliverance and restoration message – the greater horn being the great multitude that they bring in. In the 8th chapter is described a battle between good and evil – God's people and Satan's host. The first timing *explanation* came in 8:14. The 2300 evenings and mornings is tied to when God's people would be rescued – *spiritually delivered* – made holy, adjudicated. That is Daniel's "thing" – the completion of the great restoration promise.

In that *context* Daniel said the "time appointed was long" (10:1). The Hebrew word used for "long" is *saba* and relates to fighting a battle – physical or spiritual. That is exactly what Gabriel had described between the ram and he-goat, then the *little horn* against the host, and,

finally, the prince (of this world) against God's people. The *chazown* vision describes that war. The *mareh* vision began with timing language and related to when God's people would be victorious spiritually, when the battle would be done – their deliverance complete.

Daniel is saying that he now grasps these "things." They now make sense. They are wonderfully true. The great conflict between sin and right will end – at the end – when God's people become part of the everlasting covenant. They will be righteous and holy – forever. But, he adds a concept that previously eluded him – it would be a long way off (from his time). It would be at the end of time.

This is exciting. As we see things unfold for Daniel, they unfold for us! There were things sealed from his understanding – but *the great controversy theme* as it would play out at the very *end of time* was grasped. Was this insight, referred to in verse 1, from a new vision, special conviction by the Holy Spirit or simply understanding after reviewing his previous notes? Something clicked in Daniel's thinking when he finally acknowledged that it all made sense.

We are told exactly what happened to bring about this insight. And, that is a beautiful story within this incredible prophetic saga. Daniel is about to describe his most wondrous vision – one of Jesus – one that helped solidify that understanding.

HOW DANIEL UNDERSTOOD THE PROPHECY

Verse 1 is a statement of joy and excitement. Daniel wants to share how he came to understand the long periods of time and the *mareh* vision. That vision encompassed the 2300 evenings and mornings plus the 70 weeks of years. Enlightenment came also to him as to how the *chazown* vision meshed with the *mareh*, though the *full* details of the former vision were sealed from his grasp.

He now begins to share how this all came about: *"In those days I Daniel was mourning three full weeks. I ate no pleasant bread, neither came flesh nor wine in my mouth, neither did I anoint myself at all, till three whole weeks were fulfilled"* (Daniel 10:2-3).

What does all this self-inflicted fast mean? This great prophet, restless to know truth, now aged in years, wanted a full revelation of prophecy – and in addition, help for the slowed reconstruction of the Jerusalem temple. He deliberately set out to fast and grieve over this and prayed for a deeper grasp of God's will.

The Hebrew word for "mourning" (*abal*) truly means mourning like those who grieve a deceased relative. Can you imagine feeling such a depth of loss over wanting to see the beauty of truth more clearly unfolded?!

"Upon the occasion just described (Daniel 9), the angel Gabriel imparted to Daniel all the instruction that he was then able to receive. A few years afterward, however, the prophet desired to learn more of subjects not yet fully explained, and again set himself to seek light and wisdom from God. 'In those days I Daniel was mourning three full weeks. I ate no pleasant bread, neither came flesh nor wine in my mouth, neither did I anoint myself at all.'"[4]

Could this be a lesson for us? "Those who claim to be sanctified, while they have no desire to search the Scriptures or to wrestle with God in prayer for a clearer understanding of Bible truth, know not what true sanctification is."[5]

Was this to satisfy Daniel's curiosity in his later years?

"And in response to his supplications, light from the heavenly courts was communicated for those *who should live in the latter days.* With what earnestness, then, should we seek God, that He may open our understanding to comprehend the truths brought to us from heaven."[6]

This amazing prophet was mourning a lack of knowledge relative to heaven's messages. He is fasting and praying for deeper insights. As it turns out – for our benefit! What a model for us in our search of His Word!

TIMING OF THIS EXPERIENCE

A little-analyzed area of Scripture is the frequent reference to periods of time, predictions when something would occur or how an event relates to a feast or moon phase. These are fantastic interpretive tools. It is the same in this Danielic message. *"And in the four and twentieth day of the first month, as I was by the side of the great river, which [is] Hiddekel"* (Daniel 10:4).

Daniel mourned and fasted for three weeks. The vision came to him on the 24th day of the first month (Abib – Jewish; Nissan – Chaldean). This was the first month of the Jewish religious year (Exodus 12:2) of seven months (equating to the last of March and the beginning of April). It was then that the spring feasts were celebrated.

Did Daniel observe those feasts? We aren't told – but likely. His fast was only partial but would conceivably relate to the time the Passover and the Feast of Unleavened Bread occurred – and now, it is during the 50-day *waiting period!* More on this in the next chapter.

"Fasting and fervent prayer to God have moved the Lord to unlock His

---

[4] White, Ellen G.; *The Sanctified Life,* p. 49.
[5] *Ibid.,* pp. 48-49.

[6] *Ibid.,* p. 50 (emphasis added).

treasures of truth to their understanding."[7]

This was beautifully true here when Gabriel said, *"Fear not, Daniel: for from the first day that thou didst set thine heart to understand, and to chasten thyself before thy God, thy words were heard, and I am come for thy words"* (Daniel 10:12). This is a remarkable illustration of God's responsiveness to a sincere petition to grasp Biblical truth.

The expression, "three full weeks" is literally "three weeks of days," and is likely used to differentiate from the phrase "weeks of years" used in chapter 9.

A RIVER AND A VISION OF GOD!

Daniel 10–12 was given so Daniel "would understand" chapters 8 and 9! What especially needed clarifying?

1. The Medo-Persian ram link

2. The Grecian he-goat link

3. The timing of all – especially

4. The climax or deliverance from the battle between good and evil (an issue for God's/Daniel's people)

5. How the 70-week prophecy *would end*

Remember – the exciting expressions from verse 1 by Daniel affirm that he had much understanding. He is now unfolding to us what brought conviction and knowledge to him. He is sharing with us what fasting and prayer revealed. A similar understanding is to be expected by those approaching the throne of grace as Scripture is studied and analyzed.

The Hiddekel River represented God's "host" or people. The message

about to be given is for them. Daniel was promised that God's people and His church would turn back to Him and become holy (Daniel 8:14). He was given a capsule of information showing that Satan would fight that possibility. But the restoration process, the particulars of how an evil *little horn* power would be out to subvert what God set in motion and the timing when this would occur, was still very mysterious. He was told when the Messiah would arrive – but that prophecy suddenly dangled. Further details were needed.

The rest of the book is for God's people – the *mareh* part Daniel finally grasped.

THE RAM OF GOD

The ram that came from the *east* represents Medo-Persia. But God said this vision was for the time of the end, at the "appointed time" (Daniel 8:17, 19). It therefore represents something more vast than an earthly kingdom. Jesus said, "For as the lightning cometh out of the east, and shineth even unto the west; so shall also the coming of the Son of man be" (Matthew 24:27). Coming from the east, what did Medo-Persia and/or its kings represent or symbolize?

- Deliverer of Israel (Isaiah 44:28)

- God's anointed (Isaiah 45:1)

- Character development (Isaiah 45:2)

- Power that prepares for the promised land (Isaiah 44:28)

- Calling God's people out of Babylon

- Preparing for everlasting righteousness

- Victory over evil

---

[7] White, Ellen G.; *Testimonies,* vol. 2, p. 650.

That ancient power, Medo-Persia, that brought Babylon's fall is *seen* as a ram – the "deliverer." The forces that Satan wars against are its two horns – the 144,000 and the great multitude (Revelation 7).

At the end of time the great satanic forces of evil will war against the Prince and His host – Jesus and the remnant. The heavenly message has already been given by Jesus, and the 144,000 will cry with a loud voice, *"Babylon ... is fallen, is fallen, ... come out of her my people"* (Revelation 18:2, 4). The outcome of that "Medo-Persian force" – God's kingdom of people – is established. Now a mystery unfolds!

"Then I lifted up mine eyes, and looked, and behold a certain man clothed in linen, whose loins [were] girded with fine gold of Uphaz: His body also [was] like the beryl, and his face as the appearance of lightning, and his eyes as lamps of fire, and his arms and his feet like in colour to polished brass, and the voice of his words like the voice of a multitude" (Daniel 10:5-6).

In answer to Daniel's fasting and praying, the Ram of God appears personally to Daniel. If there was any misunderstanding as to who will be the ultimate Deliverer from Babylon, there can be now no question.

Daniel raised his eyes upward and saw Jesus – he "looked" (KJV) – there He was "before me" (NIV). This word "looked" is translated from the Hebrew word *hinneh*, which really suggests that he was excited about this.[8] "I gazed upward and to my amazement there was a man." But no ordinary man.

Daniel lifted up his eyes (an eschatological phrase) and saw (note the parallels):

Daniel 10:5-6	**Revelation 1:13-16**
A certain man	Son of man
Clothed in linen	Garment to foot
Loins girded with gold	Paps covered with golden girdle
Body like beryl	–
Face like lightning	Countenance like shinning sun
Eyes like lamps of fire	Eyes like flame of fire
Arms and feet like brass	Feet like fine brass
Voice like multitude	Voice the sound of many waters

The Messiah (Jesus), the Prince, the Deliverer, is before Daniel. The white linen reflects the High Priest on the Day of Atonement, the golden girdle a royal personage, the face and eyes reflect judgment. The "man" in linen will be seen again in Daniel's final vision (12:6).

This is a theophany. Daniel is in contact visually with God (just like Ezekiel in 1:26-28 and John in Revelation 1:12-16). "Daniel talked with God, ... No less a personage than the Son of God appeared to Daniel."[9] What an awesome honor for a man to look and see Jesus attired in garments of His heavenly roles. Here we see Jesus as:

- Priest – proleptic
- King – proleptic
- Judge – proleptic

proleptic = a future event seen in the present

Why is it not His role right then and there? Daniel was seeing a "prophecy of Jesus." Just as Gabriel already told us,

---

[8] Miller, Stephen R; *The New American Commentary* (Broadman & Holman Publishers), p. 280.

[9] White, Ellen G.; *The Sanctified Life,* p. 49.

these visions were for the *eth qets* – the time of the end. So the imagery presented is *when* Jesus *can be declared* a priest, a judge and a king. That would have to be after the 2300 evening and morning prophecy had ended! There is only one time in history that this occurs. It is just before Jesus returns at the deliverance of God's people. Daniel 12 elaborates more on this.

"The light that Daniel received from God was given especially for these last days. The visions he saw by the banks of the Ulai and the Hiddekel, the great rivers of Shinar, are now in process of fulfillment, and all the events foretold will soon come to pass."[10]

Here is given to Daniel the ultimate picture of the ram. In a theophany few men have ever experienced, God is conveying, as He did to John, that the Deliverer of Israel is Jesus. Yes – Medo-Persia and Cyrus are metaphors for a deliverer. But again and again the issues point to the Lamb of God in His final redemptive role as seen in Revelation. Jesus came personally envisaged in a future role to Daniel's lingering questions. "Daniel – behold the ram of God."

"And I Daniel alone saw the vision: for the men that were with me saw not the vision; but a great quaking fell upon them, so that they fled to hide themselves" (Daniel 10:7).

Daniel's companions fled. It was too much for them to encounter. So, it will be at the end. Daniel represents those who look up and are enraptured at seeing Jesus – the Lamb of God. And, those who fled symbolize those who cry, "hide us from the face of Him that sitteth on the throne."

---

[10] White, Ellen G.; *Testimonies to Ministers,* pp. 112-113.

CHAPTER 30

DANIEL'S ENCOUNTER WITH JESUS

– A Metaphor for the Remnant's Encounter with Him –

"Therefore I was left alone, and saw this great vision, and there remained no strength in me: for my comeliness was turned in me into corruption, and I retained no strength. Yet heard I the voice of his words: and when I heard the voice of his words, then was I in a deep sleep on my face, and my face toward the ground. And, behold, an hand touched me, which set me upon my knees and [upon] the palms of my hands" (Daniel 10:8, 10).

Undoubtedly, Daniel, during those three weeks of praying and fasting, honored the deliverance and restoration themes of the Passover and the Feast of Unleavened Bread. It's so amazing and divinely orchestrated to discover Jesus, the great Restorer and Deliverer, personally coming to Daniel to begin answering his prayer soon after those great events ended. Incredible as it may seem, the prophecies Daniel was seeking to clarify (Daniel 8 and 9) ended in deliverance and restoration for God's people.

It is stunning that this prophet personally sees God, in the form of a man, when He is Priest, King and Judge. Well could Daniel have said, *"Mine eyes have seen the King, the Lord of hosts"* (Isaiah 6:5b). When man encounters Jesus, something happens. The expose' of Daniel's response is a lesson for all until the end of time.

"'I Daniel alone saw the vision: for the men that were with me saw not the vision; but a great quaking fell upon them,

so that they fled to hide themselves.... And there remained no strength in me: for my comeliness was turned in me into corruption, and I retained no strength' (verses 7, 8). All who are truly sanctified will have a similar experience. *The clearer their views of the greatness, glory, and perfection of Christ, the more vividly will they see their own weakness and imperfection.* They will have no disposition to claim a sinless character; that which has appeared right and comely in themselves will, in contrast with Christ's purity and glory, appear only as unworthy and corruptible."[1]

"True holiness and humility are inseparable. The nearer the soul comes to God, the more completely is it humbled and subdued. When Job heard the voice of the Lord out of the whirlwind, he exclaimed, 'I abhor myself, and repent in dust and ashes.' It was when Isaiah saw the glory of the Lord, and heard the cherubim crying, 'Holy, holy, holy is the Lord of hosts,' that he cried out, 'Woe is me, for I am undone!' Daniel, when visited by the holy messenger, says, 'My comeliness was turned in me to corruption.' Paul, after he had been caught up into the third Heaven, and heard things that it was not lawful for a man to utter, spoke of himself as 'less than the least of all saints.' It was the beloved John, that leaned on Jesus' breast, and beheld his

---

[1] White, Ellen G.; *The Sanctified Life,* pp. 50-51 (emphasis added).

glory, who fell before the angels as one dead. *The more closely and continuously we behold our Saviour the less we shall see to approve in ourselves.*"[2]

What happened when Daniel saw Jesus? "Then was I in a deep sleep on my face, and my face toward the ground" (10:9). Later, in grand scenes in the courtroom of heaven, John saw the 24 elders "*fall down* before him that sat on the throne" (Revelation 4:10), "the four beasts and four and twenty elders *fell down* before the Lamb" (Revelation 5:8). "And the four beasts said, Amen. And the four and twenty elders *fell down* and worshiped him that liveth for ever and ever" (Revelation 5:14).

These scenes describe the ultimate response to the eternal presence – bowing down prostrate before Him – the only response that created beings can have to the Eternal. To fall prostrate before our Maker is respect, worship and honor that purity and holiness demand. To the sinner, a vision of Jesus lays bare the corruption of the heart. As that picture of our Savior becomes ever more clear, the soul longs for restoration, to be exactly like Him and yearns to come into harmony with His character.

"One ray of the glory of God, one gleam of the purity of Christ, penetrating the soul, makes every spot of defilement painfully distinct, and lays bare the deformity and defects of the human character. It makes apparent the unhallowed desires, the infidelity of the heart, the impurity of the lips. The sinner's acts of disloyalty in making void the law of God, are exposed to his sight, and his spirit is stricken and afflicted under the searching influence of the Spirit of God. He loathes himself as he views the pure, spotless character of Christ.

"When the prophet Daniel beheld the glory surrounding the heavenly messenger that was sent unto him, he was overwhelmed with a sense of his own weakness and imperfection. Describing the effect of the wonderful scene, he says, 'There remained no strength in me: for my comeliness was turned in me into corruption, and I retained no strength.' Daniel 10:8. The soul thus touched will hate its selfishness, abhor its self-love, and will seek, through Christ's righteousness, for the purity of heart that is in harmony with the law of God and the character of Christ."[3]

When one witnesses a theophany or angelic appearance (e.g., Daniel 8:16-18, Joshua 5:14, Ezekiel 1:28, Revelation 1:17), the splendor and majesty of something so much greater and more wonderful causes the human frame to sink into nothingness. When that occurs only celestial aid can rescue and restore. For those who resist and rebel, the glory of an encounter with Jesus becomes a burning fire (II Thessalonians 2:8), and they cry, "hide us from the face of him that sitteth on the throne, and from the wrath of the Lamb" (Revelation 6:16). Daniel's companions ran away and hid. Who were they? We aren't told. But they are a metaphor for all those at the very end of time who have some vision of Jesus and seek to distance themselves from Him – never to return.

A most unusual revelation continues regarding this encounter. Though he lost all his strength and was in a "deep sleep" on the ground, "Yet heard I the voice of his words"! What did Jesus say to him? (10:9). We aren't told. In the heart of this beloved prophet were hid and cherished those words that were undoubtedly very personal. Wonder of wonders! Jesus took

---

[2] White, Ellen G.; *The Signs of the Times,* April 7, 1887 (emphasis added).

[3] White, Ellen G.; *Steps to Christ,* p. 29.

time out of administering the billions of worlds and countless beings that pulsated harmony and love in His infinite realm to visit with Daniel!

"Daniel's privileged status as one especially precious to God resulted from his complete absorption in the will and glory of the Lord to whom he had yielded his heart.

"Though James 5:16 tells us that the prayer of a righteous man is powerful and effective, we may not realize the mighty forces that are unleashed when we really devote ourselves to intercession before the throne of grace."[4]

For those individuals who are day by day seeking an experience with Jesus, every encounter is one of new growth, ever more bonding and coming nearer to His heart. That is exactly what happened here. Daniel testifies that when he fell prostrate to the ground like one unconscious: "A hand touched me"! (Daniel 10:10). Jesus touched him. Amazing – indescribable. John writes exactly the same thing. Right after he fell at Jesus' feet as one "dead," He laid His right hand (the hand of covenant and promise) on him. No sooner do we fall and the precious Savior touches us, ready to help and lift us up.

Scholars aren't sure and the record isn't clear exactly when Gabriel is introduced into the scene. It is certain that when the narrative begins in verse 12 that Gabriel is speaking and Jesus (Michael) comes to help him in verse 13 during the Persian crisis. Ellen G. White gives assistance here, suggesting that the 11th verse is when Gabriel enters the scene.

"Gabriel now appeared to the prophet, and thus addressed him: 'Oh Daniel, a man greatly beloved, understand the words that I speak unto thee, and stand upright: for unto thee am I now sent. And when he had spoken this word unto me, I stood trembling.'"[5]

Daniel is on his hands and knees. Gabriel now orders him to "stand on your feet" (10:11), "Don't be afraid" (10:12, 19). Within this restoration discourse Daniel is affectionately called "greatly beloved" (10:11, 19, cf. 9:23). "No matter how ominous these messages might seem to you and your people, you are loved and the best things will eventually occur to your people." Recall the Hebrew word *dabar*? Due process will happen!

All these amazing encounters were a preamble to what Gabriel was about to reveal. There were still unanswered questions from Daniel 8. In verse 1 Daniel finally grasped the meaning of the *mareh* vision. But what about the *chazown* vision? That was to be sealed – but not before considerably more detail is given. And – that is exactly what Gabriel is about to do!

Daniel calls the vision of Jesus "this great vision." What word does he use for vision? *Mareh!* That is still part of the great theme of how God's people will corporately become part of the everlasting covenant. That vision has seen:

- 2300 evenings and mornings to

- Holiness of God's people or church (referenced in the ram)

- Their adjudication and eternal righteousness established

- The part God's people must have in that occurring

- The 70-week period of probation

- The restoration – Redeemer Jesus who is Priest (Pastor/Intercessor),

---

[4] Gaebelein, Frank E.; *The Expositor's Bible Commentary,* vol. 7, p. 24.

[5] White, Ellen G.; *The Sanctified Life,* p. 51.

Judge (metes out judgment on wicked) and King (the one in charge)

- The assurance that all legal issues will be settled in favor of God's people

In the midst of the *chazown* vision, describing the end-time hostility and opposition toward God's people, comes the beautiful message (the *mareh* vision) which assures Daniel and the reader that everlasting righteousness will come in. The presence of Jesus is an incredible affirmation through God's foreknowledge of all that will occur *after* the 2300 atonement years:

- Unfailing intercession
- Judgment
- Restoration
- Kingdom

Gabriel now tells Daniel, "Now I am come to make thee understand what shall befall thy people in the latter days: for yet the vision [*chazown*] is for many days." This "is clearly eschatological."[6] "Normally, the phrase 'the latter days' describes events that will occur just prior to and include the coming of the kingdom of God."[7]

Isn't that most interesting! Gabriel was sent to help Daniel understand the Daniel 8 *chazown* vision. He reminds Daniel and all his readers that this was for the end of time. Daniel needed to grasp the *mareh* vision of hope first. Why? Because the *chazown* vision is all about Satan's opposition to a holy people

and the everlasting covenant. It is about persecution, conflict between good and evil and the mystery of iniquity. But – at the end, God is victorious.

With uncanny insight, E. G. White saw this and warned of the trials ahead, using a theme from Zechariah.

"Zechariah's vision of Joshua and the Angel applies with peculiar force to the experience of God's people *in the closing up of the great day of atonement.* The remnant church will be brought into great trial and distress…. Satan … has gained control of the apostate churches; but here is a little company that are resisting his supremacy. If he could blot them from the earth, his triumph would be complete….

"Their only hope is in the mercy of God; their only defense will be prayer. As Joshua was pleading before the Angel, so the remnant church, with brokenness of heart and earnest faith, will plead for pardon and deliverance through Jesus their Advocate. They are fully conscious of the sinfulness of their lives, they see their weakness and unworthiness, and as they look upon themselves they are ready to despair. The tempter … points to their … defective characters. He presents their weakness and folly, their sins of ingratitude, their unlikeness to Christ, which has dishonored their Redeemer….

"But while the followers of Christ have sinned, they have not given themselves to the control of evil. They have put away their sins, and have sought the Lord in humility and contrition….

"As the people of God afflict their souls before Him, … the command is given, 'Take away the filthy garments' from them, … 'Behold, I have caused thine iniquity to pass from thee, and I will clothe thee with change of raiment.' The spotless robe of Christ's righteousness is placed upon the tried, tempted, yet faithful-

---

[6] Hartmen, Louis F. and Di Lella, Alexander A.; *The anchor Bible – The Book of Daniel,* p. 284.

[7] Miller, Stephen R; *The New American Commentary,* p. 287.

ful children of God. The despised remnant are clothed in glorious apparel, nevermore to be defiled by the corruptions of the world. Their names are retained in the Lamb's book of life, enrolled among the faithful of all ages.... Now they are eternally secure from the tempter's devices. Their sins are transferred to the originator of sin.... 'A fair miter' is set upon their heads. They are to be as kings and priests unto God. While Satan was urging his accusations and seeking to destroy this company, holy angels, unseen, were passing to and fro, placing upon them the seal of the living God. These are they that stand upon Mount Zion with the Lamb, having the Father's name written in their foreheads.... the hundred and forty and four thousand ...

"Christ is revealed as the *Redeemer* and *Deliverer* of His people."[8]

Now a sacred and awesome task lies ahead. We must study and grasp chapter 11. It shows two rises of the papacy. It outlines details of the final conflict between good and evil. But the most wonderful and hope-driven message comes early in chapter 12 (which ends the Daniel 11 vision). God's people are delivered from evil – eternally – and soon – very soon!

[8] White, Ellen G.; *Testimonies,* vol. 5, pp. 472-476 (emphasis added).

KEY SECULAR LEADERS DURING THE 490 YEARS

– Daniel 11:1-20 –

"Also I, in the first year of Darius the Mede, [even] I, stood to confirm and to strengthen him" (Daniel 11:1).

This verse is the launching *period* for this chapter. It reveals that heaven has ultimate control and influence over earthly leaders. And – it revisits key issues of Satan's hatred towards God's covenant by harming His people. Written in Hebrew, Daniel 11 describes elements of that conflict especially important for the last generation. Its storyline extends right to the end of probation, tribulation, deliverance of God's people and the special resurrection just before Jesus comes. How awesome to recognize God's deep concern for the end-time remnant way back in the 6th century B.C.!

Gabriel conveyed to Daniel the reason for his coming before he presented the message. It involved (here it is again) clarifying future *time* (10:14). Issues:

- Gabriel came to make Daniel understand

- What would befall God's people

- In the future – or latter days

The Hebrew entomological setting is different from that of chapter 8. There, the future was *tied* to the very end of *time* (*eth qets*), the *appointed time* (*mowed*), and the *future days* (*acharith*) when God's wrath would be exhibited. Collectively, that setting related to the eschaton. Those prophetic messages were the first part of the *chazown* vision – the sealed portion of Daniel. In this new vision, Gabriel's timed introduction is couched in more cautious terms, yet still part of that *chazown* vision. The use of *acharith* alone suggests a *general future*. When used with the word "days" (*yowm*) it usually refers to when Jesus comes the second time. The *context* also reveals to which era it applies. Here, the latter days refers to both the Jewish people and to the remnant at the end of the world.

REASON FOR DANIEL 11

"Now I am come to make thee understand what shall befall thy people in the latter [acharith] days [yowm]: for yet the vision [is] for [many] days" (Daniel 10:14).

Paraphrased: "I've come to make you grasp what is going to befall thy people in the *future.* Though it refers primarily to the consummation, it does also relate to what lies ahead for your people."

The *chazown* vision describes the workings of Satan and *his* people, persecuting or seeking to harm God's agents and His church. It is a divine bulletin, warning, telling the remnant what it will be like – thus, prepare.

The great timing issues of Daniel 8 *surround* the second coming of Jesus.

135

Here, Gabriel switches the *chazown* vision imagery to look at a general future that progressively moves forward to that time. Daniel 11 is unique to the whole book. Its mission is to carefully supplement what has already been presented with additional fascinating details. By the time the vision ends we will be at the very end of time. The introductory timing statement let **Daniel know** that this vision wasn't for his day. It was for God's people in the future.

First, Daniel's people are going to be put on a 490-year probation. The first part of Daniel 11 covers that period.

Secondly, Daniel 7 talked about one rise of the papacy – the *little horn* in the Dark Ages. Daniel 8 talked about a second rise of the papacy – at the eschaton – at the *appointed time*. God is extremely anxious that those distinct separate rises are not only seen but that key events surrounding each are identified.

God foresaw many scholarly opinions arising in an attempt to define the *little horn*. He sent Gabriel back to make sure there would be only one line of understanding – He gave Daniel 11 to set in stone forever the rises (plural) of the papacy! As Gabriel interacts with Daniel he urges a thought:

"I will show thee that which is noted in the scripture of truth" (Daniel 10:21).

"And now will I show thee the truth" (Daniel 11:2).

That is amazing! He is going to show truth from what was *already* revealed in the Scripture that was not understood. In other words, "I'm going to show you, Daniel, the *truth* about *truth*."

Intriguingly, *between* those two verses about truth is that verse that shows heaven's protection of the deliverer of God's people (11:1): *"Also I, in the first year of Darius the Mede, [even] I, stood to confirm and to strengthen him."*

You will be astounded – this vision ends with the deliverance of God's people (12:1)!

In other words, "I not only will give you truth but I'm the one who gave strength and courage to Darius in his first year." What does that have to do with the truth of the *little horn*? There lies a greater issue. Literalism will lead to a spin of opinions as to what Gabriel is saying. Darius was the Median monarch whose general, Cyrus from Persia, conquered Babylon. Babylon fell and God was strengthening Darius, and later Cyrus – both great Biblical symbols for *deliverers*.

The *deliverer* and *deliverance* came *from* oppressive pagan powers. "People of God, be courageous. No earthly power can hold you down forever. Deliverance *is* the *truth* for this hour! I will even use worldly powers to achieve that."

Same Symbol Sequence

Literal	Dark Ages	End of Ages
God's people in Babylon	God's people vs the Roman Catholic Church	God's people vs Babylon
Oppressed	Oppressed	Oppressed
Daniel and Ezekiel's message of deliverance and restoration	Protestants message of reformation, deliverance and restoration	144,000 Loud Cry Message of deliverance and restoration

When Daniel 11 was given, Cyrus had been in power for three years. God's people were delivered, and restoration was underway. That frames the end-time imagery of the terminal conflicts between good and evil, the deliverance of God's people and then their restoration! That is repeatedly coupled with warnings that the end of wickedness will be with *desolation.*

E. G. White saw clearly these contextual themes when she said: "The prophecy of the eleventh chapter of Daniel has nearly reached its complete fulfillment. Soon the scenes of trouble spoken of in the prophecies will take place."[1] She then quoted Isaiah 24:1-8; Joel 1:15-18, 12; Jeremiah 4:19-20, 23-26, 30:7.

GABRIEL OPENS THE "SCRIPTURE OF TRUTH"

The rest of the chapter on into Daniel 12:3 (all one flowing message) has four main parts, all dealing with future issues so very important to God's people.

Part 1 (11:2-20):

Highlights of kingdom rulers to the time of Jesus – covering the 70 weeks of years

Part 2 (11:21-27):

Papacy – first rise/fall

Part 3 (11:28-45):

Papacy – second rise/fall

Part 4 (12:1-3):

Last scenes of earth's history

Yes – there are significant time gaps between events, peoples and issues. That is not new to this book.

KEY KINGS DURING THE 70 WEEKS

"Behold, there shall stand up yet three kings in Persia; and the fourth shall be far richer than [they] all: and by his strength through his riches he shall stir up all against the realm of Grecia. And a mighty king shall stand up, that shall rule with great dominion, and do according to his will. And when he shall stand up, his kingdom shall be broken, and shall be divided toward the four winds of heaven; and not to his posterity, nor according to his dominion which he ruled: for his kingdom shall be plucked up, even for others beside those" (Daniel 11:2-4).

Gabriel is about to unfold king/kingdom highlights that lay ahead for the *Jewish people* in Part I. These details would act as *assurance waymarks* for Daniel's people during the 490-year period of probation. But Biblical history fails to show that they ever took advantage of this amazing information.

Gabriel begins his instruction in Cyrus' third year. This immediately follows Daniel's wonderful vision of Jesus in chapter 10. Three kings are to follow Cyrus (539–530 B.C.).

1. Cambyses II (529–522 B.C.)

2. False Smerdis (522 B.C.)

3. Darius I (the one who made Shushan the Medo–Persian capital — 522–486 B.C.)

Then a fourth king who was "far richer than they all" would come and fight against the kingdom of Greece. This was a task Darius I left to that fourth king as a follow-up to the *Ionian* rebellion during his reign when a Greek fleet was defeated.

4. Xerxes (Ahaseurus of Esther's time) (485–468 B.C.) is that "far richer" king.

"Now it came to pass in the days of Ahasuerus, (this [is] Ahasuerus which reigned, from India even unto Ethiopia, [over] an hundred and seven and twenty provinces:) ... When he showed the riches of his glorious kingdom and the honour of his excellent majesty many

---

[1] White, Ellen G.; *Testimonies*, vol. 9, p. 14.

*days, [even] an hundred and fourscore days" (*Esther 1:1, 4).

Xerxes was the king who, at the time of Esther, was used by God to first make and then reverse a death decree against Israel. That brought great respect and security to God's people. *"The Jews had light, and gladness and joy, and honor"* (Esther 8:16).

Because of those dramatic events, the Jews were exalted and feared, and *"many of the people of the land became Jews"* (Esther 8:14, 17).

That opened the door for the next king, though not listed in Gabriel's notables. Xerxes' son, Artaxerxes I (464–425 B.C.), became the king to issue a decree to restore the *Jewish theocracy*. This began the 2300-year (Daniel 8:14) and 490-year (Daniel 9:25) prophecies – the great *mareh* vision.

Keep in mind that the purpose of the *chazown* vision is very end-time. But within that framework, Gabriel is now simply beginning a prophetic journey that will soon wind up exactly there – at the very end of time!

Let's continue.

"And a mighty king shall stand up, that shall rule with great dominion, and do according to his will" (Daniel 11:3).

Most expositors agree that this describes Alexander the Great (336–323 B.C.) at the rise of the Grecian kingdom. But different from Daniel 2 and 7, the real issue now is *not* kingdoms but waymark *kings*. From Xerxes to Alexander was a leap of 129 years. A sequence of notable nobles is developing to honor the proleptic insight of God – and – inspire hope for God's people as each *sign* unfolds. (Each king is a sign that they are getting closer to the end of the 490-year period.)

"And when he shall stand up, his kingdom shall be broken, and shall be divided toward the four winds of heaven;

and not to his posterity, nor according to his dominion which he ruled: for his kingdom shall be plucked up, even for others beside those" (Daniel 11:4).

Exactly as the Scriptures point out, as Alexander's kingdom stood up (came into dominance), it was broken, lasting only 13 years. Alexander had no strong posterity, so the kingdom was divided among others – "plucked up" or removed from his heirs toward the four winds of heaven.

Four of Alexander's generals took up territory in four different areas:

1. Cassander – Macedonia and Greece

2. Ptolemy I Lagi (Soter) (323–285 B.C.) – Egypt, Palestine and Phoenicia (south)

3. Seleucus I Nicador (321–316) – Babylon and Syria (north)

4. Lysimachus – Asia Minor

"And the king of the south shall be strong, and [one] of his princes; and he shall be strong above him, and have dominion; his dominion [shall be] a great dominion" (Daniel 11:5).

A new term is introduced here – *king of the south* – as a literal king. In verse 25 that phrase becomes a metaphor for another power. This is often associated with the rival *king of the north*. Ptolemy I Lagi (Soter) – *king of the south* – was initially the most powerful of the four. Seleucus I Nicator (312–280 B.C.) of the north even placed himself for a time under his rule. The text was fulfilled exactly as God had predicted. Eventually, Seleucus became the strongest. He then became the first *king of the north* mentioned in chapter 11. Eventually he took the lands of Cassander and Lysimachus. He truly was in charge of all northern kingdoms, leaving only a southern kingdom.

"And in the end of years they shall join themselves together; for the king's daughter of the south shall come to the king of the north to make an agreement: but she shall not retain the power of the arm; neither shall he stand, nor his arm: but she shall be given up, and they that brought her, and he that begat her, and he that strengthened her in [these] times" (Daniel 11:6).

This is an amazing prophecy. Antiochus II Theos (280–246 B.C.) (from the north), son of Antiochus I Soter (324–261 B.C.) and grandson of Seleucus I Nicador (north), inherited a state of war with Egypt (the "Second Syrian War"). During the war he was given the name "theos," meaning "God" in Greek. Peace eventually came "in the end of the years ... they shall join themselves together." Antiochus II gave up his first wife and half-sister Laodice and married Bernice (yes, as Gabriel had revealed), the daughter of Ptolemy II of Philadelpheus, Egypt (south). Bernice didn't retain any power or authority because Laodice had Bernice and her son murdered. Thus, Laodice's son Seleucus II Callinicus took the throne of the north by a "northern declaration."

"But out of a branch of her roots shall [one] stand up in his estate, which shall come with an army, and shall enter into the fortress of the king of the north, and shall deal against them, and shall prevail: And shall also carry captives into Egypt their gods, with their princes, [and] with their precious vessels of silver and of gold; and he shall continue [more] years than the king of the north" (Daniel 11:7-8).

A family "branch" of Bernice's, from "her roots," her brother Ptolemy III

Euergetes now ruled Egypt. In revenge at his sister's death, he took the fortified northern kingdom and brought back with him 2500 gold and silver idols, precious vessels and prisoners. Exactly the details the Scriptures portray! Laodice was killed in the attack.

"So the king of the south shall come into [his] kingdom, and shall return into his own land" (Daniel 11:9).

If this referred to Ptolemy III, it would be *repeating* information contextually. Here are a few other translations that suggest the King James Version is in error:

"And he shall come into the realm of the king of the south, but he shall return into his own land" (American Standard Version).

"Then the latter shall come into the realm of the king of the south but shall return into his own land" (Revised Standard Version).

"Also [the *king of the north*] shall come to the kingdom of the king of the South, but shall return to his own land" (New King James Version).

"But the latter will invade the kingdom of the king of the south, then retire to his own country" (Jerusalem Bible).

"The king of the north shall then invade the realm of the king of the South, but he shall retreat to his own country" (Moffatt's Translation).

The context and flow of ideas invite the insights of these four examples.

Seleucus II Callinicus of the north wanted to get back at Ptolemy III for his military carnage. He tried to take Egypt in 240 B.C. but suffered a major defeat, including loss of his navy and "returned to his own land."

"But his sons shall be stirred up, and shall assemble a multitude of great forces: and [one] shall certainly come,

and overflow, and pass through: then shall he return, and be stirred up, [even] to his fortress" (Daniel 11:10).

Seleucus III Ceraunus Soter (226–223 B.C.) and Antiochus III the Great (223–187 B.C.), sons of Seleucus II, decided to continue the revenge against the south to avenge their father's failure. Seleucus III was killed. Antiochus III took up the northern banner, recaptured the port of Antioch, then set out on a systematic campaign (219 B.C.) to conquer Syria and Palestine from the now new Egyptian head, Ptolemy IV Philopator (221–203 B.C.).

It is noteworthy that God's people in Judea, at this moment in time, are nearly half way through their 490-year probation – the 70 weeks. Why is the Bible silent during this period regarding God's people? One must conclude that the probation was not going well – with God waiting in silence. Apostasy led God to have Palestine crisscrossed with repeated military campaigns between the kings of the north and the kings of the south.

The only prophetic warning God would now give is found right here in Daniel 11. Each military fray and each king was a reminder of a sovereign God who had predicted it all beforehand. Alas, when God came (and Daniel 9 clearly tells when), they didn't recognize him. This is all a metaphor of exactly what it will be like at the end between the *King of the north* and the *king of the south*. When Jesus comes, He will not have been anticipated by most of those who claim to be His followers.

"And the king of the south shall be moved with choler, and shall come forth and fight with him, [even] with the king of the north: and he shall set forth a great

multitude; but the multitude shall be given into his hand" (Daniel 11:11).

An enraged Ptolemy IV brought 68,000 foot soldiers, 5000 cavalry and 73 elephants against Antiochus III's – "assembled multitude" of 75,000 men. Antiochus III lost 17,000 of his men and suffered defeat with 4000 prisoners being taken: "the multitude shall be given into his hand." This all culminated at the battle of Raphia in Palestine on June 22, 217 B.C. Ptolemy was the victor.

As these prophetic details unfolded, a book of destiny was developing. Israel is being reminded with the saga of each king that their probation time is running out – 248 years now remained.

"[And] when he hath taken away the multitude, his heart shall be lifted up; and he shall cast down [many] ten thousands: but he shall not be strengthened [by it]" (Daniel 11:12).

Ptolemy IV (south) was proud of his victory. But in his administrative indolence he failed to secure the empire. He became careless and was not strengthened by his military exploits. This weakened his kingdom. His dynasty began to rapidly decline. Then Egyptians began to rebel against their Greek leaders. In 203 B.C. Ptolomy IV and the queen died mysteriously.

"For the king of the north shall return, and shall set forth a multitude greater than the former, and shall certainly come after certain years with a great army and with much riches. And in those times there shall many stand up against the king of the south:" (Daniel 11:13-14a).

Antiochus III the Great (north) sixteen years after Raphia (201 B.C.) took advantage of a weakened Egypt now under Ptolemy V Epiphanes, a ten-year old boy. Antiochus mounted a vicious attack and regained Syria and Palestine and pushed the conquest as far as India.

Internal strife within Egypt against the Greek Ptolemy leaders deepened. Philip of Macedonia joined Antiochus III and threatened to divide the empire. Rome became involved and crushed Philip's westward push. While that went on Antiochus III pushed hard against a defenseless Egypt and made extensive military gains.

"... also the robbers of thy people shall exalt themselves to establish the vision; but they shall fall" [Daniel 11:14 (last part)].

As noted in the commentary under verse 10, this was the time for the final, last-chance probation ever to be given to the Jewish people. Those phrases (vs 14) are a commentary insert to let God's people know that they are the issue in the heart of this prophecy.

God foretells, in spite of battles and conflicts crisscrossing "their" land, that this would fail to refine, humble and change them. Their leaders were robbing the people of truth, making themselves the ultimate losers of the battle. How did God react ahead of time? "They shall fall." God's cleaver of justice soon would fall on the Jewish nation – forever – just as we saw in Daniel 9.

"So the king of the north shall come, and cast up a mount, and take the most fenced cities: and the arms of the south shall not withstand, neither his chosen people, neither [shall there be any] strength to withstand" (Daniel 11:15).

Antiochus III seized the fortified cities of Gaza (201 B.C.) and Sidon (198 B.C). Palestine fell to his control. Rome, Italy, had been invited by Egyptian authorities to help protect the young Ptolemy V. They had warned Antiochus III not to attack – but he did anyway. Rome was contending with Philip of Macedonia and unable to help. During the reign of Antiochus III, the Jewish religion was nearly exterminated.

It wasn't long before Antiochus IV (Epiphanes – 175-164 B.C.) ruled Syria (king of north).

In a spirit of deep anger he organized an expedition against Jerusalem. He wanted to destroy the Jews and exterminate all worship of their God. For all those who kept the seventh-day Sabbath to any Jew who refused to worship his idols, death was imminent. The temple was desecrated by sacrificing and worshiping a pig within its precincts. All these were reminders to God's people that their covenant with Him was being desecrated and their probation time was being squandered. The Jews had been at peace with the Ptolomies. During Ptolomy IV's reign they had translated the Torah from Hebrew into Greek for the royal library at Alexandria. This was called the Septuagint translation.

Of intense providential warning, Antiochus IV murdered any infant found circumcised along with its mother – because circumcision symbolized that they were a covenant-keeping people. Alas, it was only outward show. Their hearts were far from God.

"But he that cometh against him shall do according to his own will, and none shall stand before him: and he shall stand in the glorious land, which by his hand shall be consumed" (Daniel 11:16).

This began a series of battles instigated by Rome ("he [Rome] that cometh against him [initially, Antiochus III – but more so Antiochus IV]"). In 191 B.C. Rome conquered Antiochus III's forces. Rome is now beginning to "do according to his own will." At the battle of Pydnain in 168 B.C. under Antiochus IV, the vestiges of the Greek empire began to crumble. In 64 B.C. the Roman General Pompey invaded Palestine – "the glorious land." The Hellenistic age was at an end. Rome was now in control.

"He shall also set his face to enter with the strength of his whole kingdom, and upright ones with him; thus shall he do: and he shall give him the daughter of women, corrupting her: but she shall not stand [on his side], neither be for him" (Daniel 11:17).

The phrase "and upright ones with him" is in question. It appears to represent an administrative stance of Rome where their rule of conquered lands was equitable to the conquered peoples – "Thus shall he do."

Rome continued its world conquest under the command of Julius Caesar. The then king of Egypt, Ptolemy XII Auletes Philadelphus, gave Julius Caesar his daughter Cleopatra VII as a mistress. They never married – "she shall not stand with him, or be for him."

"After this shall he turn his face unto the isles, and shall take many: but a prince for his own behalf shall cause the reproach offered by him to cease; without his own reproach he shall cause [it] to turn upon him. Then he shall turn his face toward the fort of his own land: but he shall stumble and fall, and not be found" (Daniel 11:18-19).

"He," Julius Caesar, conquered many islands along the north coast of Africa and Asia Minor, and he invaded Great Britain twice.

In his final military exploits to expand the empire into Europe, Julius embarked on brilliant campaigns, conquering northern France, Belgium and Southern Great Britain, subjugating the Celts.

Pompey, who had been a loyal general (*prince*) had remained at Rome during the European campaign. He turned the Senate against Julius [the *prince* who was originally part of "his own behalf" brought "reproach" on him (contextual

meaning)]. There is dispute among translators as to how this part of the verse should be worded. It appears as though the *prince* will bring reproach against him, but the reproach will be turned against the *prince*. That would describe what occurred with Pompey. They declared Julius an enemy of the state. They ordered Julius to turn over his lands and generalship.

Julius Caesar attacked. Now General Pompey was on the opposite side. In 48 B.C. Pompey was defeated, having had to retreat to Pharsalus, Greece.

Julius Caesar then turned "his face toward the fort of his own land." By 46 B.C. the Roman Senate appointed him dictator for life.

Brutus, his adopted son, and his friend Cassius, plotted and killed Caesar in 44 B.C. – "he shall stumble and fall, and not be found."

"Then shall stand up in his estate a raiser of taxes [in] the glory of the kingdom: but within few days he shall be destroyed, neither in anger, nor in battle" (Daniel 11:20).

The great-nephew of Julius Caesar, Octavius, succeeded him and became Caesar Augustus. Under his leadership the Roman Empire saw its zenith of power and influence.

He brought to that kingdom universal taxes. This helped to fulfill prophecy by bringing Joseph and Mary to Bethlehem for a census (Luke 21:1), where the Messiah of Israel was born.

This now brings us to the point where a major break comes in the prophecy. Many symbolic issues are now to be taken up. Gabriel is about to take another leap of several hundred years to a fearful king – a *vile person* (vs 21).

Once again, in this summation prophecy, the issue of kingdoms, beast images and powers give way to key world leaders of notable importance to God's people.

- Cyrus – deliverer

- Xerxes (Ahasuerus) – deliverer

- North and South rivalry – metaphorical picture of what happens during the final probation

- Caesar Augustus – facilitated the way for the Deliverer and Restorer – Jesus.

"As in old time Cyrus was called to the throne of the world's empire that he might set free the captives of the Lord, so Caesar Augustus is made the agent for the fulfillment of God's purpose in bringing the mother of Jesus to Bethlehem. She is of the lineage of David, and the Son of David must be born in David's city. Out of Bethlehem, said the prophet, 'shall He come forth ... that is to be ruler in Israel; whose goings forth have been from of old, from the days of eternity.' Micah 5:2, margin."[2]

Part two of this vision now must begin. Of utmost importance is that God's people recognize the two rises of the evil power, the papacy. It will be part of the third angel's message of Revelation 14. Its nuances must be clear, its ultimate curse of God understood.

God's people have been in a probationary time. These kings were *clear* waymarks through that time, revealing God's sovereign power through prophecy. Daniel 11 should have humbled them to their knees and led them to an unswerving commitment to complete Daniel 9:24. Their minds were numbed by prejudice and tradition. The Messiah – Immanuel – came, and they knew Him not.

Now we look at the first rise of the papacy – a visible expression of the *mystery of iniquity.*

---

[2] White, Ellen G.; *The Desire of Ages,* p. 44.

CHAPTER 32

THE RISE OF THE PAPACY

– Daniel 11:21-27 –

We now enter the part of Gabriel's vision that reveiws briefly a theme already introduced in chapters 7 through 9. Everything in chapter 11 unfolds what was a preamble in previous chapters. There are two rises of the papacy! – one in chapter 7 and the second in chapter 8. Each is depicted as a *little horn*, but they exist in two vastly different eras of time. God wanted to make certain that Biblical expositors understood this – thus chapter 11. Verse 21 begins the account of the first rise. The rest of the chapter is "just to make sure" that those two rises remain distinct in our thinking.

The reason there are so many differing views of this vision lies in the diverse assumptions that commentators have already formed from chapter 8. Exegetic and contextual clues have been ignored, compounding interpretive errors as the narrative continues. Gabriel made it clear in his introductory remarks that this vision was for the "last days" (*acharyth*) (10:14) – "future days to come." Daniel already went a step further and said the *acharyth* would be at the very end of time (*eth qets*) (8:17, 19). Yet, in face of these contextual revelations, the *majority* of commentators tenaciously hold to the *vile person* or *little horn* as Antiochus IV Epiphanes who died in 163 BC! That is an interpretative disconnect.

The vision ranges from Daniel's day in the 6th century B.C., with special anchor points, all the way to the resurrection (Daniel 12:2). Just preceding this is a period of distress and unparalleled tribulation (Daniel 12:1). Jesus said that that time of trouble would occur just before He returns (Matthew 24:21, 29-30). Thus, we view a vision in Daniel 11 that transects time into key segments, covering more than 2500 years.

The resurrection noted in Daniel 12:1-2 is preceded by the demise of the tyrant *king of the north* – same as the *little horn* and *vile person*. Is the theological "hero" Antiochus Epiphanes going to survive centuries? Jesus said the evil work of the *king of the north* would cease at the time of the wonders of the resurrection and when God's people were delivered (Daniel 12:1-2, 7) – at the end of a 1260-day or three and a half year period.

In addition, the Maccabean theory states that the "abomination of desolation" of Daniel 11:31 applied exclusively to the Syrian leader Antiochus Epiphanes (175–164 B.C.). Yet Jesus said the abomination of desolation was one of the "timing signs" just preceding His coming (Matthew 24:15-30). Who's right? Jesus or tradition? Daniel 12 makes it clear that the abomination that leads to desolation would last only 1290 days, ending in the deliverance of God's people.

Correct bonding of Biblical clues reveals not only a beautiful and simple end-time picture but Jesus personally becomes involved in the understanding of Daniel's book. When the disciples ask about the end of time, He refers them back to Daniel – of all things!

Another thematic issue reveals the rise and fall of many kings from Daniel 11:2-20. This stops when the vile king emerges. Then something different happens. Daniel 11:21-45 collectively reveals the actions of a single individual – though in two eras. There is no successor recorded at the very end of time or to that individual.

The "power" of that *vile person* parallels the *little horn* of Daniel 8. Also, Gabriel refers to that power, there, as "he" or "his" thirteen times. Daniel 9:26-27 speaks of the one who becomes desolate.

LITTLE HORN (CHAPTERS 7 AND 8) AND VILE KING (CHAPTER 11)

"And in his estate shall stand up a vile person, to whom they shall not give the honour of the kingdom: but he shall come in peaceably, and obtain the kingdom by flatteries" (Daniel 11:21).

A vile (*bazah* – contemptible) person, acting against God's will, appears firmly established but without a kingdom. He comes to power peaceably – not through military might. In the end he will have a kingdom through deceit and flattery.

Daniel 11:21-27, in a brief expose, dramatizes the first papal reign of power. How do we know? It *follows* the sequential history noted in verses 2-20, ending with Caesar Agustus (with a time gap we have seen frequently in this chapter). Secondly, this power enters the stage of history peaceably through deceit.

- "Obtains the kingdom by flatteries" (11:21)

- "Mouth speaks great words" (7:11, 20, 25)

- "Changes times and laws" (7:25)

The papacy entered the world scene peaceably. Justinian (Flavius Anicius Juianus Justianus) was a Roman Emperor for 38 years (527–565 A.D.) working out of Constantinople. He had a brilliant carrier in securing the Byzantine empire, immortalizing Byzantine architecture and developing legal codes. The latter became a lasting legacy to Western civilization.

His ecclesiastical genius recognized the importance of religious peace to civil order. The Justinian Codes of law had their origins through a commission of ten lawyers that he appointed. They drew from the teachings of four economic councils[1] and became "Corpus Juris Civilis." This, in turn, later guided the development of canon law by the Roman Catholic Church.

Justinian's general, Belisarios, arranged for Pope Vigilius to be the head of the Roman Church by banishing a competitor, Silverius. This changed the way ecclesiastical leaders were previously appointed by religious councils. Justinian also appointed a bishop in Constantinople, which began a schism that fully developed by 1035 A.D. and remains today.

The "papal kingdom" emerged through gifts, endowments and outright transfer of land by Pepin the Short in 754 A.D. Its power reached its zenith in the 16th century as part of its Counter Reformation with excommunication, inquisition, bans, index of books and censorship became its *modus operandi*.

"And with the arms of a flood shall they be overflown from before him, and shall be broken; yea, also the prince of the covenant" (Daniel 11:22).

The use of the word "flood" (*sheteph*) suggests *judgment* or *wrath*. Here is depicted a scene where going before this

---

[1] http//cappsfamily.hypemart.net/justian.htm

vile person is his overwhelming wrath, crushing those before him. Who are "they" that are "broken" (*shabar*) or crushed? The explanation of Gabriel makes it clear that it is God's people, because he says, "Yea, also the prince of the covenant." He is the Prince Messiah [the same as the "prince of the host" (8:11), the "Prince of princes" (8:25) and "Messiah the Prince" (9:25-26)]. In those verses the *little horn* stands up against the *Prince of princes*. The *little horn* and the *vile person* both represent the *papal system*.

When did wrath go before the papacy to crush God's people and, figuratively, Jesus? The Dark Ages stands as a rebuke to the fiendish hatred of the Roman Church – the papacy – towards them.

The "arms" (a symbol of military power) came through civil governments, doting to the hateful commands of the papacy.

"And after the league [made] with him he shall work deceitfully: for he shall come up, and shall become strong with a small people" (Daniel 11:23).

The word for league (*chabar*) means an agreement based on charm. Many countries bowed to the wishes of the papacy. In fact, many emperors and kings felt a guilt obligation to render allegiance to papal Rome – especially in France, Germany and Spain.

Indeed, this verse expresses what is apparent all along – "he shall work deceitfully." The Hebrew word for "deceitful" is the same word for "craft" in Daniel 8:25. How is this league formulated? Through crafty associations, using civil powers to enforce its dogma. In Revelation 13 the sea-beast *also* represents papal power. There, the "image to the beast" symbolizes those ecclesiastical agencies that copy this papal technique by manipulating civil power to further its

ends. There, the earth-beast representing apostate Protestantism (the false prophet) imitates the papacy.

Does the papacy use "a small *number* of people?"[2] Its ecclesiastical administrative body, the Holy See, has always been small.

"He shall enter peaceably even upon the fattest places of the province; and he shall do [that] which his fathers have not done, nor his fathers' fathers; he shall scatter among them the prey, and spoil, and riches: [yea], and he shall forecast his devices against the strong holds, even for a time" (Daniel 11:24).

This continues a description of the horrible practices of the papacy. Always in an air of peace and pompous godliness, the papacy comes even to wealthy people and areas, doing what the church fathers dared not do: taking among themselves the riches, spoils and even people from their *exploits* while they cause the martyrdom of millions of God's people. This added to the wealth of the church and became land known as "papal states."

This verse ends with an insightful statement. The *vile person* will forecast (*chashab*), meaning contrive his devices (*machashabah*) or his cunning plans against the strongest. Yet, it would only continue for "a time." What time? Daniel 7:25 says for a "time and times and the dividing of time." This is seen to represent 1260 years. Its machinations would be time-limited by God's sovereign will.

"And he shall stir up his power and his courage against the king of the south with a great army; and the king of the south shall be stirred up to battle with a very great and mighty army; but he shall not stand: for they shall forecast devices against him" (Daniel 11:25).

---

[2] Quoted by Robert Wood, Prophecy Research Initiative document – 2004, p. 15.

The *vile person* stirs up his power against the *king of the south* with a great army. Egypt, as a *kingdom of the south*, became a *historical* issue long before. It symbolizes an anti-Christian, anti-God power. This now brings new meaning to the "king of the south." How did the papacy enter into military exploits and by default now become the *king of the north*?

In the 7th century A.D. Arab Muslims conquered Palestine. During the 11th century the fierce Seljuk Turks from central Asia invaded the near east and became conquers of the Byzantines (Battle of Manzikert in Asia, 1071 A.D.), capturing many lands, including Palestine, from the Arab Muslims. They then blocked all Christian pilgrimages to the area.

The Byzantine Emperor Alexius Commenus (1048-1118 A.D.) asked Pope Urban II for the help of the Catholic Church in fighting the Muslim Turks. Urban II was competing with a rival "pope" and thought this a unique way to consolidate his power and prestige.

In the autumn of 1095 A.D. he met with church leaders in Clermont, France, and appealed to his European parishioners to unite and fight to regain Palestine. He offered spiritual and physical rewards, including forgiveness of sins, if they joined this crusade.

From 1096 A.D. through 1270 A.D. Crusades against the Turks were conducted. Knights and princes, the common people and the wealthy joined. This added greatly to the trade and economic growth of Europe. Their immediate goals were reached. With a "very great and mighty army," Palestine was retaken. Biblical prophecy was fulfilled. But the Ottoman Empire continued to resist. Their control of the "glorious land" was regained and then lost again. By 1453 A.D. the Byzantine Empire fell and the Muslim

Turks were permanently in charge.[3] This anti-Christian power was for a time the "king of the south."

The battle between the Christian world and the Muslim world is a type of what will occur at the end of time as the latter verses of this chapter unfold. That will reveal, once again, a battle between the Christian world and the Muslim world.

The *little horn* of Daniel 8, representing the end-time papal power, "waxed exceeding great, toward the south and toward the east, and toward the pleasant land." Palestine will once again be a focal point of the Christian world and papal power (the latter owns most of the land of Christian *shrines* already). As this manuscript is being written, not only is the Vatican negotiating with Muslims and Jews regarding "peace" in the "pleasant land," the whole evangelical world believes Palestine is part of the prophetic end game before the "rapture." The "glorious land" is clearly seen in prophecy (Daniel 11:41, 45) – but not depicted as they believe – as will unfold later.

"Yea, they that feed of the portion of his meat shall destroy him, and his army shall overflow: and many shall fall down slain" (Daniel 11:26).

This verse introduces an important note from history. The Crusades were successful initially, especially the first one. But Palestine was recaptured by the Muslims. The subsequent history through nine crusades shows many local victories and defeats. The "Christian" Crusaders not only plundered Muslim areas during this time but freely massacred Jews.

But the Muslims repeatedly showed their resiliency. Their goal was to conquer the European Christian world. The Crusades were, in part, an attempt to

---

[3] *The World Book Encyclopedia,* 1996 Edition (World Book Inc, a Scott Fetzer Company; Chicago, London, Sydney, Toronto), 1995.

turn back those conquests. But they were by and large poorly organized, without a central leader and, ultimately, ended in defeat.

Who shared with the papacy the same interest in defeating the Islamic world? Initially France, then Spain and, later, Germany – then back to France. They all "fed" with the papacy the shared religious cause of the Crusades, bearing the symbol of the Cross in their exploits. But the text says that those who were part of the *vile person* "destroyed him." His support and defense was "overflown" (*shataph* – inundated, under judgment) or came under wrath, and many were slain.

This occurred in 1798 when General Louis A. Berthier, upon Napoleon's orders, was sent to Paris to take Rome. A Roman republic was established, and Pope Pius VI was taken captive. He later died in France. "They that feed" with him "shall destroy him." That would be called later in Revelation 13 a "deadly wound."

"And both these kings' hearts [shall be] to do mischief, and they shall speak lies at one table; but it shall not prosper: for yet the end [shall be] at the time appointed" (Daniel 11:27).

The *vile person* was destroyed in the previous verse but is now alive. This verse is a commentary insert adding additional information to the previous verses (20-26).

Because of the continued fighting, the Crusaders and Muslims entered into treaty after treaty to bring peace or peaceful coexistence. But the Muslims wanted to control and coerce.

The armies on both sides repeatedly experienced defeat and victory, with land being gained and lost. In the meantime tens of thousands of people were slain.

The *vile person's* representatives and Muslim leaders spoke lies by conveying interest in peace. Those "mischievous treaties" were for their survival and temporal convenience only. They did "not prosper" or last.

The final part of verse 27 brings in an interesting turning point. At the *appointed time* (*mowed*) the end (*qets*) will occur. Does this suddenly refer back to 8:17 and 19? Context is everything to our understanding. This is the end of the *vile person*. Daniel 7:25 makes it clear that the *little horn* power was predestined to end at the termination of 1260 years. That end or *qets* was at an appointed time. Why the use of the Hebrew word *mowed* for the appointed time here – a word often denoting a sacred appointment? It was a sacred decree appointment in God's calendar. Thus, there are two appointed times in Daniel – one that deals with the end of the 1260 years, the other the 1260 days (the two times the papacy was in power). The next three verses clarify what occurred.

A significant turning point now comes in the vision that goes right to the end of the chapter. It begins to describe the *vile person* as having great riches and against the *treaty of God* – the "holy covenant." So thing has changed, and new imagery is being introduced. This begins to describe the second period when the papacy will be a world power.

What happened in the interim between these rises? The papacy struggled and maintained its ecclesiastical authority. Its secular rule was taken away through a series of vacillating moves on the part of France and later by the Italian people. On March 17, 1860, Italy became a full-blown "kingdom" state. By September 20, 1870, Rome fell to Italian troops and the papal states became part of Italy. The "kingdom" of the papacy came to its end. The papacy was reigned into 109 acres within Rome – the Vatican.

It is to be noted that at this time some of the most treacherous ecclesiastical decisions were made that defied the God of heaven. It was also during this period that the first Vatican Council was convened (1869) by Pope Pius IX. It was then that the doctrine of papal infallibility was adopted through coercive pressure of the pope on the delegates.

In the next chapter we will begin to deal with the final history of the *vile person*. There, the *king of the north* will be adopted. Why the change? God is helping us to see that the same power continues to be presented – but now in a different era. The north was where God, the great King, was tabernacled on Mount Zion (Psalm 48:2). Satan aspired to exalt his throne above the stars of God to that "mount of the congregation, ... I will be like the most High" (Isaiah 14:13-14). The *king of the north,* as Satan's representative, attempts to do this at the end of time. Thus, the name is apropos and descriptive.

CHAPTER 33

THE "VILE PERSON" RISES AGAIN

– Daniel 11:28-35 –

In the last chapter the *vile person* is destroyed by a country that had previously been its ally (vs 26) – France. This occurred when Pope Pius VI was taken prisoner by Napolean's General Berthier in 1798. Pius VI died shortly thereafter in France. The *secular rule* of the papacy began its downward plunge in that year and was complete by 1870. Its *ecclesiastical power* was clipped but not destroyed. Its "deadly wound" would later be healed (Revelation 13:3). This linguistic play simply reveals a *lethal* secular blow and *bruising* of its ecclesiastical authority.

"Then shall he return into his land with great riches; and his heart [shall be] against the holy covenant; and he shall do [exploits], and return to his own land. At the time appointed he shall return, and come toward the south; but it shall not be as the former, or as the latter. For the ships of Chittim shall come against him: therefore he shall be grieved, and return, and have indignation against the holy covenant: so shall he do; he shall even return, and have intelligence with them that forsake the holy covenant" (Daniel 11:28-30).

These verses use the word "return" five times (first noted by Wood[1]). That word is *shuwb* in Hebrew. In this context "he," the "vile person," *returns from exile* (cf. Ezekiel 2:1, Nehemiah 7:6, Isaiah 10:22, Jeremiah 22:10, 12:15). This means he is restored to what had been before.

He "returns" into "his land with great riches" (vs 28).

The self-imposed *imprisonment* by Pope Pius IX to the Vatican formally began in 1870 when it lost all of its *papal states.* The pope refused to recognize the existence of the Italian government. This picture was terminated during the time of Pope Pius XI by the Lateran Treaty on February 11, 1929, and confirmed by the Italian constitution in 1948.

The signatures on that first historic document were Cardinal Pietro Gasparri for the Holy See and Premier Benito Mussolini for the kingdom of Italy. With a stroke of two pens the Holy See was reestablished – and with great riches:

1. Church–State authority of the Holy See was recognized (they legally became a civil *and* ecclesiastical power).

2. The city of Rome was conveyed as the center of the Catholic world and a place of pilgrimage.

3. Italy recognized the validity of Catholic marriage and that all such issues were to be settled by Catholic Canon Law.

4. Catholic religious instruction would be permitted in public schools. Textbooks were to be approved by the Church.

---

[1] Wood, Robert, M.D.; Daniel 11 – 2500 Years of Religious History, p. 19.

151

5. Up until 1985 Roman Catholicism was to be the Italian State religion.

6. There was Church sovereignty over the 109 acres of the Vatican (an internationally recognized *state*).

7. There were payments of cash and bonds to the church from Italy for the state land they had lost.

8. Many free (forever) civil services were given – from railroad to postal.

The record says that his heart shall be *against the holy covenant* (vs 28). Psychoanalyst and Jesuit-trained E. Boyd Barrett wrote a book in 1935 that outlined the sinister plans of Pope Pius XI to become once again a world power! This book not only contained language to influence a major social agenda but permitted anything to further its power.[2] It is sinister and belies its claim to be a Christian church. The document ends with the words "Rome will stoop to conquer – even to sin."

Thus its name, "Rome Stoops to Conquer." This was the shot that went around the world, depicting this power as evil and willing to deceive – typifying the antichrist. This "prince" is portrayed as warring against the covenant. This parallels the *little horn* power in chapter 8 – "a king of fierce countenance" – one who was deceptive, "understanding dark sentences" (8:23), who would "cause craft to prosper" (8:23-25). Most remarkable – he is the one who stands up against Christ ("the Prince of princes"), seeking to undermine His work and people (8:24-25).

This is amazing because in 11:22 we learned that the *vile person* warred

against the Messianic "Prince of the covenant" during the Dark Ages. Here, he is doing exactly the same thing in a different era! The papacy hasn't changed. Gabriel early on depicts this power as anti-God. It fights the redemptive plans that God has made with mankind. It defies the everlasting covenant.

"... and he shall do [exploits] and return to his own land" (Daniel 11:28).

The word "exploits" is not in the original. Scholars have felt it better expresses the meaning of having its own way or doing its own pleasure. Since it says "he" returns to his own land, it suggests the papacy was away and then returns to the Vatican – its own land *by now*. This matches exactly what modern popes have done, making trips to foreign lands outside of Rome and Italy. Pope John Paul II was the most traveled papal head in history. He made over 100 foreign trips as a public image gesture to Catholic people. But through the sheer numbers that came out to see him, the whole world "wondered." Some gatherings reached over a million people in attendance.

Another form of "exploit" occurred. Since 1929 there has been increased meddling in world affairs. This began with Pope Pius XI, who made aggressive moves to infiltrate and control the political machinery in America. Pope Pius XII, his successor, was active in working with Hitler in treacherous plans against the Jews (something the Vatican is working hard to cover up). Pope John Paul II, in one of the greatest secret alliances of all time between himself and President Ronald Reagan (beginning on June 7, 1982), brought the Soviet bloc and its communistic regimes to an end.

"At the time appointed he shall return, and come toward the south; but it shall

---

[2] Barrett, E. Boyd, *Rome Stoops to Conquer*, p. 125 (Julian Messner, 1935).

not be as the former, or as the latter" (Daniel 11:29).

The "time appointed" or *mowed* was recently used for the time the papacy came to its Dark-Ages end (11:27). The *final end-time* meaning is noted here and in 8:19, 11:28-29, 11:35 and 12:7. These relate to the three and a half years when God's people are persecuted and ends with their deliverance (12:7, 1) just before Jesus comes.

Pope John Paul II had for years been courting a friendship with the Islamic world. Many of their leaders visited him in the Vatican and many attended a world peace conference in Assissi, Italy (January 24, 2001). In return, the pope visited the Syrian Omayyad mosque May 5, 2001 – the first papal head to ever do so.

The *vile person* is seen also as the *king of the north*. Though the papacy is its prophetic head, it represents – at the end – Babylon, and draws into its fold apostate Protestantism and spiritualism (as defined in Revelation, chapters 12–13 and 16–18). In 11:40 there is aggressive imagery of the *king of the south* "pushing" or warring against the *king of the north*. Here in verse 29 he is not aggressive. He comes towards the south in peaceful imagery.

It appears that the *vile person* comes into the Islamic world at the onset of this appointed time. What is happening?

For many years the papacy under Pope John Paul II had offered to be a neutral party or leader in Jerusalem and mediate the Jewish–Muslim–Christian conflict. The papacy succeeds in this verse to administer this wish. He comes "into the south" and acts as a buffer of peace. The foundational work towards this began in earnest with Pope John Paul II. This is one of several reasons

that we know from Revelation 17:10 that the king "which is" refers to this specific pope. It draws on many prophecies. Now, the one that "is to come" has arrived.

Daniel notes that it won't be "as the former or *as* the latter" (vs 29). The former represents the Crusades. The latter is when open war is ongoing and the Muslim countries are defeated (vs 40).

"For the ships of Chittim shall come against him: therefore he shall be grieved, and return, and have indignation against the holy covenant: so shall he do; he shall even return, and have intelligence with them that forsake the holy covenant" (Daniel 11:30).

This verse has stimulated creative theories as to its meaning. Few expositors have tried to contextually analyze its thoughts *within* the *sequence* of ideas.

The previous verse reveals a "southward" influence by the *vile person*. The Islamic world, competing with the Vatican in power and global membership, is courted by the papacy in its ecumenical outreach. Whatever the "ships of Chittim" specifically do, it intimidates and directly threatens the *vile person* – "he shall be grieved."

Ships (*tsiy*) simply refers to boats. Chittim (*kittiy*) is used in a variety of ways in the Scriptures. Balaam prophesied that ships would come from the *coast of Chittim*, afflicting Assur (Assyrians) and Eber (Hebrews) (Numbers 24:24). Isaiah refers to the "land of Chittim" (Isaiah 24:1, 12). Jeremiah noted the "isles of Chittim" (Jeremiah 2:10), referring to the coasts of Cyprus. Ezekiel refers to the "isles of Chittim" (Ezekiel 27:6), also alluding to Cyprus.

The two common things from these texts are the island of Cyprus and the *westward direction* from Daniel and

Palestine. "In Daniel's day the word referred … to the lands and peoples of the west."[3] That appears to be the key here.

There is a significant emphasis on directional symbols ever since the ram who was pushing "westward and northward and southward" in 8:4. What influence coming from the west would threaten the papacy (the *vile person* or the *king of the north*)?

"Since *north* and *south* portray the forces hostile to God (see verse 27), it stands to reason that *east* and *west* illustrate those who meet with God's approval. There are a number of texts that also indicate the correctness of this concept: 'Fear not: for I *am* with thee: I will bring thy seed from the *east,* and gather thee from the *west;* I will say to the *north,* Give up; and to the *south,* Keep not back: bring my sons from far, and my daughters from the ends of the earth.' (Isaiah 43:5, 6).

"'Thus saith the Lord of hosts; Behold, I will save my people from the *east* country, and from the *west* country.' Zechariah 8:7 (cf. Revelation 7:2; 16:12 where, although no mention of 'west,' 'east' bears favorable symbolic significance)."[4]

Symbolically, what would be west of Rome that would cause it to grieve at the end of time? Without equivocation, the *remnant,* as their forces begin to consolidate under the banner of the everlasting covenant. There is an anecdotal story about a Seventh-day Adventist lady who worked for Pope John Paul II. He purportedly told her that he wasn't concerned about the influence or power of the Adventist church (as reflected in Malachi Martin's book *Keys of this Blood,* p. 286). But he went on to express grave

concern when he noted, "the 144,000 we don't yet know how to deal with." We will shortly note that "people that do know their God shall be strong, and do exploits" (vs 32). They are symbolized by the *remnant* in prophecy – the white horse of the first seal, who goes out to conquer, to finish the work (Revelation 6:1-2).

As the end of time unfolds and the appointed time comes, first noted in 8:17 and 19, the spectacle of those committed to God will increasingly contrast with the ecumenical thrust of a papal coalition with apostate Protestantism. The pinnacle will be reached when moves *against* the covenant agreement will become law. That will signal the last bastion of resistance to the geopolitical goals of the Vatican.

The ships of Chittim symbolize *the remnant people coming from the west,* specifically beginning in the United States, who oppose the *vile person.* E. G. White referred to this verse, then quoted verses 31-36 and concluded that these "scenes" will "take place" when Satan assumes "control of human minds who have not the fear of God before them. Let all read and understand the prophecies of this book."[5] She saw these events as part of the end-of-time scene.

What is the papal power's response to this? He exhibits open indignation against the holy covenant, which embodies God's law and man's allegiance to the great principles it conveys. "So shall he do" Gabriel says. Do what? Do something to repudiate its sacredness. That will be seen, as we've noted before, as the transgression or abomination that will bring it to its desolating end.

[3] White, Ellen G.; Seventh-day Adventist Bible Commentary, vol. 4, p. 873.

[4] Wood, Robert, M.D.; *Daniel 11 – 2500 Years of Religious History*, pp. 20-21.

[5] White, Ellen G.; *Manuscript Releases,* vol. 13, p. 394.

"... he shall even return, and have intelligence with them that forsake the holy covenant" (Daniel 11:30).

This fearfully portrays an element of ecumenism based on unity of common beliefs – here, distinctly against the holy covenant. This represents the bonding that is now going on between apostate Protestantism and Catholicism.

This started on January 25, 1959, when Pope John XXIII announced that the Second Vatican Council would take place. *Catholics and Protestants Together* was a golden thread that wove its way through its subsequent proceedings. Documents of unity between the two have since been signed. Dialogue continues as they hold hands together in an ever closer bond.

They have intelligence (*biyn*) with one another. They have understanding with each other over forsaking or setting aside the holy covenant or law. What area of the law once held in the Ark of the Covenant do Protestants and Catholics mutually reject? The fourth commandment, regarding the Sabbath. That is the issue that is now coming to the fore in this chapter! Recall that the "transgression" or *pesha* of 8:13 was against (1) God's authority, (2) His law and (3) His covenant. All these issues are embodied in the fourth commandment.

"And arms shall stand on his part, and they shall pollute the sanctuary of strength, and shall take away the daily [sacrifice], and they shall place the abomination that maketh desolate" (Daniel 11:31).

The arms (*z@rowa*) that support what the *vile person* does symbolize military or political forces. This suggests that nations or governments will stand behind the papacy during this end-time rise to power. That is exactly what is portrayed in Revelation 17:12 where ten horns/ kings are described, who share power with the beast (papacy–Babylon) for a short time. Also, this parallels Revelation 13:12 where the earth-beast (apostate Protestantism) causeth the earth and them which dwell therein to worship the first beast (sea-beast – papacy). The world's civil infrastructure comes to the support of the Vatican right at the end.

Long after Gabriel's message to Daniel, Jesus talked about the abomination that leads to desolation (Matthew 24:15, Mark 13:14). In that dual prophecy Jesus related this decreed curse to the destruction of Jerusalem and the end-time desolation of the world.

"The Saviour's prophecy concerning the visitation of judgments upon Jerusalem is to have another fulfillment, of which that terrible desolation was but a faint shadow. In the fate of the chosen city we may behold the doom of a world that has rejected God's mercy and trampled upon His law."[6]

"As the siege of Jerusalem by the Roman armies was the signal for flight to the Judean Christians, so the assumption of power on the part of our nation [the United States] in the decree *enforcing the papal Sabbath* will be a warning to us."[7]

"The first day of the week is to be exalted and presented to all for observance. Shall we be partakers of this *cup of abomination*? Shall we bow to the authorities of earth and despise God? The powers of darkness have been gathering their forces to bring this crisis about in the world, so that the man of sin may exalt himself above God."[8]

An important note: Since Jesus ties the abomination of desolation to the fall

---

[6] White, Ellen G.; *The Great Controversy,* p. 36.

[7] White, Ellen G.; *Testimonies,* vol. 5, p. 464.

[8] White, Ellen G.; *The Review and Herald,* April 15, 1890. *The Signs of the Times,* March 3, 1890.

of Jerusalem and the end of the world, which meshes with Daniel 8–12, the popular interpretation of Antiochus Epiphanes (~165 B.C.) to the *little horn*, *vile person* and *king of the north* simply doesn't fit. It's a concept that is against Jesus' clear teaching.

"And such as do wickedly against the covenant shall he corrupt by flatteries: but the people that do know their God shall be strong, and do [exploits]" (Daniel 11:32).

This verse is a dramatic statement by Gabriel. This ecumenical bond between Catholicism and Protestantism against God's holy law and covenant is driven by deception and seductive actions, conveying what they are not. This insight began in chapter 8 – a king "understanding dark sentences, shall stand up" (8:23) and "he shall cause craft to prosper in his hand" (8:25).

The last half of this verse is beautiful. In contrast to the corrupt covenant breakers are those who "know their God." They are strong (*chazaq*) and cleave to the holy principles of heaven. It then states that they do *exploits.* That word, again, is not in the original Hebrew text. But the implication that is made in this last thought means that they follow through or act upon their conviction and loyalty to God. This draws upon a remarkable theme found in Revelation 6, where it depicts the unswerving dedication of the 144,000 in the white horse. At that time, when the history of the world is coming to a close, God's remnant will be active, going out to conquer and conquering.

"And they that understand among the people shall instruct many: yet they shall fall by the sword, and by flame, by captivity, and by spoil, [many] days" (Daniel 11:33).

This verse and the last part of verse 32 should have been topically together. They that understand (*sakal*) have an intelligent grasp of God and His truth based upon reason. His people (the remnant) shall instruct many. This last group of people will be teachers. This is when the spread of the gospel crescendoes around the world into the *Loud Cry.* It comes at the time of the oppressive abomination. As Satan corrupts the world, God's people will be "instructing many." This is, again, beautifully depicted in the first Seal (Revelation 6) when the white horse (God's purified, holy people) goes out to conquer.

Another contrasting picture is here painted. Those loyal people will fall by the sword and flame, be imprisoned and have their belongings taken away. This is persecution and parallels the second, fourth and fifth Seals (Revelation 6:3-4, 8-9) where a group of vengeful people (red horse) are associated with others to harm and kill (pale horse), resulting in martyrdom.

The King James Version of the Bible says "many days." In Hebrew it is simply days (*yowm*). A similar phrase was used in 8:26 that referred to an indefinite time in the future. Here it is used without the word "many." *Yowm* refers to literal days as used by Daniel. It suggests a short, indefinite time period. The next chapter will tell us exactly how long that will be – three and a half years – the time of trouble or tribulation.

"Now when they shall fall, they shall be holpen with a little help: but many shall cleave to them with flatteries" (Daniel 11:34).

When God's people shall fall (*kawshal* – suggesting stumble or totter from weakness or weariness from the pursuit of persecution), they will be assisted with some help. God sustains His people. He never leaves or forsakes them.

"Those who are loyal to God's law will not always find the way smooth. God has not promised his people exemption from trials, but he has promised that which is far better. He has said: 'As thy days, so shall thy strength be.' 'My grace is sufficient for thee; for my strength is made perfect in weakness.' 'The God of all comfort, who comforteth us in all our tribulation.' 'As the sufferings of Christ abound in us, so our consolation also aboundeth.' All who love and fear God will suffer persecution. But Jesus will be near to sustain everyone who is afflicted for the truth's sake. When in the prison of Philippi, the scourged and heavily-manacled servants of Christ had such divine consolation that they sang praises to God, and the walls resounded with their triumph. To these faithful messengers, that cold dungeon, reeking with dampness, was made as the gate of heaven. The glory of the Sun of Righteousness beamed forth into that inner prison, making it radiant with a divine effulgence. Christ, the royal messenger, came to John when on his sea-bound isle, and gave him the most wonderful revelations of himself, and of what was to take place in the world's history prior to his second appearing. Jesus revealed himself to Stephen while he was surrounded with pitiless foes. The martyr was given a view of the glory of God with Jesus standing at his right hand to give help to his suffering servant."[9]

"Through centuries of persecution, conflict, and darkness, God has sustained His church. Not one cloud has fallen upon it that He has not prepared for; not one opposing force has risen to counterwork His work, that He has not foreseen. All has taken place as He predicted. He has not left His church forsaken, but has traced in prophetic declarations what would occur, and that which His Spirit inspired the prophets to foretell has been brought about. All His purposes will be fulfilled. His law is linked with His throne, and no power of evil can destroy it. Truth is inspired and guarded by God; and it will triumph over all opposition."[10]

Sadly, many of those who claim loyalty to God, when under threats, will join with or cleave to those who have been deceived by "smooth" teaching. They are attracted to the flatteries of the wicked. This is a description of many who will leave or be shaken out of God's fold at the end of time.

"As the controversy extends into new fields and the minds of the people are called to God's downtrodden law, Satan is astir. The power attending the message will only madden those who oppose it. The clergy will put forth almost superhuman efforts to shut away the light lest it should shine upon their flocks. By every means at their command they will endeavor to suppress the discussion of these vital questions. The church appeals to the strong arm of civil power, and, in this work, papists and Protestants unite. As the movement for Sunday enforcement becomes more bold and decided, the law will be invoked against commandment keepers. They will be threatened with fines and imprisonment, and some will be offered positions of influence, and other rewards and advantages, as inducements to renounce their faith."[11]

"I was pointed to the providence of God among His people and was shown that every trial made by the refining, purifying process upon professed Christians

---

[9] White, Ellen G.; *The Signs of the Times,* March 3, 1890.

[10] White, Ellen G.; *The Acts of the Apostles,* p. 11.

[11] White, Ellen G.; *The Great Controversy,* p. 607.

proves some to be dross. The fine gold does not always appear. In every religious crisis some fall under temptation. The shaking of God blows away multitudes like dry leaves. Prosperity multiplies a mass of professors. Adversity purges them out of the church. As a class, their spirits are not steadfast with God. They go out from us because they are not of us; for when tribulation or persecution arises because of the word, many are offended."[12]

"And [some] of them of understanding shall fall, to try them, and to purge, and to make [them] white, [even] to the time of the end: because [it is] yet for a time appointed" (Daniel 11:35).

The wording of this verse is confusing. It is a verse of hope, however, and has been included to show that at the very end many backsliders will return to the fold.

The clearest rendition of this text comes in a transliteration, *The Berkeley Version in Modern English*: "On the part of some teachers their stumbling shall be for their refinement and purification to make them white, preparatory to the final period which is delayed until the appointed time.

"When the storm of persecution really breaks upon us, the true sheep will hear the true Shepherd's voice. Self-denying efforts will be put forth to save the lost, and many who have strayed from the fold will come back to follow the great Shepherd. The people of God will draw together, and present to the enemy a united front.... The love of Christ, the love of our brethren, will testify to the world that we have been with Jesus and learned of Him. Then will the message of the third angel swell to a loud cry, and the whole earth will be lightened with the glory of the Lord.–Testimonies, vol. 6, p. 401 (1900)."[13]

This verse is filled with the most helpful information regarding the end of time. We've already seen in 8:19 that the end of time (*eth qets*) is at the appointed time (*mowed*). Daniel 12 has shown us that this is the *chazown* vision in the last three and a half years of time. That is when God's people are "trodden underfoot," "cast down" or persecuted.

The wording in the last half of this verse strongly suggests that when many backsliders return to the loyalty of the remnant noted in verse 34, the dross of this world is purged and they become white – just like the 144,000 noted in the white horse of Revelation 6:1-2. What a message! From the seeds of harm come a renewed commitment to Jesus Christ at the end.

---

[12] White, Ellen G.; *Testimonies,* vol. 4, p. 89.

[13] White, Ellen G.; *Evangelism,* p. 693.

CHAPTER 34

PRETENDING TO BE LIKE GOD

– Daniel 11:36-39 –

"And the king shall do according to his will; and he shall exalt himself, and magnify himself above every god, and shall speak marvellous things against the God of gods, and shall prosper till the indignation be accomplished: for that that is determined shall be done" (Daniel 11:36).

This "king" is clearly the *king of the north* or *vile person* by the description given (similar to the *little horn* of chapter 8).

- He exalts himself (8:11, 25)

- He magnifies himself above every god (8:25)

- He speaks against God (8:23, 25)

- He prospers (8:12, 8:24-25)

This cross-references with II Thessalonians 2:4.

- Exalteth himself

- Exalteth himself above all that is called God

The *king of the north* had indignation (*zaam*) against the holy covenant (11:30). But at the appointed time the indignation or wrath (*zaam*) of God will turn against him. He prospers until then. Again, in Daniel 8:19 it is at the *appointed time* when God's wrath is exhibited. It says the *little horn* will come to its end – "he shall be broken without hand"

(8:25). Only God intervenes. No man, army or political force brings it to its end. That is exactly what is described in Revelation 16:19. Babylon comes into remembrance before God "to give unto her the cup of the wine of the fierceness of his wrath."

The final phrase, "that is determined shall be done," simply means that what God has already decreed will be done. The *vile person*, the *little horn* and the *king of the north* are destined for destruction. God has foretold its final demise. That was declared a second time in Daniel 9:26-27.

Expositor White understood Daniel 11. She applied verses 31-36 to the emerging time of tribulation, future to 1904, when her thoughts were penned. This is what she observed: "We have no time to lose. Troublous times are before us. The world is stirred with the spirit of war. Soon the scenes of trouble spoken of in the prophecies will take place. The prophecy in the eleventh of Daniel has nearly reached its complete fulfillment. Much of the history that has taken place in fulfillment of this prophecy will be repeated. In the thirtieth verse a power is spoken of that 'shall be grieved, and return, and have indignation against the holy covenant: so shall he do; he shall even return, and have intelligence with them that forsake the holy covenant.' [Verses 31-36 quoted.]

"Scenes similar to those described in these words will take place. We see evidence that Satan is fast obtaining the control of human minds who have not the fear of God before them. Let all read and understand the prophecies of this book, for we are now entering upon the time of trouble spoken of: [Dan. 12:1-4 quoted.]"[1]

This insight helps us to put into perspective the setting and meaning of the last third of this remarkable chapter.

"Neither shall he regard the God of his fathers, nor the desire of women, nor regard any god: for he shall magnify himself above all" (Daniel 11:37).

This verse sequentially flows from the previous one. The *king of the north* – the papacy – has no regard for the God of his fathers – nor any god. The Apostolic Church had a pure faith and unswerving interest to uphold the God of truth. As Rome gradually became the center of administrative Christian power, anti-Semitism and pagan influences tainted truth. Compromise and tolerance brought terrible changes to a church still in its youth. The seeds of apostate Christianity, of "Romanism," sprouted into Catholicism. Bishops, and later popes, were elevated as God. Finally, they ruled against the very Being they claimed to represent. Salvation was deemed only through the church. The priest became the arbiter of forgiveness and the gatekeepers to heaven or hell.

"Let no man deceive you by any means: for [that day shall not come], except there come a falling away first, and that man of sin be revealed, the son of perdition; Who opposeth and exalteth himself above all that is called God, or that is worshipped; so that he as God sitteth in the temple of God, showing himself that he is God" (II Thessalonians 2:3-4).

The disregard for women is reflected in the coercive rule of celibacy, the de-

nial of women's role in the priesthood and prohibition of marriage to tens of thousands of nuns who serve the church, often in a state of forced poverty.

Celibacy was instituted by the early Roman Church – not as an issue of purity but to preserve property. Many kings and nobles donated property to priests (who were married) for their long and devoted spiritual services. When they died, the wives would be the heirs. Thus, the church would lose out. In celibacy the church became the heir. This became church dogma, finally eliciting guilt, sin and sacrilege on the part of anyone who opposed or broke a celibacy vow.

Keeping the nuns single became a tool to control and extract loyalty to the church or its priest leadership. This coercive administrative ploy automatically rejects women's ordination. Ordination would make women equal to men, something the Catholic Church functionally resists.

Reviewing Catholic literature, one is struck with the moral and elevated spiritual values they see in being celibate and single. All those were an afterthought to the original financial and power objectives of Rome. "For he shall magnify himself above all" – an arrogant theme that Scripture reminds us of repeatedly. They control and manipulate lives, acting as God but representing the character of Satan.

"But in his estate shall he honour the God of forces: and a god whom his fathers knew not shall he honour with gold, and silver, and with precious stones, and pleasant things" (Daniel 11:38).

The context flows from the previous verse where in the parting thought it noted that the papacy magnified itself (himself) above every god/God. This new verse transcends even that horror by noting that he honors or promotes the god (the King James Version's capitalizing of "God" here is incorrect) of strongholds.

---

[1] White, Ellen G.; *Manuscript Releases,* No. 13, p. 394.

This setting implies that because of the papal arrogance, power and elevated honor by the world, it assumes it is its own fortress – impervious to any opposition or powers that might seek to curtail its authority.

Once again, a negative point is made that this power has deviated from the God of heaven and paid loyalty to a god the early Christian church did not know. Immediately, this introduces gods from paganism/mysticism, and what follows confirms this insight.

The papacy honors gods of gold, silver, precious stones and pleasant things. This conjures up the massive system within Catholicism of idols, icons, expensive ornaments, opulent clothing, jewelry and churches that cost many times that of Protestant edifices. The Catholic Church readily admits its rites and worship styles have come heavily from pagan traditions.

Perhaps most reprehensible is the transference of worship from the God of heaven to man himself – the pope. This theme continues what was introduced in verse 37. The pope is seen as, worshiped as and declared to be "god on earth."

The New York Catholic Catechism says: "The Pope takes the place of Jesus Christ on earth ... by divine right the pope has supreme and full power in faith and morals over each and every pastor and his flock. He is the true Vicar of Christ, the head of the entire church, the father and teacher of all Christians. He is the infallible ruler, the founder of dogmas, the author of and the judge of councils; the universal ruler of truth, the arbiter of the world, the supreme judge of heaven and earth, the judge of all, being judged by one, God himself on earth."

In his encyclical, *The Reunion of Christendom* (1885), Pope Leo XIII stated that the pope holds "upon this earth the place of God Almighty."

The Council of Trent declared: "Sitting in that chair in which Peter, the prince of the Apostles, sat to the close of life, the Catholic Church recognizes in his person the most exalted degree of dignity, and the full jurisdiction not based on constitutions, but emanating from no less authority than from God Himself. As the Successor of St. Peter and the true and legitimate Vicar of Jesus Christ, he therefore, presides over the Universal Church, the Father and Governor of all the faithful, of Bishops also, and of all other prelates, be their station, rank, or power, what they may be."

The Catholic book, *My Catholic Faith*, which is based on the Baltimore Catechism, says on page 251, "The Pope can make and unmake laws for the entire Church; his authority is supreme and unquestioned. Every bishop, every priest, every member of the Church is subject to him."

"The Pope is of so great dignity and so exalted that he is not a mere man, but as it were God and the vicar of God...."

"The Pope is as it were God on earth, sole sovereign of the faithful of Christ, chief of kings, having plenitude of power, to whom has been intrusted by the omnipotent God direction not only of the earthly but also of the heavenly kingdom...."

"The Pope is of so great authority and power that he can modify, explain, or interpret even divine laws...."

"The Pope can modify divine law, since his power is not of man but of God, and he acts as vicegerent of God upon earth with most ample power of binding and loosing sheep." (Translated from Lucius Ferraris,

Papa II, Prompts Bibliotheca, vol. VI, pp. 25-29).

That is blasphemy of the highest order against the sovereign God of the universe!

"Thus shall he do in the most strong holds with a strange god, whom he shall acknowledge [and] increase with glory: and he shall cause them to rule over many, and shall divide the land for gain" (Daniel 11:39).

The wording of this verse is difficult to grasp. In the context of the previous verse the papacy will continue with those deeds, using the cover of their *strong holds* (their great cathedrals and churches, which they claim to be Christian) as their protection. The mysticism of that cover and its rites and traditions will safeguard the strange god of the papacy – the pope. The world will be enamored with him. This ties to "Who is like the beast? Who can make war against him?" (Revelation 13:4). The mysticism of the papacy so intrigues the minds of the world that they capitulate to it, feeling it all-powerful.

Whoever acknowledges him is allegedly rewarded with glory (*kabowd*), honor or a *sense* of moral security.

These dynamics were effective in the past and will be repeated in a far more persuasive and deceptive manner at the end: "As her power increased, the darkness deepened. Faith was transferred from Christ, the true foundation, to the pope of Rome. Instead of trusting in the Son of God for forgiveness of sins and for eternal salvation, the people looked to the pope, and to the priests and prelates to whom he delegated authority. They were taught that the pope was their earthly mediator and that none could approach God except through him; and, further, that he stood in the place of God to them and was therefore

to be implicitly obeyed…. Thus the minds of the people were turned away from God to fallible, erring, and cruel men, nay, more, to the prince of darkness himself, who exercised his power through them. Sin was disguised in a garb of sanctity. When the Scriptures are suppressed, and man comes to regard himself as supreme, we need look only for fraud, deception, and debasing iniquity. With the elevation of human laws and traditions was manifest the corruption that ever results from setting aside the law of God."[2]

Catholicism creates a psychological magnetism that ensnares millions of minds. Verse 39 portrays a magnetic attraction the world will have for that authority. It reveals an intriguing dependency in a coercive, submissive bond.

"And this is the religion which Protestants are beginning to look upon with so much favor, and which will eventually be united with Protestantism. This union will not, however, be effected by a change in Catholicism, for Rome never changes. She claims infallibility. It is Protestantism that will change. The adoption of liberal ideas on its part will bring it where it can clasp the hand of Catholicism.–RH June 1, 1886.

"The professed Protestant *world* will form a confederacy with the man of sin, and the church and the world will be in corrupt harmony. – 7BC 975 (1891)."[3]

The final thoughts of this verse reveal that this *vile person*, the *king of the north*, the papacy, will reward land and kingship over the masses (many) to those who have been loyal to its authority. Not only will the religious world give submissive honor to the papacy, but here, the secular world experiences gain. We must turn to Revelation 17 for added understanding.

---

[2] White, Ellen G.; *The Great Controversy,* p. 55.
[3] White, Ellen G.; *Last Day Events,* p. 130.

The harlot (that blasphemous woman), symbolizing Babylon (the Roman Catholic Church), makes the "inhabitants of the earth ... drunk with the wine of her fornication" (17:2). The world is enamored with her deceptive, abominable teachings. These are depicted by the "abominations" in the "golden cup in her hand" (17:4). It doesn't stop there. The scarlet beast or papal power upon which she rides has ten horns, which are "ten kings" which haven't received their kingdom as yet (the time in which this prophecy begins to unfold). BUT — they will "receive power as kings one hour with the beast" (17:12).

When does that occur? At the very end of time, which is described here in Daniel 11:39! The world has already been divided into ten great divisions for a future time by the United Nations and The Club of Rome. Those are the ten horns depicted here soon to become future "kingdoms" that rule under the administrative guise of the papacy.

CHAPTER 35

THE PAPACY COMES TO ITS END

– Daniel 11:40-45 –

"And at the time of the end shall the king of the south push at him: and the king of the north shall come against him like a whirlwind, with chariots, and with horsemen, and with many ships; and he shall enter into the countries, and shall overflow and pass over" (Daniel 11:40).

The *little horn, prince, vile person* and *king of the north* parallel the *man of sin* in II Thessalonians. These descriptive narratives of Daniel have been presented in the *chazown* vision through its several parts. Repeatedly, we have been reminded that it was for the end of time (*eth qets*) at the appointed time (*mowed*). At the end of time this power – the papacy – would arise and confront God by defying the core truths of His Word. Even more defiant would be his claim to be like God by assuming many of His prerogatives.

Within that end-time framework, the message of Revelation 13 introduces an earth-beast ("false prophet," the United States and apostate Protestantism), who will give fiendish support *right at the end* to the sea-beast (the papacy) to the point of taking the life of any opposition. These two powers, along with the dragon, are called "Babylon" in Revelation. This is the broader meaning of the *king of the north*. A more focused view is the papacy – the central earthly apostate power.

Against that end-time backdrop a "king of the south" is reintroduced. Many expositors have defined the "south" to be Egypt and interpret it to mean atheism. This designation has been taken to ex-treme views with frequent statements that since it is atheism, it must be *atheistic communism*. These designations have brought confusion and have left wide gaps in our understanding.

The *king of the south* "pushes" (*nagach*) against the *king of the north*. *Nagach* means likely to gore with horns. It symbolizes warring against. What could this refer to in an end-time setting?

We already noted in verses 2-20 fierce competition between the Seleucids' northern kings of Syria and the Ptolomy's southern kings of Egypt. North and south were directional images of competition and conflict. In the middle of this conflict was the "glorious land." All that timed imagery was a metaphor for the very end of time.

During the Dark Ages the conflict, as portrayed here in this chapter, was between the "Christian" papacy and the Muslim world through the Crusade wars. The center of the conflict was Palestine. That, too, was a portrayal of the future.

Once again we have a battle between the north and the south. We already noted that the *little horn* of Daniel 8 came from the north and pushed worldwide. But it specifically said "towards the pleasant land" or Palestine (8:9). Shortly, we will see that the *king of the north* – Babylon – will plant its center of worship "between the seas in the glorious holy mountain" (Isaiah 45). That is, once again, Palestine – the "glorious land."

What power would fight against "Christianity" – the papacy and Protestantism (though in apostasy)? There is only one significant world power that "gores" or "wars" specifically against Christianity – and that is the Muslim world.

It is fascinating that the Koran identifies all non-Islamics as "unbelievers." Islam is the antithetic force opposing the "symbolic center" of Christianity – the papacy and the United States/Protestantism. The history of this sect reveals intermittent armed conflict against Christians since 674 A.D.[1]

Islam's spirit of war and hatred has its broad roots in the Koran: "I will instill terror into the hearts of the *unbelievers*: smite ye above their necks and smite all their finger-tips off them" (*Koran* 8:12).

In 1979 the Iranian Revolution exploded, giving birth to a new form of radical Islamic thinking. Ayatollah Khomeini convinced the Islamic world that the United States was the "Great Satan." Seventy of the world's 184 countries are now part of *Dar al Islam* or the House of Islam. Six of these are active sponsors of terrorism.

In the setting of the 40th verse of Daniel 11, at the *eth qets* or time of the final end, when judgment occurs, conflict between the *king of the south* (which *initiates* the war of hate) and the *king of the north* will occur. The latter becomes the conqueror.

The imagery portrays the type of "pushing" (*nagach*) seen in growing numbers of terrorist attacks against Christians. Sudan, under Islamic rule since 1988, has murdered upwards of

two million Christians. Their ultimate goal is liquidation of all Christians.

The aggression by Islamic "radicals" is a Koran-directed and -instigated *order* to all the Muslim World.

"Fighting is prescribed for you, and ye dislike it. But it is possible that ye dislike a thing which is good for you, and that ye love a thing which is bad for you. But Allah knoweth, and ye know not" (*Koran* 2:216).

"The punishment of those who wage war against Allah and His Messenger, and strive with might and main for mischief through the land is: execution, or crucifixion, or the cutting off of hands and feet from opposite sides, or exile from the land: that is their disgrace in this world, and a heavy punishment is theirs in the Hereafter" (*Koran* 5:33).

"For the Rejecters we have prepared Chains, Yokes, and a Blazing Fire" (*Koran* 76:4).

"Nor take life – which Allah has made sacred – except for just cause. And if anyone is slain wrongfully, we have given his heir authority (to demand Qisas or to forgive): but let him not exceed bounds in the matter of taking life; for he is helped (by the Law)" (*Koran* 17:33).

Apocalyptic issues suggest that this is a great diversionary tool of Satan's to unite the United States, at the center of world power, with the papacy and apostate Protestantism in a moral forefront of humanitarian concerns in their opposition to Islam.

The response of the *north* is like a "whirlwind" or terrible storm. The description of chariots, horsemen and ships entering many countries and going through them is descriptive of military action that we are beginning to see against radical Islam. The Biblical description suggests that it will become a terrible conflict, far exceeding what we see today (2005).

[1] Westerman, Toby; "The Historic Spread of Islam," "Jihad, The Radical Islamic Threat to America," *Whistle Blower,* Nov. 2001, vol. 10, No. 11, pp. 8-9.

"He shall enter also into the glorious land, and many [countries] shall be overthrown: but these shall escape out of his hand, [even] Edom, and Moab, and the chief of the children of Ammon" (Daniel 11:41).

The *king of the north* will enter the glorious land – Palestine.

Some believe the *glorious land* is the United States, but there is nothing to support that assertion. It is the same country also depicted as "the glorious land" in verse 16, and the "pleasant land" in Daniel 8:9. This can only be Palestine. Its parallel is also found in verse 45 of this chapter where it is called a "glorious holy mountain." This suggests that the *vile person* will eventually occupy Palestine in some manner.

Others have argued that the glorious land represents God's church when the papal *north* tries to impose her dogma and will upon it. The context, however, shows that the military might of the *north* (Babylon) is a reaction to the harm the *south* brought against the *north*. That reactionary focus is against Islam (*south*). However, the powers for right will be specifically introduced in verse 44! We are given an overview in these verses of two end-time evil powers in an earthly conflict. Some have tried to pin prophetic messages to specific countries such as Iran or Iraq in association with Daniel 8. The imagery is only general. To add what is not specifically noted is speculation and *adds* to the prophecy.

There is a spiritual application discovered in verse 45 that we must emphasize. Though this prophecy has been and is difficult, we are reminded of Gabriel's warning of another end-time prophecy: *"If any man shall add unto these things, God shall add unto him the plagues that are written in this book"* (Revelation 22:18).

"Glorious land" or "pleasant land" in several places in the Old Testament refers to Palestine – the promised land to the Jewish people (Psalm 104:24, Jeremiah 3:19, Zechariah 7:14, Deuteronomy 8:7-10, 11:12). In one place only does it allude to God's people being like "delightsome land" (Malachi 3:12). The weight of evidence encourages a Palestinian application.

The papacy and its ally, apostate Protestantism, symbolized as the United States in Revelation 13, enters Palestine. Enter (*bow*) has broad meaning. In the context of this verse where it says "many countries shall be overthrown," *bow* means that Palestine will be besieged at a time of a massive military campaign, presumably in the mid-eastern theater. This all follows the "pushing" or terror the Muslim world has against the *north*.

This is an interesting verse in light of what is occurring today. The papacy owns all the major Christian sites related to the birth of Christianity in Palestine. For over a decade Pope John Paul II had been offering to mediate a Palestinian solution, even to the point of administering the land – especially Jerusalem. In addition, the evangelical world, through a novel view of the seventy-week prophecy of Daniel 9, believes that the Jews will rebuild the temple on the Temple Mount. They also see the antichrist coming in the middle of a seven-year period to seize power in that temple. Though believing this because of a serious error in their Biblical understanding, the majority of Protestants now feel Palestine is crucial to the fulfillment of end-time prophecy. Regardless of whether the deceptive views of dispensationalism are entertained or the contextual exposition propounded here, Palestine appears to be a prominent focal point in this end-time drama.

Thus, this verse unfolds a point in time where military operations will occur against the Islamic world, securing Palestine, and, perhaps in the Protestant mind, fulfill prophecy through might. God, however, guides the play and interplay of events to assure that His final will of earth's happenings will contrast right with wrong – good with evil.

The last half of this verse is fascinating and requires contemplative study. Edom, Moab and the chief of the children of Ammon will escape the destructive onslaught. Is this referring to people related to these three groups or do we have a land area symbolized by Edom, Moab and Ammon? Or will the land of Moab and Edom be protected and only the "children" of Ammon escape the sword?

Since we are dealing with a very end-time scenario, the first point to observe is that the country of Jordan now occupies what was once Ammon, Moab and Edom. Intriguingly, they have been able to maintain a position of remarkable neutrality among the mid-eastern hostilities. Though that literalism brings great risk when addressing prophecy, the use of the symbols for war in verse 41, then the word "countries" in the same verse, along with other such words, contextually focus on the literal mid-east. It appears that Jordan is singled out as a land area not involved in this strife.

Edom was the southernmost group of the three. These people were descendants of Esau. Prophecy revealed that they would cease to exist. God said he hated Esau (Malachi 1:3). Babylonian armies early in the 6th century B.C. attacked them, and the "curse of Esau" led to the termination of this people. They no longer exist. Spiritually, they would not be a desirable *people* to be represented here. Thus, the *land/country* previously known as Edom must be symbolized.

Moab was the name of Lot's son from his elder daughter from an incestuous relationship. The central area of the three lands under review here was called after him – Moab. They were a powerful people and had intermittent conflict with Israel. Ruth was a Moabitess (Ruth 1:4), and her great grandson was King David (Ruth 4:13-22). Moab was where Moses died (Deuteronomy 34:1-8) and Israel mourned there for thirty days.

Isaiah 15, 16 and 25:10-12 predicted the annihilation of the Moabites. That came true. Today, Moab no longer exists, and its people have disappeared. Thus, the *land/country* previously known as Moab must be meant here, not the people.

Ammon was the northernmost country of the three. The people were descendants of Ammon, Lot's son by his younger daughter (Genesis 19:38). Along with the Moabites, they hired Balaam to curse Israel (Deuteronomy 23:4). Solomon had many Ammonite wives. One, Naamah, was the mother of King Rehoboam (I Kings 14:31, II Chronicles 12:13). Fearful judgments were prophesied against them because of their hostility towards Israel (Zephaniah 2:8; Jeremiah 43:1; Ezekiel 25:1, 10; Amos 1:13).

They were apparently a numerous people at the time of Justin Martyr (*Dial. cum Tryph.,* sec. 119). Over the course of the next century they vanished from the view of history. No bona fide ties exist today to the Ammonites of old. They symbolized a predatory group of people who were pagans. God told Israel not to meddle in the affairs of the "children of Ammon" (descendants of Ammon) because their land would not be given to them.

In an end-time prophecy (Jeremiah 25:15-38) God's wrath comes and desolates the nations of the earth. Edom, Moab and Ammon are listed among many others. These three are judged as evil. Why are they listed and "chief of the children of Ammon" singled out?

It appears, once again, that within the context of "countries" being specifically addressed, the nation of Jordan is addressed. The capital of Jordan is Amman. That is in the northern area of the country where the *leaders of the people* exist. This understanding is tentative but draws on the Biblical record, history and context of this area within Daniel 11:40-45.

There are many spiritual themes in the Old Testament that are drawn from these three countries. Though some "good" comes through various incidents, the ultimate fate results from their evil:

"The Ammonites" will "not be remembered among the nations" (Ezekiel 25:10).

"Moab shall be trampled down under him as straw is trampled down for the refuse heap" (Isaiah 25:10).

The "House of Edom" would become "stubble" (Obadiah 18).

"He shall stretch forth his hand also upon the countries: and the land of Egypt shall not escape" (Daniel 11:42).

The first part of this verse reiterates in different words what was said in verse 40: *"He shall enter into the countries, and shall overflow and pass over"* (Daniel 11:40). *"He shall stretch forth his hand also upon the countries"* (Daniel 11:42).

A new thought is introduced by identifying Egypt specifically as not escaping the warring *king of the north.* In prophecy Egypt symbolizes the world from which God's people are delivered as they journey to the promised land. Egypt also represents paganism/atheism, an anti-God power. Egypt represents today one of the Muslim nations in the Middle East.

They are part of the *king of the south* imagery. Yet, it is singled out here as if to say "even Egypt, that God-defying nation who wielded so much power, is going to be harmed – even they won't escape."

There is another important theme that is introduced by singling out the land of Egypt. The verse uses "he," which again and again in this prophecy refers to the papacy or spiritual Babylon. The words not only reiterate what was said in verse 40 of his exploits, but the Hebrew word for "countries" and "lands" in this verse is the same as in verse 40 – *erets* or *eres.* This is a frequently-used word in the Old Testament. Its primary imagery is "the earth" in a cosmological sense – the world. The way the King James Version (and most others) translates it leaves the meaning of the next two verses isolated to Egypt or with its surrounding countries. That introduces a confusing picture and fragments the flowing theme in these final verses.

If we observe the greater meaning of the words in context, this thought emerges: The *king of the north* shall also stretch his hand of power over the earth, and the wicked, God-defying world will not escape his grip.

This not only makes more sense but parallels the thoughts in Revelation 13.

Sea-beast – papacy

- Blasphemes God's name, His church and all heavenly beings (Revelation 13:6)
- Power was given him over **all** kindreds, and tongues, and nations (Revelation 13:7)

Earth-beast

- Exercises **all** the power of the first beast (Revelation 13:12)

This also ties with the world power it wields with "ten kings" at the end (Revelation 17:12). This now opens a clearer meaning for the next verse.

"But he shall have power over the treasures of gold and of silver, and over all the precious things of Egypt: and the Libyans and the Ethiopians [shall be] at his steps" (Daniel 11:43).

The *king of the north* (generally portraying "Babylon") will have power over the treasures of gold and silver, and over all the precious things of Egypt (representing the world). The Hebrew word for power is *mashal.* It means "to rule" or "have charge over."

The Vatican (representing the papacy) associated with the United States (representing apostate Protestantism) will be in control of the world's finances and monetary system. This is intriguing. The Vatican Bank is an international institution. Yet, it is the only bank that is not required to report its operations to the world financial community. Though denied by the Vatican, credible reports have been circulated that when Pope John Paul I became pope he wanted to clean up the corruption of the Vatican Bank. Internal hostilities broke out, and he *died* shortly after taking office. This raises questions as to how much monetary control is being exercised already in "Babylon."

The United States, through the IMF (International Monitory Fund) and World Bank, holds major control of the flow of world money. These two together (*king of the north*) could easily fulfill the intent and prophecy foretold here. Revelation 13 makes clear that the dual cooperative power of the two beasts (sea-beast and earth-beast) will unite at the end in completing Satan's work.

"The papacy will appear in its power"[2] at the end.

"As we approach the last crisis, it is of vital moment that harmony and unity exist among the Lord's instrumentalities. The world is filled with storm and war and variance. Yet under *one head*–the papal power–the people will unite to oppose God in the person of His witnesses.

"What is it that gives its kingdom to this power? Protestantism, a power which, while professing to have the temper and spirit of a lamb and to be allied to Heaven, speaks with the voice of a dragon. It is moved by a power from beneath.

"'These have one mind.' There will be a universal bond of union, one great harmony, a confederacy of Satan's forces. 'And shall give their power and strength unto the beast.' Thus is manifested the same arbitrary, oppressive power against religious liberty, freedom to worship God according to the dictates of conscience, as was manifested by the papacy, when in the past it persecuted those who dared to refuse to conform with the religious rites and ceremonies of Romanism.

"In the warfare to be waged in the last days there will be united, in opposition to God's people, all the corrupt powers that have apostatized from allegiance to the law of Jehovah. In this warfare the Sabbath of the fourth commandment will be the great point at issue; for in the Sabbath commandment the great Lawgiver identifies Himself as the Creator of the heavens and the earth."[3]

What could the Libyans and the Ethiopians following in his footsteps mean? There is virtually no Biblical in-

---

[2] White, Ellen G.; *Manuscript Releases,* vol. 4, p. 330.

[3] White, Ellen G.; *Maranatha,* p. 187 (emphasis added).

formation to guide us on the Libyans or Libya. Ethiopia is mentioned several times in the Old Testament (Psalms 68:31, 87:4; Amos 9:3; Zephaniah 2:12, 3:10). Scholars have concluded it symbolizes "remote lands." One must conclude that "Libyans" refers to the same.

Contextually, then, we see this verse ending with the thought that not only does the *king of the north* control the world's financial assets but also *remote lands* such as Ethiopia and Libya.

"But tidings out of the east and out of the north shall trouble him: therefore he shall go forth with great fury to destroy, and utterly to make away many" (Daniel 11:44).

The tidings (*sh@muwah*) in this context means disquieting reports. They come out of the "east" and the "north." This directional symbolism is of great importance.

The "east" was where the tribe of Judah was camped in relation to the tabernacle (Numbers 2:3). That tribe was represented by the first of the living creatures in heaven (Revelation 4:7) and by the white horse of the first Seal (Revelation 6:1-2). Those apocalyptic symbols are associated with the last work of the 144,000. Since we know this setting in Daniel 11 is end-time (*eth qets*), what is represented here by "tidings" can be none other than the Loud Cry of the 144,000, coming from the "east." It is having an influence, an effect (*bahal*). That is, he is "alarmed," even to the point of being terrified.

What does the "north" represent? North is where Mount Zion is, where God's people will associate with Him and where Satan seeks to enthrone himself (Isaiah 14:13-14). The *king of the north* is called that because he wanted to be *like* God.

What "tidings" or message might come from God's throne? In this setting it would have to be the power of the Holy Spirit in the work of the Latter Rain, giving power to the Loud Cry. Though the *king of the north* persecutes, God's people receive power and, clearly, are under the blessing of heaven. This directly relates to the fifth Trumpet when Satan and his host are warned to hurt not the *grass, green thing* or *tree* (Revelation 9:4). At the time of the Loud Cry, God's people are under special protection, symbolized by these living items.

The reaction to all this is that "he" goes forth with great fury to exterminate and utterly destroy "many."

"The heavenly sentinels, faithful to their trust, continue their watch. Though a general decree has fixed the time when commandment keepers may be put to death, their enemies will in some cases anticipate the decree, and before the time specified, will endeavor to take their lives. But none can pass the mighty guardians stationed about every faithful soul. Some are assailed in their flight from the cities and villages; but the swords raised against them break and fall powerless as a straw. Others are defended by angels in the form of men of war."[4]

"Fearful is the issue to which the world is to be brought. The powers of earth, uniting to war against the commandments of God, will decree that no man may buy or sell, save he that has the mark of the beast, and, finally, that whoever refuses to receive the mark shall be put to death. [Rev. 13:15, 17.] The word of God declares: 'If any man worship the beast and his image, and receive his mark in his forehead, or in his hand, the same shall drink of the wine of

---

[4] White, Ellen G.; *The Great Controversy*, p. 631.

the wrath of God, which is poured out without mixture into the cup of his indignation' [Rev. 14:9, 10.] But not one is made to feel the wrath of God until the truth has been brought in contact with his mind and conscience, and has been rejected. There are many in the churches of our country who have never, even in this land of light and knowledge, had an opportunity to hear the special truths for this time. The obligation of the fourth commandment has never been set before them in its true light. Jesus reads every heart, and tries every motive. The decree is not to be urged upon the people blindly. Every one is to have sufficient light to make his decision intelligently. The Sabbath will be the great test of loyalty; for it is the point of truth especially controverted."[5]

"As Nebuchadnezzar the king of Babylon issued a decree that all who would not bow down and worship this image should be killed, so a proclamation will be made that all who will not reverence the Sunday institution will be punished with imprisonment and death…. Let all read carefully the thirteenth chapter of Revelation, for it concerns every human agent, great and small. – 14MR 91 (1896)."[6]

"And he shall plant the tabernacles of his palace between the seas in the glorious holy mountain; yet he shall come to his end, and none shall help him" (Daniel 11:45).

There is a temptation to interpret this verse literally and see the *king or ruler of the north* planting (*nata*) or establishing his tabernacles (*ohel*) or tents in Palestine, the glorious land. Though interpreted this way by many expositors and though it may represent a minor applica-

tion, it is out of context to a greater message.

This verse continues the thought of the previous verse. The papacy is troubled by what is occurring and, in his fury, sets out to destroy God's people in an end-time Loud Cry setting. In *that* context comes the report that he is fastening or establishing his (*appenden*) tents or palace.

The implication means that the papacy is fixing its authority or leadership role between the seas and the glorious holy mountain. Most scholars understand that the word "in" noted in the King James Version should be "and" – thus, between the seas "and" the mountain.

Seas represent people, nations of the world (Revelation 17:15; cf. Isaiah 17:12, Jeremiah 46:7). The glorious holy mountain draws from a rich history of the highest and southernmost mounts in Jerusalem. This was the area of the "City of David," Solomon's temple and, today, part of the *Temple Mount*. It was and remains a sacred place and is often called Mount Zion (Psalm 48:2, 12-13). In Revelation Mount Zion is seen as the place where God's people – the 144,000 – are gathered with the Lamb (Revelation 14:1).

Once again, shall we view this as literal or symbolic? If literal, which seas? Is it the *Temple Mount* in Jerusalem, represented by the "holy mountain?" Literalism invites never-ending mid-eastern speculation that exists today in the evangelical dispensationalist world.

Perhaps most importantly, we see Mount Zion here representing the seat of the true church on earth and in heaven (Jeremiah 8:19, Hebrews 12:22, Revelation 14:1). It is intriguing that this mount is located on the "sides of the north" (Psalm 48:2), the very place that the *king*

---

[5] White, Ellen G.; *Spirit of Prophecy,* bk 4, pp. 422-423.

[6] White, Ellen G.; *Last Day Events,* p. 3.

of the north receives "tidings" that bring fear and terror to him!

The imagery presents a picture of the papacy and its supporting "host" with its imposing power, fixing its authority between the people of the world and God's holy people. There is already action against God's remnant seen in the previous verse. Now it is firmly established that this *king,* the second rise of the *little horn,* the *vile person,* is in a central world power position.

"Under one head – the papal power – the people will unite to oppose God in the person of His witnesses."[7] The setting is one of battle, one of opposition, one of force against God's people. It is as if Satan said to God's people, "In the evangelizing of the world by your Loud Cry, you're not going to get near my people. I dare you to try to pass the fortress I've set up between us!"

Well – God has the last word. The *king of the north* comes to his end (*qets*), his *final end* and no one will help him.

When does that occur? It begins when the River Euphrates is dried up under the sixth Plague (Revelation 16:12). Babylon's support is finished. Why? One of the final steps for Jesus and His followers already reigning with Him, in the symbol of the 24 elders, is to return from the east. The final blow comes when "God remembers" the hatred and treachery of the papacy, the earth-beast and the dragon. When it is separated and finally subject to His wrath (Revelation 6:16-17, 16:19), the battle is over.

That is exactly the terminus of Daniel 8:1-13! That is the promised timed prophecy of Daniel 12:7. That is the end of papal power that brings the deliverance of God's people (Daniel 12:1-3, 6-13).

Finally – at last – Daniel 8–12 has all beautifully come together. The only details remaining are those in Revelation. We have just been given a great prologue/preface/introduction to that final Biblical book – which, too, is **all** very end-time.

---

[7] *Ibid.,* p. 132.

Other End-Time Materials Available
from the
Christian Heritage Foundation

Ten Volume Commentary on the Book of Revelation. Phrase by phrase analysis of each verse in the Book of Revelation in light of the end of time. Over 1400 pages [Wire-0].

End-Time Secrets of Daniel 8-12. Over 500 years before Jesus' first advent, He appeared three times to Daniel, opening up amazing events that would occur at the end of time. Those prophecies were based on special timing periods, which we now know tell why Jesus is about to come! 55 pages [Perfect bound paperback].

"Strange Work" of the Seven Trumpets. The blast from the first four tribulation Trumpets is God's response to the saints' cry, "How long?" That is when He begins His "strange work." Then Satan is given his last chance to "influence" the world in Trumpets 5–7. His actions are so fiendish, the Bible calls them "woes." The Trumpets are God's final statement against sin before He returns and Satan's last revelation of his character. This is one of the most amazing apocalyptic studies! [Paperback – 146 pgs – Perfect Bound].

God's Great Week of Time. Within the great redemptive sevens, God designed that sin would last no longer than 6,000 years. That Biblical message is the Great Week of Time. 150 pages [paperback].

Sequence of Earth's Final Events. Penetrating sequence of events as outlined in the writings of expositor E. G. White. Complete with all references. Her incredible insights as to the *steps* or *sequence* of all significant end-time events are given in depth. 55 pages [Wire-0].

Workshop Workbooks:

End-Time Secrets of Daniel – Workbook **One** *(Teaching outline covering Chapters 8 & 12)* – 70 pages [Wire-0].

End-Time Secrets of Daniel – Workbook **Two** *(Teaching outline covering Chapters 9-10:7)* – 60 pages [Wire-0].

The Seven Seals of Revelation *(Teaching outline covering Chapters 6 & 8:1)* – 70 pages [Wire-0].

Revelation 17:1-11 *(Teaching outline with narrative article)* – 40 pages [Wire-0]

Revelation 17:1-11 DVD – Is Pope Benedict XVI the last pope? – 2 hours.

Revelation 17 & 18 -- Babylon's Final Years – *(Teaching outline covering Revelation 17 & 18)* – 30 pages [Wire-0].

Additional books on the end of time are coming.

To order: Send check or money order to following address:

Christian Heritage Foundation, CS
4256-B Mockingbird Lane
Banning, California USA
E-mail: christianheritagefo@earthlink.net
Web: www.endtimeissues.com